TRADE AND HUMAN RIGHTS

To
I. L. F.

Trade and Human Rights

The ethical dimension in the U.S.-China relations

SUSAN C. MORRIS
Old Dominion University, USA

Ashgate

Aldershot • Burlington USA • Singapore • Sydney

Published by
Ashgate Publishing Limited
Gower House
Croft Road
Aldershot
Hampshire GU11 3HR
England

Ashgate Publishing Company
131 Main Street
Burlington,VT 05401-5600 USA

Ashgate website: http://www.ashgate.com

British Library Cataloguing in Publication Data
Morris, Susan C.
    Trade and human rights : the ethical dimension in
    U.S.-China relations
    1. International trade - Moral and ethical aspects 2. Human
    rights - China 3. United States - Commerce - China 4. China -
    Commerce - United States 5. United States - Foreign
    relations - Moral and ethical aspects
    I. Title
    337.7'3'051

Library of Congress Control Number: 2001095428

ISBN 0 7546 1837 4

Printed in Great Britain by Antony Rowe Ltd, Chippenham, Wiltshire

Contents

List of Figures

List of Tables

Preface

Amid the globalization of markets and the interdependence of states, human rights violations throughout the world still persist. China, for example, still maintains one of the worst human rights records in the world. The Freedom House Annual Survey of Freedom (2000) recently rated China at its lowest point.[1] Yet despite China's ongoing human rights transgressions, economic relations between the United States and China continue to expand.

This book attempts to establish a relationship between the economic interdependence of nations and the moral responsibilities of nations by examining the case of the 1994 decision by the Clinton administration to sever the ties between China's human rights practices and most-favored-nation status. The 1994 decision is a particularly significant one because it represents a decisive change in how human rights issues are — and will be — addressed in U.S. foreign policy. The decision brings to the fore both the conflicting and complementary issues of states' moral responsibilities to the protection of universal human rights and states' economic interests. In dissecting the U.S.-China relationship within the context of the 1994 U.S. decision, this book has a much broader objective. That is to provide some insights into the state of human rights throughout the world as we embark on the 21st century and to offer some policy options that can advance the cause of human rights not only in China but in every country where human rights violations are found.

The three major competing theoretical paradigms of realism, liberalism, and radicalism are applied to the question of why the Clinton administration considered it no longer useful to condition trade on China's respect for human rights. The findings suggest that each paradigm alone was theoretically limited in explaining the motives for the decision, and therefore an alternative explanation that considers the complexities of the post-Cold War era is advanced.

This endeavor would not have been possible without the assistance, guidance, and expertise of many people. My main debt, however, is to Dr. Francis Adams whose thoughts on style, content, and structure throughout the writing process helped to shape and sharpen this work. I am in gratitude to Dr. Regina Karp, for her guidance and suggestions regarding my research. To Dr. Gilbert Yochum, professor of economics, I extend my appreciation for taking the time to provide economic and political insights into my research, for the privilege of experiencing his inspiring lectures on economics, and for his spiritual support as well.

I am equally grateful to Dr. Simon Serfaty, professor and program director of the Center for Strategic and International Studies (CSIS), for his ever-insightful observations on U.S. foreign policy. The early lectures of Dr. Xiushi Yang were also influential in shaping the methodology. Dr. Friedrich von Kirchbach, chief of Market Analysis Section at ITC UNCTAD/WTO, gave me the opportunity of a "birds-eye" view of world trade and development and was influential in the early formation of my academic interests.

I would like to extend my many thanks to Dr. David P. Forsythe, the Charles J. Mach Distinguished Professor of Political Science at the University of Nebraska, for his willingness to provide outside commentary on this book. I am also grateful to Dr. Ramesh G. Soni, whose friendship and support helped to sustain me through the difficult moments as well as the more joyous ones. Additionally, I would like to thank Ms. Billie Fedyszyn of the GPIS office for her kindness and help throughout my time at Old Dominion. Ms. Sue Wallace of the Office of the Dean was instrumental in providing administrative support.

I am forever grateful to my parents, Dr. Morton Morris and Mrs. Abigail Morris, who helped to make this book a reality. I also extend my appreciation to Ms. Gytelle Bloom and Mr. Arthur Gold. Thanks are due to Ms. Elizabeth Shiverdecker, Ms. Barbara George, Ms. Kait Stright, and Ms. Casey Harlow, for lending an ear. Ms. Sarah Charters, Assistant Desk Editor at Ashgate, tactfully conveyed many useful changes to the manuscript. Special thanks are due to my commissioning editor, Ms. Kirstin Howgate, and to Ms. Elaine Dawson for the preparation of the manuscript. While this book has been framed from the teachings and discussions of many of the individuals named above, its imperfections are my own.

Susan C. Morris

Endnote

1   On a scale of 1 to 7, where 1-2.5 are considered to be "Free", 3-5.5 "Partly Free", and 5.5-7 "Not Free", China received a rating of 7.6, "Not Free".

List of Abbreviations

AMM	ASEAN Ministerial Meeting
APEC	Asia Pacific Economic Cooperation
ASEAN	Association of Southeast Asian Nations
ATMI	American Textiles Manufacturers Institute
BEM	Big Emerging Market
CDP	China Democratic Party
COCOM	Coordinating Committee for Multilateral Export Controls
CSCE	Conference on Security and Cooperation in Europe
EC	European Community
ECOSOC	United Nations Economic and Social Council
EPZ	Export Processing Zones
EU	European Union
EXIMBANK	Export-Import Bank
FDI	Foreign Direct Investment
GATT	General Agreement on Tariffs and Trade
GDP	Gross Domestic Product
GSP	Generalized System of Preferences
IBRD	International Bank for Reconstruction and Development
ILO	International Labor Organization
IMF	International Monetary Fund
ITO	International Trade Organization
JV	Joint Venture
MFA	Multi-Fiber Arrangement
MFN	Most-Favored-Nation
MILS	Minimum International Labor Standards
MNE	Multinational Enterprise
MOU	Memorandum of Understanding
NAFTA	North American Free Trade Agreement
NATO	North Atlantic Treaty Organization
NBC	National Broadcasting Communications
NEC	National Economic Council
NGO	Nongovernmental Organization
NIC	Newly-Industrialized Countries
NIE	Newly-Industrialized Economies

NRF	National Retail Federation
NSC	National Security Council
OECD	Organization for Economic Cooperation and Development
OPIC	Overseas Private Investment Corporation
PNTR	Permanent Normal Trade Relations
PRC	People's Republic of China
SEZ	Special Economic Zone
SRI	Socially Responsible Investing
TDP	Trade and Development Program
TFI	The Fertilizer Institute
TMA	Toy Manufacturers of America
UNCTAD	United Nations Conference on Trade and Development
UNDP	United Nations Development Program
UNEP	United Nations Environmental Program
UNRISD	United Nations Research Institute for Social Development
UR	Uruguay Round
USTR	United States Trade Representative
VOA	Voice of America
WTO	World Trade Organization

1 Introduction

One of the major ideas to emerge from the twentieth century is human rights. Flagrant human rights violations that occurred before and during World War II served as the catalyst for the human rights and fundamental freedoms stipulated in the 1945 United Nations Charter (Humphrey, 1990).[1] From this charter grew an international law which superceded the traditional rights of states and acknowledged the rights of individual men and women.[2] The international system of rights expanded to include the Universal Declaration of Human Rights, adopted by the U.N. General Assembly on December 10, 1948.[3]

Signed in 1966 and entered into force by ratification by states in 1976 were the two International Covenants on Civil and Political Rights,[4] and Economic, Social, and Cultural Rights.[5] A number of regional conventions on human rights had also been formed, most prominently, the European Convention on Human Rights, drafted by the Council of Europe in 1953. All of these major proclamations, combined with a growing number of international, regional, and national organizational human rights conventions, constitute the "New World Law of Human Rights" (Humphrey, 1990, pp. 119-21).

The human rights revolution has evolved dramatically, particularly during the last thirty years or so. In the 1960s, for example, human rights groups were unwelcome in most parts of the world and found difficulties finding a voice in government. Today, human rights activists and advocates meet regularly with government, and most foreign aid programs contain stipulations for democracy building and the protection of human rights (Rieff, 1999, p. 38). The wars in Bosnia and Kosovo, for example, were waged in the name of moral principles rather than strategic interests (p. 37). The universality of application for the respect for individual human rights has been evidenced in Spain's request for the extradition of former Chilean dictator, Augusto Pinochet, to face trial for thousands of "disappearances" of political opponents during his regime. Human rights offenders throughout the world are now being brought to trial for crimes against humanity.

The U.S. government has rhetorically and often actively affirmed its commitment to human rights over the last half century.[6] One recent U.S. affirmation to human rights was addressed at the 1993 World Conference on Human Rights in Vienna, Austria. U.S. Secretary of State Warren Christopher articulated:

My delegation will support the forces of freedom — of tolerance, of respect for the rights of the individual — not only in the next few weeks in Vienna, but every day in the conduct of our foreign policy throughout the world. The United States will never join those who would undermine the Universal Declaration and the movement toward democracy and human rights. (Christopher, 1993)

In May 1994, however, the policy shifted when President Clinton announced that there would no longer be a connection between China's human rights record and most-favored-nation (MFN) status.[7] The Clinton administration maintained that one of the ways to promote human rights in China was to encourage market reform and trade. Stapleton Roy, former U.S. ambassador to China, asserted in 1993:

If you look at the 150 years of modern Chinese history . . . you can't avoid the conclusion that the last 15 years are the best in terms of prosperity, individual choice, access to outside sources of information, freedom of movement within the country and stable domestic conditions. (American Electronics Association, 1996)

Although there have been significant human rights improvements throughout the world, there remain governments which continue to repress dissidents and engage in torture without trial. In 1998, for example, the international human rights organization Amnesty International reported that there were a significant number of Chinese still in prison for participating in the peaceful, prodemocracy protests of 1989, and many others for listening to the Voice of America. Many of China's prisoners were jailed without charge or trial under "reeducation through labor" provisions (U.S. Congress, House, 1998 [Rickard], pp. 22-26). Amnesty also reported that of 1,625 executions worldwide in 1998, 80 percent (1,067) were in China.[8]

The 1.2 billion people in China cannot speak out, do not have freedom of expression, and there is no independent public advocacy on social, political, religious, environmental, or economic issues. There is no independent judicial system that can defend the victims of human rights, and there is no free press for the people. (pp. 22-26)

Despite ongoing reports of China's human rights transgressions, economic relations between the United States and China continue to expand.

The dissolution of the Soviet Union has resulted in a major global transformation. National borders, once closed, have now opened, and new and untapped markets are ripe for the first takers. More cross-national political and economic contacts have become possible since the fall of the Berlin wall. Yet, in light of these geopolitical and economic transformations, systematic human rights violations persist throughout the world. Notorious examples include the human rights atrocities of the former Yugoslavia, and the Rwandan genocide of 1994.[9] The most recent outrage is in Chechnya, where civilians have become the targets of persecution and summary executions in the name of Russian nationalism.[10] As the twentieth century comes to a close, the list of human rights violations continues unabated.

Against this backdrop, this study attempts to establish a relationship between the economic interdependence[11] of nations and the moral responsibilities of nations by examining the U.S.-China case of the 1994 Clinton administration decision to delink China's human rights practices from most-favored-nation status.[12] In further delineation, this research asks the question why the Clinton administration decided to separate China's human rights record from most-favored-nation trading status.

The 1994 decision is a particularly salient one because it represents a decisive change in how human rights issues are — and will be — addressed in U.S. foreign policy. The decision brings to the fore both conflicting and complementary interests of states' moral obligations to the protection of universal human rights and state economic interests. This adds insights not only into Sino-American relations, but also into the broader relationship between global market forces and ethical principles. Can corporate profit and morality[13] coexist, for example? Human rights activists have expressed concern that future world governments may only be willing to uphold human rights principles where economically unimportant countries like Serbia or Burma are involved (Rieff, 1999, pp. 38-40).

By examining specifically the U.S.-China case of the 1994 decision, new insights may be obtained into the consequences and implications of economic instruments as tools for human rights improvements. The issue raises substantive questions, such as will expanding human rights, globally, undermine the free market mechanism by applying externalities[14] that could affect jobs and prices of goods and services? Or, would the free market mechanism help to further the progress of human rights? Which of the many policy options recommended by scholars and practitioners would improve human rights conditions in China and in other countries? The case also brings to light the continuing question of the sovereign rights of states as protectors of human rights and the protection of human rights under international law.

The United States' 1994 decision to end the connection between China's human rights record and most-favored-nation status is particularly significant because of China's increasing role in the international political economy. "It is predicted that if China's economy continues to grow at the annual rate of 10 percent, and if it acquires advanced technology capabilities, China's impact on the international economic system will dwarf that of Japan during its most influential period of the 1970s and 1980s" (Ross, 1996, p. 19). As the only "developing" nation[15] with a permanent seat on the United Nations Security Council, China exerts considerable influence on world affairs.

The 1994 decision is also important because of the role the United States and China have to one another. The United States is China's second largest trading partner, for both exports and imports. In 1998, for example, China's exports to the U.S. amounted to $38 billion, second only to Hong Kong, at $39 billion. Comparably, in 1998, China's imports from the U.S. amounted to $17 billion, second only to Japan, at $28 billion.[16] And bilaterally, both the United States and China offer major market entry and growth potential for each others' firms. In particular, however, to the United States and to U.S. firms, China offers the opportunity to sell to what potentially could be the world's largest market, home to approximately one fifth of the earth's population.

The U.S.-China trade and human rights issues encompass political, economic, and ethical concerns that are interwoven into the discourse and actions of both countries, and ultimately into the international economic and political arena. "The MFN treatment, granted reciprocally, is the most important clause in the Sino-U.S. Trade Agreement, and is the foundation for the development of Sino-U.S. trade and economic cooperation" (Wenjing Chen, 1996, p. 20). Despite the 1994 decision to delink trade and human rights, the issue of MFN and human rights continues to raise considerable debate in the U.S. Congress.

Research Design

The three major competing paradigms,[17] realism, liberalism, and radicalism are utilized as foundations for testing alternative hypotheses. Alternative theories or approaches may be useful, but have not been chosen as a framework for the present analysis. The bureaucratic politics approach, for example, may be applicable to a degree, but intrinsic to the model are some weaknesses. The increasing influence of externalities on the bureaucratic process in the U.S. government may not lend itself to the intricacies involved in present day foreign policy decision making. The growing interdependence of states and the increased role of the private sector and international governmental bodies in governmental decision making have created complexities that reach beyond the bureaucratic network of the Congress, executive branch, and intra-governmental agencies. Fast-paced global forces such as the speed of international financial transactions and political upheaval may call into question the applicability of the bureaucratic decision-making model as a basis for analyses due to the slowness of the bureaucratic decision-making process. "The general literature on government bureaucracies has paid much greater attention to how organizations respond to incremental changes in their external environments than to revolutionary changes. Yet U.S. foreign policy agencies now face revolutionary changes in their external environment" (Lindsay and Ripley, 1997b, p. 9).

The psychological approach to foreign policy analysis perhaps may be useful. Theories of cognitive psychology provide insights into the way individual decision makers think and perceive situations. Cognitive knowledge, or beliefs about the world and their images, are the key explanatory variables in foreign policy behavior. However, the psychological approach may be limited as well. The psychological approach, for instance, does not consider the influence of the environment on the beliefs of the decision maker. For example, there is the potential for inaccurate predictions of one's own behavior by miscalculating the degree to which an event may stir emotions. In this approach, the pre-existing belief system of the decision maker may deter the ability to predict political outcomes that are guided by beliefs that are different. As well, today's global environment is in constant transformation. This makes human patterns of perception or misperception difficult if not impossible to follow and decipher when interpreting the decisions of foreign policymakers.

Moreover, the market mechanism, on which trade patterns rely and operate, is a significant factor in the 1994 MFN decision. The market mechanism is structured on the interactions of economic units, such as the interactions between savings, financial institutions, investment, income, wages, consumer and government expenditures, land, labor, and capital, rather than on the beliefs or perceptions of individual government leaders. For these reasons, the psychological approach to foreign policy has not been chosen as a framework for analysis.

Other theories have been considered by scholars as a basis for investigation. Nonetheless, it is of the opinion of the present writer that the three major traditional theories of realism, liberalism, and radicalism provide a broad scope for analysis of the issue.

Deriving from the previous literature on the subject, to be further expounded upon in chapter 2, the following hypotheses are suggested:

H1   Based upon the realist perspective, it is proposed that the U.S. intent to sustain and increase power[18] in the Asian region influenced the 1994 U.S. decision to separate China's human rights record from most-favored-nation status (Krauthammer, 1990/91; Segal, 1996; Haass, 1997; Mastanduno, 1997).

H2   Based upon the liberal perspective, it is proposed that the U.S. intent to improve respect for human rights in China through economic engagement influenced the 1994 U.S. decision to separate China's human rights record from most-favored-nation status (Harland, 1994/95; Lilley, 1994/95; Levine, 1996; Simon, 1996).

H3   Based upon the radical perspective, it is proposed that corporate influence is associated with the 1994 U.S. decision to separate China's human rights record from most-favored-nation status (Shambaugh, 1991; Streeten, 1992; Wallerstein, 1994; William Robinson, 1996; Silbey, 1997).

The hypotheses speculate three causal relationships among the variables. The first causal relationship is between the U.S. quest for power in the Asian region and the 1994 decision to delink China's human rights record from most-favored-nation status. The second causal relationship is between the U.S. intent to improve respect for human rights in China and the 1994 decision to separate China's human rights record from most-favored-nation status. The third causal relationship is the influence of the corporate sector and the 1994 decision to separate China's human rights record from most-favored-nation status.

The above hypotheses indicate one dependent variable and three independent variables. The dependent variable is identified as the 1994 U.S. decision to delink China's human rights record from most-favored nation status. The independent variables are identified as:

1.   the U.S. intent to sustain and increase power in the Asian region;
2.   the U.S. intent to advance human rights in China through economic engagement; and
3.   corporate interests.

The preceding hypotheses, although worthy of testing, may be oversimplifications of the problem, however. The New World Order has ushered in new complexities into the world system. A multitude of post-Cold War evolutionary and revolutionary events have taken place. Such dynamic events have included newly forming states and boundaries, cross-border state alliances, transnational corporate mergers, a new monetary union on the European continent, and the expansion and solidification of international and regional trade regimes, such as the World Trade Organization (WTO), the North American Free Trade Agreement (NAFTA), the European Union (EU), and the expansion of international nongovernmental organizations (NGOs).

With the demise of the Soviet Union, the bipolar, "balance of power" Cold War structure has been broken. The Cold War arrangement that had been the basis for international political analyses for nearly half a century is no longer applicable. These global transformations, coupled with the global spread of information technology, may bring into question the plausibility of traditional theories as explanations for social phenomena in the postmodern era.

Realism, for example, with its emphasis on state power, may overlook explanations in international relations that arise from a changing world of complex interdependence.[19] Liberalism, with its emphasis on international trade as a means for peaceful relations among countries, may underestimate the significance of state survival as a motivation for behavior. Finally, radicalism, in its assumption that the international social order is guided by an elite ruling class that is fueled by the hands of multinational corporations (MNCs), may overlook human values, consumer sovereignty, public opinion and independent social groups as influential factors in foreign policy decisions.

Because of these global transformations, each hypothesis, in and of itself, may not be sufficient in explaining the U.S. 1994 decision to delink China's human rights record from most-favored-nation status. Each of the three stated hypotheses may serve as a partial explanation of the decision. But even in combination, the hypotheses may not be sufficient explanation as to the reasoning of this critical turning point in U.S. foreign policy on human rights. Environmental factors that reach beyond the U.S.-China bilateral relationship may have affected the decision to separate human rights and trade.

In light of the above considerations, an alternative hypothesis, **H4**, is proposed. The fourth or alternative hypothesis draws upon elements of past approaches but places the U.S. foreign policy decision on China in the context of complex interdependence. The independent variables therefore include:

1. the U.S. intent to sustain and increase power in the Asian region;
2. the U.S. intent to advance human rights in China;
3. corporate interests; and
4. complex interdependence.

The dependent variable is the 1994 U.S. decision. Thus a fourth causal relationship would be between all four of these factors and the 1994 U.S. decision.

This study employed primary and secondary sources from available data, utilizing a content analysis approach to research. Primary sources included public documents and official records, such as the proceedings of U.S. government bodies[20] and testimonies of major actors that surrounded the 1994 decision. These key actors include government officials, corporate executives, human rights organizations and specialists, business and interest groups, and academicians. Secondary sources, such as previous research, the media, and opinions of analysts on the subject, were also consulted.

Central Contributions

A significant amount of the literature on the U.S.-China MFN debate, and the resultant 1994 U.S. decision on China analyze the issue from a journalistic standpoint, a legal standpoint, or a marketing standpoint. Many scholars and practitioners have engaged in fruitful policy analysis of the 1994 decision. All of these approaches are indeed valid and appropriate to the subject and are incorporated into the analysis of the present study. Fewer studies, however, have examined the 1994 U.S. decision from a theoretical perspective. By applying the U.S. decision to the three major alternative theoretical schools of realism, liberalism, and radicalism, this study attempts to expand the knowledge of the current scholarship.

The case study of the U.S. 1994 decision contributes to theory by questioning, confirming, or improving upon existing theoretical constructs as explanations for political and economic outcomes. These insights contribute not only to a theoretical understanding of the problem, but also to a practical understanding. The practical value of researching the 1994 MFN decision is that by expanding on the available literature, policymakers may gain further insights into the relationship between trade and human rights, and the social consequences and implications that trade policy has on the progress of international human rights.

Through empirical investigation and analysis, this research study offers insights into the motives of major decision makers that surrounded the 1994 decision. Implicitly, the research study contributes to the understanding of the bilateral U.S.-China relationship. A more thorough understanding may be gained as to the political and economic consequences of the 1994 decision on the U.S.-China relationship, thereby contributing to the knowledge that can be applied to U.S. policy choices on China. Explicitly, the research attempts to provide some answers into the future status of universal human rights. For instance, which mechanisms will be utilized to address and ensure global human rights in the future? And what role will the United States play as guarantor of universal human rights?

Organization of the Research

The research is presented in six chapters. Chapter 2 consists of a review of the relevant literature within the context of three major political paradigms; realism, liberalism, and radicalism. Each school of thought is briefly reviewed, followed by a discussion of the viewpoints of major analysts within each school. The strengths and limitations of each theoretical school as applied to U.S. foreign policy behavior are assessed. The chapter begins with a discussion of the literature on realism, which focuses on scholars whose opinions are suggestive of the importance of the U.S. national interest and the acquisition of national power. Realists suggest that the best way for the United States to maintain and increase power in the world is to engage in international trade. U.S. economic power would be gained through close economic ties with other countries.

The liberal perspective of U.S. foreign policy, briefly stated, is that foreign trade is a conduit for world peace and higher standards of living among nations. The chapter draws upon traditional scholars of economic and social liberal thought. These liberal forefathers include, among others, Immanuel Kant, Adam Smith, Woodrow Wilson, John Rawls, and David Ricardo. The chapter then proceeds to discuss the views of current liberal thinkers and how their views relate to the interpretation of U.S. foreign policy decisions. Particular reference is given to U.S.-China policy.

Finally, the radical paradigm is brought forward in the chapter. The philosophies underlying radical thought, which are founded in the works of Karl Marx, Frederick Engels and Vladimir Ilich Lenin, are introduced and discussed within a foreign policy context. The chapter unfolds to discuss some of the major modern day followers of radical theory. Slight differences of opinion are found in the current radical literature. Most radical opinions, however, evince the fundamental Marxist/Leninist tenets of class conflict and imperialism. All three of these competing theoretical viewpoints, which will be more thoroughly considered in the literature review, have significant implications for U.S.-China policy and for U.S. trade and human rights policy in general.

The third chapter consists of an historical view of the issue. The chapter is divided into two sections. The first section of the chapter details the evolution of U.S.-China trade policy, beginning with the first U.S. commercial contacts with the Mainland, in the eighteenth century, and ending with the 1994 Clinton administration decision to separate trade policy and human rights. The trade policies of past U.S. presidential administrations, and the international and domestic political and economic events that affected those policies are discussed.

The third chapter continues to provide an historical perspective of the relationship between trade and human rights in U.S. foreign policy. Major U.S. trade acts that have been linked to U.S. human rights policy throughout the centuries are discussed. The chapter highlights the institutional mechanisms through which the United States has exercised economic leverage to further the progress of human rights. The chapter concludes with a synopsis of the decision making process and the major events that led up to the U.S. 1994 decision.

The first three hypotheses are empirically tested in the fourth chapter. The hypotheses include:

H1   The U.S. intent to sustain and increase power in the Asian regions influenced the 1994 U.S. decision to separate China's human rights record from most-favored-nation status;

H2   The U.S. intent to improve respect for human rights in China through economic engagement influenced the 1994 U.S. decision to separate China's human rights record from most-favored-nation status; and

H3   Corporate influence is associated with the 1994 U.S. decision to separate China's human rights record from most-favored-nation status.

The hypotheses are placed and analyzed within one of the competing theoretical arguments. Each section begins with a brief description of the theory to be applied. The strengths and limitations of the theoretical findings are also discussed.

Chapter 5 analyzes and discusses the theoretical findings of the fourth hypothesis, which draws upon elements of past approaches while considering complex interdependence as a causal factor in the U.S. decision to delink trade from human rights in 1994. Elements of the first three hypotheses are synthesized, along with external factors that had affected the 1994 decision. Major transnational forces come into play and are addressed as part of the findings. These environmental influences include linkages between multilateral corporations, international organizations and cross-national alliances between businesses and governments. The chapter highlights how economic interdependencies can influence political decisions.

Finally, the sixth chapter serves as a review and conclusion of the overall research findings. The chapter reviews the findings of each theoretical argument, offering further insights into the strengths and weaknesses of each proposition. The chapter focuses on the implications of the research results. These include theoretical implications and implications for U.S.-China economic policy.

The broader implications of the research findings are also discussed, with specific reference given to the effects of U.S.-China policy on the global political economy and on universal human rights. Recommendations for U.S. trade and human rights policies are proposed, and suggestions for future research are offered.

Endnotes

1   The 1945 United Nations Charter formed the legal basis for the Nuremberg trials, the Genocide Convention, and the 1948 Universal Declaration.

2   "WE THE PEOPLES OF THE UNITED NATIONS DETERMINED . . . to reaffirm faith in fundamental human rights, in the dignity and worth of the human person, in the equal rights of men and women and of nations large and small, and to establish respect for the obligations arising from treaties and other sources of international law can be maintained, and to promote social progress and better standards of life in larger freedom" [emphasis added]. United Nations, *Charter of the United Nations and Statute of the International Court of Justice* (New York: United Nations Department of Public Information, 1945), signed June 26, 1945, in San Francisco at the conclusion of the United Nations Conference on International Organization.

3   As Humphrey explains, the Declaration did not acquire legal force, as resolutions of the General Assembly have only the force of recommendations, but because the Declaration has been invoked repeatedly throughout the years, it has become part of the customary law of nations (Humphrey, 1990, p. 120).

4   Civil and political rights include "the right to life, liberty, security, freedom from torture, freedom of thought, religion, and opinion" (United Nations, 1986, p. 303).

5   Economic, social, and cultural rights include "the right to equal pay for equal work, to education, social security and an adequate standard of living" (United Nations, 1986, p. 304).

6   For this project, I use the concept of human rights, taken from Kenneth A. Bollen. Bollen (1992) identifies three categories of human rights: 1) political rights and liberties; 2) rights to protect the integrity of a person (or civil rights), and 3) social and economic rights. This project focuses on political rights and liberties because of their importance in influencing other rights. The justification for this is that when political rights and liberties are strong, there is greater potential to bring about social and economic rights and personal integrity. "Political rights exist when the national government is accountable to the general population and each individual is entitled to participate in the government directly or through Representatives. Political liberties exist when the people of a country have the freedom to express any political opinions in any media and the freedom to form or participate in any political group". Ultimately and ideally, all of these rights are mutually reinforcing.

7   The guiding principle of the World Trade Organization is the concept of most-favored-nation, which assures that member countries "have the benefit of any advantage, favor, privilege or immunity granted by any other country to any product originating in or destined for any other country". Protocol of Provisional Application, 61 Stat. (5), (6), T.I.A.S. No. 1700, 4 Bevans 639, 55-61 U.N.T.S.; current amended version, BISD vol. IV (concluded at Geneva, October 30, 1947, entered into force January 1, 1948). The concept of most-favored-nation status has existed, in a bilateral form, at least since the seventeenth century.

"To reduce the impact of protectionist trade measures, countries have long concluded international agreements providing reciprocally for the favorable treatment of each other's merchants". In recent decades, most-favored-nation status has been granted through the multilateral mechanism of the General Agreement on Tariffs and Trade, formed in 1947, now known as the World Trade Organization (Janis, 1988, pp. 206-7). The term "most-favored-nation" may be somewhat misleading in the sense that it implies that one nation is favored over another. From the U.S. point of view, MFN is not a privilege or reward, nor is MFN actually the most favored tariff treatment the United States provides. For example, special tariff treatment more favorable than MFN has been provided to more than 100 countries under a number of special tariff programs such as the General System of Preferences (GSP) and North American Free Trade Agreement (NAFTA). The tariff rates under these agreements have been lower than most-favored-nation rates (American Electronics Association, 1996).

8   It was further reported that "Amnesty believes that the true totals for China are higher than those reported. The death penalty remains most entrenched in East Asia. China alone regularly accounts for more executions than the rest of the world combined and applies it to a wide range of crimes beyond murder" (*Economist*, 1999a, p. 95).

9   Over half a million people were exterminated in this genocide. For further explanation, see Human Rights Watch (1999).

10   "Human rights are no reason to interfere in the internal affairs of a state", said Russia's foreign minister, Igor Ivanov. Quoted by Craig R. Whitney (1999, p. 1). Also refer to Human Rights Watch (2000a).

11   Robert O. Keohane defines interdependence as "situations characterized by reciprocal effects among countries or among actors in different countries. Interdependence, most simply defined, is *mutual* dependence". Keohane contrasts interdependence with complex interdependence, the latter being a far broader issue because it involves the entire international arena and a network of multilateral institutions (Keohane and Nye, 1989, pp. 8, 206).

12   Eckstein tells us that "the type of study most frequently made in the field is the intensive study of individual cases. Case studies run the gamut from the most microcosmic to the most macrocosmic levels of political phenomena. Case studies are valuable at all stages of theory building, and most valuable at the stage at which candidate theories are tested" (Harry Eckstein, 1975, pp. 79-80).

13   The definition of morality is often a matter of conjecture. Morality is understood here as "a commitment to protecting human rights, raising living standards and democratization", as defined by David Little (1991, p. 3). An alternate definition is provided by Robert J. Meyers: "Morality can be seen as deriving from four sources: 1) religion, 2) utilitarianism, 3) deontology, 4) human virtue. The four sources of morality are the basic stuff of ethics, ethics being the rules of conduct" (1991, p. 30). This work also takes the utilitarian approach to morality, as described by Meyers — that is, "a particular policy or action that is guaranteed to produce the greatest good for the greatest number".

14   Externalities refer to "the costs or benefits of a transaction that are incurred or received by members of the society but are not taken into account by the parties to the transaction" (Lipsey and Steiner, 1981, p. 424, as quoted by Cheung, 1998, p. 9).

15   The question of whether China can be classified as a "developing" nation has been challenged by political and economic analysts when applying purchasing power parity (PPP) to the level of development. Cheung, for example, points out that in March 1995, China's GDP per capita was $435, but using PPP, the figure soared to $2,428. Cheung recommends that because of "the increasing internationalization of China and opening of its economy, PPP

would be a more precise and appropriate unit of measurement" (Cheung, 1998, pp. 307-8).

16 PRC General Administration of Customs, China's Customs Statistics 1997, 1998, as quoted by the U.S. China Business Council (1998). Note that China's export figures to the United States for the year 1998 differ from the U.S. imports from China figure (as shown in Table 2 of Chapter 3) for the year 1998. For example, the United States, for the year 1998, reports imports from China in the amount of US$71.2 billion, whereas China reports exports to the United States, for the year 1998, as $38 billion. This statistical discrepancy is due to the different reporting methods used by the PRC General Administration of Customs and the U.S. Department of Commerce. According to the PRC, trade with the United States is classified as trade with Hong Kong if it passes through Hong Kong ports.

17 As Eckstein explains, "the most powerful way to test and improve a theory is to be hard on your own approach and be easy on the alternatives. Theorists must be ready to tolerate some of the propositions of the opposite camp" (Harry Eckstein, 1975, p. 88).

18 "Ray Cline divides power into two components, tangible and intangible. The formula is:
$$Pp = (C+E+M) * (S + W)$$
where Pp = perceived power; C = critical mass = population + territory; E = economic capability; M = military capability; S = strategic purpose; W = will to pursue national strategy. C, E, and M are tangible, while S and W are intangible" (Cline, 1977, p. 11 as noted by Cheung, 1998, p. 107).

19 "Complex Interdependence refers to a situation among a number of countries in which multiple channels of contact connect societies, where states do not monopolize these contacts. These channels of contact include informal ties between governmental elites, as well as foreign office arrangements and channels between transnational corporations. Complex Interdependence consists of multiple issues that are not arranged in a clear consistent hierarchy. The absence of hierarchy means that military security does not consistently dominate the agenda" (Keohane and Nye, 1989, pp. 24-25).

20 "Hearings are good ways to look at not only the practitioners' viewpoints but also the other opinions drawn from the society at large. More often than not, people from business groups, academic circles, and 'careerists and ins-and-outers,' including foreign policy elites, the executives of large firms, and academic professionals, are substantially influential in foreign policy-making" (Thomas McCormick, 1995, quoted by Cheung, 1998, p. 9). Cheung further asserts that "although congressional hearings cannot reveal everything about U.S. foreign policy, they indicate the discourse of the U.S. foreign policy. Like the political party, the hearing functions as the articulation of ideas and the aggregation of opinions".

2 Theoretical Perspectives

This work is an inquiry into the relationship between the economic interdependence of nations and the moral responsibilities of nations by examining the 1994 decision by the Clinton administration to separate China's human rights record from most-favored-nation status. By employing the case study method of analysis, insights are gained into the complementary and conflicting issues of ethical principles and global market forces.

The proceeding chapter examines the relevant literature by drawing on a wide variety of scholarly opinions that, for the most part, were representative of major theoretical traditions. A small but significant number of viewpoints did not fall exclusively into one theoretical tradition or another, but rather reflected a combination of traditional theoretical approaches, or perhaps even new approaches to discovery, particularly as they pertained to the post-Soviet era. These views are briefly discussed.

The chapter focuses on literature that is relevant to the 1994 U.S. decision to end the linkage between international trade and human rights. The literature covers a broad perspective on U.S. foreign policy, with a particular emphasis on U.S. foreign economic policy. Opinions of analysts are derived from both political and economic areas, as both overlap and are ultimately intertwined into the making of U.S. foreign policy.[1]

Because it is assumed that some moral imperative is involved when making decisions on human rights issues, moral considerations and their role in U.S. foreign policy are also reviewed in the literature. The literature review places the opinions of analysts within the context of the competing schools of thought of realism, liberalism, and radicalism, with specific focus given to U.S.-China policy. A brief description of each theoretical school is provided at the beginning of each section. The strengths and weaknesses of these theoretical approaches are then evaluated.

Realism

In realist theory the central actors in a political system are the nation-states. "The function of states are similar, and distinctions among them arise principally from their varied capabilities" (Waltz, 1986, pp. 92-93). Political realism maintains that "the primary obligation of every state — the goal to which all other objectives should be subordinated — is to promote the national interest, defined as the acquisition of power" (Kegley, 1995b, pp. 92-93).[2] True to the Machiavellian and Hobbesian concept that humankind is sinister by nature, the goal of the state is to survive by any means, such as by military might, war, and the conquering of other states. Structural anarchy, or the absence of a central authority, is assumed, and therefore a state's relative capabilities are a measure of survival within an anarchic system (Holsti, 1995). It is also assumed in realist theory that states behave rationally "and are guided by the logic of the national interest" (p. 37).

Hans Morganthau, in his notable work *Politics Among Nations*, professed that "the limitless aspiration of power drives all nations" (Morganthau, 1967, p. 202). The economic policies of nations are therefore "judged primarily from the point of view of their contribution to national power" (p. 29). Klaus Knorr underscored the importance of a nation's economic capabilities in terms of relative power gains, where he pointed to the fact that national economic capabilities can be used as a lever to gain advantage over another nation (Knorr, 1977). "Economic valuables", Knorr contended, "can be used as direct leverage over the outside world" (p. 99).

After the fall of the Berlin wall, many realist scholars stressed the importance of maintaining the U.S. hegemony or the "unipolar moment" (Krauthammer, 1990/91; Mastanduno, 1997; McLennan, 1997). Charles Krauthammer noted that "the immediate post-Cold War world was unipolar. The center of world power was the unchallenged superpower, the United States, attended by its Western allies" (Krauthammer, 1990/91, p. 23). From Krauthammer's point of view, U.S. foreign trade and investment was a means to sustain and increase U.S. power. In support of Krauthammer's argument, Mastanduno referred to Stephen Walt's neorealist "balance of threat" theory, which held that the dominant state would deal with potential challengers in order to maintain the hegemonic position (Mastanduno, 1997, citing Walt, 1987). Specifically with regard to China, Mastanduno observed that increased U.S. interests in penetrating the China market explained U.S. efforts to mobilize for national economic competition against other major economic powers. In the realist sense, then, Mastanduno maintained that the U.S. policy of economic engagement with China was "threat" driven.

Similarly, Brzezinski warned that Russia continued to be a threat to U.S. security after the Cold War and that former Soviet officials still desired to control the former satellite states (Brzezinski, 1997/98). The emergence of a foreign military and economic superpower on the Eurasian continent must therefore be deterred through international economic linkages and convergence (p. 51). True to his belief in a lingering post-Cold War communist threat, Brzezinski argued that China may grow economically, but may not democratize, thus posing a threat to the U.S. hegemony in the Asian region, and beyond (pp. 52-54).

Affirming the opinion of Brzezinski, Mearsheimer (1990) warned of a Soviet return to expansionism, and Ariel Cohen (1996) cautioned of centuries of Russian imperial rule and the "Russification" of ethnic minorities. Concomitantly, McLennan (1997) argued that socialism on the Asian continent had not dissolved, and that newly privatizing states were no assurance that autocracy would abate or that democracy would ensue. In further explanation of U.S. foreign policy from the realist perspective, Haass argued that "alliances among like-minded governments and the support of liberal trade and multilateralism helped to assure the U.S. military and economic hegemonic position" (1997, pp. 43-45).[3]

With an underlying realist threat and its principle of relative power, McLennan (1997) noted that it was in the national interest of the United States to maintain strategic hegemony in East Asia. One way of maintaining the U.S. hegemony was through economic ties with China while maintaining a cautious relationship in order to assure that U.S. national security interests would be protected (Ross, 1997). Such U.S. security interests included the reform of China's economic system so that the system would allow for U.S. free market values, particularly as they affect U. S. economic policy (pp. 44-45).

Following the realist school of thought, Segal (1996) asserted that the lack of balance of power stability[4] in the post-Cold War era was all the more reason China should be contained through "constrainment". More specifically, increased U.S. economic relations with China would decrease the possibility of China's economic ascendancy in the Asian region because China's leaders would be prevented from making economic decisions unilaterally.[5]

In the broader perspective, Stremlau (1994/95) proposed that U.S. economic relations with big emerging markets (BEMs)[6] would promote a convergence of U.S. national interests by creating jobs for citizens, by increasing domestic productivity and by reducing trade and fiscal deficits. Stremlau further noted that "U.S. foreign policy would increasingly revolve around commercial interests, and that economic diplomacy would be essential to resolving the great issues of our age" (p. 18). Stremlau's observation is evidenced in the increased emphasis on the U.S.-China commercial relationship in U.S.-China policy.

Contrary to the aforementioned viewpoints that considered U.S. economic relations with other countries to be an assurance of the U.S. hegemony after the Cold War, Muravchik (1995) disparaged U.S. economic relations with other countries at the expense of decreasing defense capabilities. Muravchik, for example, concluded that with regard to China, the United States favored economics over military and human rights issues to the point of "coddling China" (p. 39). Muravchik's opinion was indicative of the traditional realist principle that the primary means to obtaining national power is by the build up of a nation's military capabilities.[7] Kagan (1997), as did Muravchik, recommended increased U.S. military capabilities in the Asian region, as opposed to increased economic ties, to assure the U.S. hegemonic position.

More specifically, Kagan argued that only tough U.S. trade sanctions against China would pressure China's leaders to incorporate U.S. values into its economic and political system (p. 27). Joseph S. Nye, in referring to Ledeen, wrote of the realist contention that "China is the one nation capable of mortally challenging the United States over the next ten or twenty years" (Nye, 1997/98, p. 69, citing Ledeen, 1997). Engaging China (economically and militarily) while establishing alliances with Japan and South Korea, Nye believed, would further the U.S. security interest in the Asia-Pacific region (Nye, 1995).[8]

An extension of the realist school of thought is isolationism,[9] or what is also referred to as protectionism. For isolationists, the economic *independence* of the state is threatened by trade with and investment in other countries (Knorr, 1973). Realists who advocate isolationism believe that ideally, a state's economy should be self-sustaining, and that the *interdependence* of states increases the probability of conflict among them (Waltz, 1971). Deriving from these beliefs, Mastel and Szamosszegi (1997) argued that China's increased wealth and technological knowledge gained from trading with the United States could be used to strengthen China's military, which could then threaten the United States.

The isolationist perspective was further advanced by Hawkins (1997) in his policy statement that "China's trade surplus with the United States provided the country with the wealth to buy weapons, and that the revocation of China's most-favored-nation status would help to deter the flow of U.S. dollars that could feed China's aggressive military ambitions". Similarly, one author contended that greater U.S. commerce with China was an empty goal because it would assist China's rise to domination in the East Asian region ("A New China Strategy", 1997).

Advancing the isolationist perspective, Caldwell and Lennon (1995) expressed that China's economic prosperity gained by trade with the United States would fuel China's military growth, which would eventually allow the country to threaten most parts of the globe. The opinions of Caldwell and Lennon suggested that U.S. economic relations with China posed a threat to U.S. security, driven by realist underpinnings of the ever-present potential of war.[10] Advocates of isolationism (Knorr, 1973; Caldwell and Lennon, 1995; Hawkins, 1997; Mastel and Szamosszegi, 1997) argued that subordinating the pursuit of security to the pursuit of trade, on the premise that increased trade with China would lead to democracy and improved human rights practices, was mistaken. Rather, the U.S. national interest should be the prevention of a potentially hostile power from usurping the U.S. hegemonic position. Isolationist theorists and practitioners therefore viewed U.S. economic engagement with China as a zero-sum proposition. Gains would be made for China only at the expense of U.S. security. Realist thinkers (Nye, 1995; Segal, 1996; Haass, 1997; Mastanduno, 1997; Ross, 1997), on the other hand, viewed U.S. economic engagement with China as a means to assure U.S. economic and strategic hegemony in the Asian region.

Reflecting the realist perspective of morality, Morganthau, in *Politics Among Nations* (1967), dismissed morality as a viable foreign policy tool because he believed that seemingly altruistic concerns for morality could conceal ulterior motives for actions in international politics. Morganthau maintained that "the state has no right to allow moral concerns to interfere with successful political action of the national survival and the quest for relative power".[11] The earlier work of Hobbes (1994), however, formed the basis of the realist view of morality. Hobbes defined the true worth of humankind in relative terms. That is to say, "the true worth of man is his price, or how much he would be given for the use of his power" (pp. 51-52).

Similarly, Brzezinski (1997/98) did not view human rights as a positive force for the well-being and betterment of humankind, but rather as a manipulative tool to sway other countries to act in the U.S. interest (pp. 51-55). Realism, in the contemporary world, was exemplified by Doyle, who ascertained that even today realist scholars doubt the basis for a "global cosmopolitan international morality" (1997, p. 434). George Kennan, one of the principal proponents of realist theory, for example, expressed that "the interests of the national society are those that only concern itself with military security, the integrity of its political life and the well-being of its people" (1991, pp. 60-61). These needs, Kennan asserted, "have no moral quality" (p. 60).

An underlying premise of Kennan's viewpoint, as discussed by Little (1991), was that there was nothing universal about morality because the concept of morality differed from society to society. "The moral claims of one culture, therefore, can be doubted by another" (pp. 3-6). Based on these traditional realist perspectives, morality and human rights concerns would not be an influential factor in U.S. foreign policy decision making.

The strength of the realist argument, in its emphasis on interstate power and military capabilities, is that it can readily explain U.S. behavior in actions pertaining to perceived or real security threats. Realism's unyielding foundation that in order to achieve peace, it is necessary to prepare for war,[12] has explained previous U.S. political actions, particularly during the bipolar Cold War years.[13]

A weakness of the realist argument, however, is that it does not account for the present changing world of complex interdependence and geopolitical reordering. The post-Cold War global expansion of international organizations and transnational corporations make realist theory static as a singular explanation for U.S. policy choice. In its emphasis on states' self-interests of survival, security, power, and relative capabilities, realist theory overlooks that state behavior can be influenced by such critical factors as international law, economic interdependence, multilateral institutions and agreements, international regimes,[14] and/or nongovernmental organizations. A further weakness of realist theory is that the intricacies involved in bureaucratic politics can undermine rational actions by key decision makers.

Although the national interest is a major determinant of realist theory, it is often difficult to discern exactly what the national interest is in light of competing domestic interests. Moreover, realist theory overlooks the human dimension of the values of freedom and individualism that have been ingrained in the political culture of U.S. society since the end of colonial rule.

Realist theory, as an explanation for U.S. behavior, fails to acknowledge that the power of human ideology and public opinion can influence the actions of states. Liberalism, on the other hand, although acknowledging the realist emphasis on the state system, paints a much different picture of global events and structures, as discussed in the following section.

Liberalism

To the liberal school of thought,[15] economic relations among and between states is viewed as a pacifying force.[16] Grounded in the theoretical and practical philosophies of Kant (1795) and Wilson (1918),[17] liberals envisage that the peace and prosperity of nations would be furthered by the removal of economic barriers. As in realism, liberal thought extends across both political and economic spheres. Neoclassical economist David Ricardo affirmed the ideologies of Kant and Wilson in his seminal work *On the Principles of Political Economy and Taxation*:

> Under a system of perfectly free commerce, each country naturally devotes its capital and labor to such employments as are most beneficial to each. This pursuit of individual advantage is admirably connected with the universal goof of the whole. By stimulating industry, by rewarding ingenuity, and by using most efficaciously the peculiar power bestowed by nature, it distributes labour most effectively and economically, while, by increasing the general mass of productions, it

diffuses general benefit, and binds together, by one common tie of interest and intercourse, the universal society of nations throughout the civilized world. (Ricardo, 1953, pp. 133-34)

Within the framework of liberalism, a global human rights regime has emerged in the twentieth century, which has been witnessed in the evolution of such international governmental and nongovernmental groups as the U.N. Human Rights Commission, the International Court of Justice, Amnesty International, and other organizations that promote the cause of human rights throughout the world. From the liberal perspective, humanitarian values drive foreign policy.

With these liberal principles in mind, Simon noted that "the United States, under President William Clinton, had formulated a new foreign policy; the enlargement of free-market democracies to replace the containment of Soviet communism as the centerpiece of U.S. foreign policy" (Simon, 1996, p. 5). Simon contended that the interests of all nations were met under liberalist principles (p. 5). The promotion of free-market democracies, according to Simon, would enhance the welfare of all nations by promoting peace and prosperity (p. 5).

In an empirical study of the impact of China's rapid trade growth on various countries for the year of 1992, for example, Arndt, Hertal, Dimaranan, Huff, and McDougall (1997) demonstrated that welfare gains of 0.1 percent change were realized by North America as China's growth increased. Their findings reflected the liberalist economic principle that international commercial exchange increases the welfare of those countries involved in the exchange.[18] In another statistical study, Solomon W. Polachek (1997) employed a cross-sectional and longitudinal regression analysis of countries, and concluded that "the fundamental factor in causing cooperation among countries was trade". This is because, Polachek conceded, "countries seek a peaceful means to protect the wealth gained through international trade" (p. 306).

The liberalist argument was further advanced by Berger, who wrote that "if a socialist economy is opened up to increasing degrees of market forces, a point will be reached at which democratic governance becomes a possibility" (Berger, 1986).[19] Lampton affirmed the view of Berger (Almond, 1991) in his assertion that U.S. trade sanctions against China would only alienate those political factions in China who were supporting political and economic reform (Lampton, 1997).

Liberalism's embracement of free market capitalism was emphasized by Caporaso and Levine, who noted that "the market is designed to free individual initiative and self interest while assuring that choice replaces coercion" (Caporaso and Levine, 1992, p. 160). Historically, the views of Caporaso and Levine were epitomized in the work of Schumpeter, in his thesis that "the discipline of industry and the market train people in economic rationalism" (1955, p. 68). Economic rationalism, Schumpeter asserted, also individualizes, and rational individuals demand democratic governance. Comparably, in present time, Donlan (1997) maintained that "the world's freedom requires open borders for business — that mass markets require consumer sovereignty and the freedom to choose products. The freedom of choice, then, becomes natural" (p. 62). With regard to U.S.-China policy, Harland (1994/95) and Simon (1996) maintained that the most effective way to promote U.S.-China relations was through the reciprocal opening of markets and the freedom to conduct business in those markets. Following the liberalist tradition, Harding (1994/95) recommended that U.S. economic engagement with China was the most viable measure to promote political reform in China and to sustain U.S.-China bilateral relations. Increased economic relations with China would then serve as a catalyst for the expansion of China's political, human rights, and economic reforms. The opening of peaceful relations among countries through economic exchange was also highlighted in the U.S.-China policy position of Laura D'Andrea Tyson (1997), who argued that U.S. revocation of China's MFN status would impede the progress of China's democratic reform.

The idea of freedom of choice through a free-market enterprise system is not new, however. In 1776, Adam Smith introduced the concept of free choice through a free market in his economic and moral treatise *The Wealth of Nations*, where he professed that "commerce allows the exercise of moral liberty — the freedom to choose — in a civil society" (Doyle, 1997, p. 233). More than two centuries later, James Lilley (1994/95) expressed that rapid economic growth and Sino-U.S. joint business ventures had done more to improve human rights in China than repeated threats and unilaterally-imposed conditions (p. 37).

Concurring with Lilley, Garten and Zoellick (1998) emphasized that U.S. trade with and investment in China would pave the way to private enterprise, free markets, and the rule of law in China. The authors called this the "soft power" approach because of the indirect effects of U.S.-China commercial interactions that reach beyond the control of government (p. 13). Levine (1996) also accentuated the positive benefits of integrated markets in his opinion that deepened economic integration among countries created a "convergence of economic systems organized along similar lines and moving toward similar levels of development" (p. 54).

An extension of the liberal paradigm was the globalization approach. Simply put, globalization[20] entails the international expansion of laissez-faire[21] capitalism, or "deepened" economic interdependence among nations.[22] Drawing on the work of Ohmae, the major conduit of globalization was the multinational corporation. "Globalization, with its well-run multinationals, looks for good markets, good workers, and they bring in exchange not private deals for officials but the promise of a better life for the people" (Ohmae, 1991, p. 195). As far back as 1916, however, Clark addressed the social obligations of corporations in noting that "the responsibility of business in a democracy was to uphold the social obligations which are defined by the whole community"(Clark, 1916).

Similarly, in 1967, Kaysen (1967) posited that "the large business corporation is in many ways the characteristic institution of American society". The corporation, Kaysen stipulated, reflected three underlying social features: 1) its open, egalitarian character, 2) the rationalization and transformation of production technologies, and 3) the growth of aggregate and per capita income, which together have created a mass middle class over the past generations (p. 210). These American values are extended into the global market by way of the corporation, Kaysen asserted. More precisely, what is good for America is good for the rest of the world.

Based on the opinions of Clark (1916) and Kaysen (1967), Garten (1997) recommended that firms serve as facilitators for improved human rights practices in countries in which they are located. Bernstein and Dicker (1994/95), as well, underscored the positive role of corporations in promoting democratic values of individual freedom and human rights. The authors asserted that "Washington must press the corporate community to act on its claim that business can be a positive force for human rights" (p. 45). In consonant, Graham (1996) found that most studies on the impact of national policy on globalization alluded to the potential benefits global firms could bring to societies, and that "national policies could even disrupt or interfere with those benefits" (p. 42). As Ohmae noted, the age of the superpower has past and has been replaced with an economic interdependence[23] of nations, which allows individuals access to the best and cheapest goods and services (Ohmae, 1991).

One of the outcomes of market liberalization has been the deepening of U.S.-China economic relations through the U.S. private sector, as explained by Lardy (1994). Lardy discerned that over the past decade, U.S. corporations have exported advanced machinery and transportation equipment to China to help forward China's marketization and modernization plans. Reciprocally, China's industries have exported finished consumer goods to the United States at prices the average U.S. consumer can afford (p. 116-17). According to the economic principles of the division of labor and specialization, professed by Adam Smith,[24] the U.S.-China economic relationship is a win-win proposition.

Unlike realism, which claims that morality is relative and subject to the interpretations of different societies, morality in liberalism is thought to be absolute (Kant, 1970). In Kant's first proposition on morality, he explained that an unqualified "good will" was sufficient by itself, and that it made no difference whether or not one's actions of "good will" were a success or a failure.[25] "Kantian moral theory assumes the existence of a single pattern of moral reasoning. The abstract rational process is presumed to bear a single and universal result, irrespective of different cultures" (Renteln, 1990, p. 50).

The universalist conception of human rights was strongly illustrated in the work of John Rawls who held the opinion that human rights were of the civil and political kind (Ben Rogers, 1999).[26] The basis for Rawls' liberalist perspective on human rights was that he believed that "the most distinctive feature of human nature is our ability to choose our own ends". Rawls distinguished that "our most fundamental duty in dealing with our fellow citizens is to respect this capacity for autonomy" (Ben Rogers, 1999, p. 58). In the tradition of Kant (1970) and Rawls (1971), Doyle (1997) insisted that "the liberal priority of freedom sets the parameters for global justice" (p. 435).

Jeffrey Isaac (1996), in examining the political philosophy of Hannah Arendt, uncovered Arendt's liberal universalist perspective on human rights. Isaac explained that Arendt, in her discussion of the politics of human dignity, theorized that "local, regional and global forms of citizenship were equally possible and equally real". Isaac further observed that Arendt's vision of a global collective empowerment, central to such groups as the Helsinki Citizens Assembly[27] and Amnesty International, would call attention to human rights abuses and would empower citizens to act collectively to further the expansion of universal human rights. Arendt's political theory, as interpreted by Isaac, underscored the universality of moral actions professed in the teachings of Kant.

Morality in liberal theory was further evidenced in the human rights position of Neier (1993), who argued that press freedom, prohibition of detention without trial, and the right of all persons to be free from cruel and arbitrary punishment, were fundamental rights of all human beings. Van Ness (1996), in speaking of human rights issues in Sino-American relations, recommended that policymakers from the United States and China give the same priority to human rights issues as they do to economic and strategic issues. The author reflected the liberal universalist perspective that state governments comply with international human rights treaties in a collective effort to protect human rights throughout the globe.

Moral issues, of course, cross into the economic realm, as Adam Smith defined in his moral and economic philosophy. In his 1776 treatise, *The Wealth of Nations,* Smith addressed morality in his assertion that "free commerce allows the exercise of moral liberty" (Doyle, 1997, p. 233). Smith's view on morality served as the foundation for those liberal scholars and practitioners who were of the opinion that free trade would lead to a freer people, and more specifically, that greater U.S. economic ties with China would hasten China's political and human rights reforms.

Kidder (1994) discussed morality from the perspective of the market and concluded that the moral obligations of states in the future demand a focus on the way corporations and markets should be regulated, and that these regulations should lie in a body of international law that would encompass a "global code of ethics" (p. 34). According to these liberal views, morality and its encompassing concern for human rights can influence U.S. foreign policy decisions.

The strength of the liberalist argument is that, in its principle that free trade leads to peace among nations, liberal theory reaches beyond the strictly power-based motives of realism. Liberal theory, in its focus on international institutions and economic interdependence opens the parameters for evaluating state behavior because it reaches beyond a state-centered analysis. The liberalist argument, therefore, with its focus on the economic and political interdependence of states, is useful in explaining decisions made by U.S. policymakers where international cooperation and multilateral solutions are required.

The liberalist argument may be useful in explaining U.S. policy decisions pertaining to pressing transnational issues as human rights violations, ethnic conflict, migration, environmental decay, refugee crises, as well as the personal security of individuals and groups. Such personal securities include the security of food, shelter, personal safety, and employment. These personal securities, of course, can be considered universal to all societies. They extend across nations and across national borders.

U.S. policymakers who base their decisions on the liberalist argument may have such idealistic notions in mind as the liberal tenets of a global village of peace, freedom, and harmony achieved through the avenues of international economic exchange. Through economic exchange, global consumers benefit from the freedom of choice of products and services. The products and services they choose effect which products corporations produce, suggesting that citizens, as consumers, are an influential part of the global market-driven economy. Liberalism, for example, because of its emphasis on international trade as a carrier of peace, may have strong utility in explaining U. S. decisions on foreign trade policy.

The weakness of the liberalist argument, however, is that it may underestimate the importance of the concern of survival as a motivation for state behavior. This survival would include perceived or real security threats. Thus liberal theory may lack explanatory power for U.S. decisions on national security. Further, as Morganthau (1967) has warned, ulterior motives of some policymakers may be hidden under the guise of liberal altruism. Additionally, liberal theory, because of its universalist foundation that "what is good for one is good for all", may not fully be useful in explaining U.S. foreign policy behavior. The theory, for example, may be too idealistic in its belief that all nations have the same shared mutual interests and values. For example, who is to determine what is best for all? Not every country is democratic, nor wishes to be followers of the U.S. free market version. As Haass explained:

> The active promotion of democracy is a luxury policymakers cannot always afford. The United States has no choice but to overlook a lack of democracy with friends of the Persian Gulf, where energy and security take precedence. At the same time, a foreign policy predicated on spreading democracy can be difficult to implement vis-à-vis our foes, either because we lack the means to influence them or because we have more pressing concerns. Thus, a democratic North Korea would be nice, but in the meantime we had better focus on Pyongyang's nuclear ambitions. Similarly, we would like to see China demonstrate greater respect for human rights, but for now we need China's help with North Korea while we seek access to its enormous market. And even when it is agreed that promoting democracy should take precedence, the fact remains that engineering foreign societies is an always difficult and often dangerous business. (Haass, 1997, p. 46)

Furthermore, economic and political liberalists may exaggerate the role of corporations in their ability to enhance the standard of living of global citizenries through economic exchange, or investment. The liberalist argument, for example, may overlook the fact that international economic exchange may not serve to enhance the welfare of all. Macroeconomic policies of individual states can affect — both positively and negatively — a state's internal distribution of resources.

Richardson (1991), for example, elaborated on this view. "Global commerce is undergoing a transformation as firms are becoming mobile, sharing technologies and management, and forming alliances with competing multinational corporations. The liberal theory of international political economy has not confronted these new realities of corporate behavior".[28] Unlike the pacifying effect of commercial relations that liberal theory espouses, "the new corporate patterns are occasionally interstate rivalry and conflict" (Richardson, 1991).

Radicalism

Grounded in subtheories of class conflict, exploitation of labor, and imperialism, espoused in the teachings of Karl Marx and Frederick Engels (1994) and V.I. Lenin (1947),[29] followers of radicalism analyze U.S. foreign policy behavior from the classic Marxist-Leninist sense. Like the utopian world envisioned by Woodrow Wilson, radical thought also holds its own utopian vision, one in which there is a "socialist future of abundance, no markets, no money, no wages, and no production for exchange. The division of labor would be overcome, and the state would wither away. The administration of men would be replaced by the administration of things" (Karl Marx, as discussed by Nove, 1992, p. 39). Marx viewed international economic exchange as a form of exploitation of wage laborers (the proletariat) by the bourgeoisie:

> It [the bourgeoisie] has resolved personal worth into exchange value, and in place of the numberless indefeasible chartered freedoms, has set up that single, unconscionable freedom — Free Trade. In one word, exploitation, veiled by religious and political illusions, it has substituted naked, shameless, direct, brutal exploitation. (Marx and Engels, 1994, p. 11)

Economic relations among states, according to Marx, were nothing more than the satisfaction of ever-increasing wants that require the products of distant lands (p. 12). Similar to the realist school of isolationism, Marx believed that international commerce destroys the foundation of national industries and the self-sufficiency of nations.[30] Radical theory is guided by the relationship between capital and labor, whereby capital gradually displaces and usurps labor. Radical theorists believe that there is a constant struggle between labor and owners of capital which create class divisions and inequalities within an economic system.

David Shambaugh (1991) explained that "the primary focus of Marxian analysis is economic. The principal actors are monopoly capitalists and their multinational corporations, creating an international dominant elite class. The main geographical targets of an imperialist agenda are the developing countries" (pp. 235, 226-27). Based on this view, for example, radicals portray the U.S.-China economic relationship as exploitative, with China as a target of a U.S. imperialistic expansion in the search for more wealth by exploiting the Chinese labor force and subverting the Chinese regime.[31]

In accordance with radical theory, Streeten (1992) criticized liberalism in his contention that the predatory state inevitably acts in its own self-interest and that of powerful pressure groups; that there is no place for disinterested, benign, altruistic government policies; only the forces of the free market are capable of advancing the society (pp. 24-25). Streeten denigrated market-based liberalism because he thought that in its own successful function, the market overlooks the inequitable distribution of resources and power (pp. 34-35). He referred to Amartya Sen to clarify his point, where Sen analyzed famines and concluded that even though total food supply was adequate, the purchasing power (or entitlements) of the poor had declined. "In those conditions the market was all too successful while the people starved" (pp. 24-25).

Radical theory was discussed in the context of post-Cold War globalization by William Robinson (1996, pp. 625-33). Robinson maintained that the United States, as the global hegemon, was leading an emergent transnational elite backed by the power of transnational capital concomitant with a decrease in state power. "Economic globalization generates pressures for integration into a single political regime. Polyarchy is the emergent global political superstructure" (p. 654). Robinson further observed that this emergent superstructure provides the basis for a new world order patterned after the Gramscian[32] model of hegemony (p. 654). In the radical interpretation, U.S. foreign policy is predicated on competing elite groups that create a global structure of social inequalities and imbalances.

Radical theory was further conveyed by Rogowski (1987), who, in applying the Stolper-Samuelson theorem,[33] argued that increased international trade activity created domestic and political class cleavages. Rogowski defined his theory of political and class cleavages within regional areas.

The land rich and still underdeveloped economies of Latin America find that expanding trade displaces "populist" coalitions of labor and capital and bring renewed influence to the landed sectors. The areas of Asia and southern Europe that are economically backward and abundant only in labor, experience labor militancy, and in a few cases, revolutionary workers movements. The few economies rich in both capital and land — principally those of North America, Australia and New Zealand, experience class conflict and a suppression of labor as international trade increases. (pp. 1130-31)

Noam Chomsky (1997) also reflected the radical ideology of an international capitalist class as the dominant global power. An international class war and a north-south divide fueled by "supranational" corporations and financial institutions, dominated the world economy. In his essay, "NAFTA: The Masters of Mankind", Chomsky labeled supranational corporations and financial institutions as the "masters" that dominate the world economy, including international trade regimes. Serving the interests of corporations and financial institutions, Chomsky contended, were the International Monetary Fund (IMF), the World Bank, the Group of Seven industrialized nations, the GATT/WTO and various other institutions, all together shaping a new "de facto world government and a new imperial age".

Similarly, Bienefeld (1994) examined globalization during the post-Cold War era and concluded that globalist policy was "a new form of imperialism"

(p. 31). An imperialism that is "dominated by a single hegemonic power seeking to establish a liberalized global economy, though, one in which the hegemonic power maintains the right to make exceptions when it so chooses" (p. 45). Bienefeld qualified that the imperialism of the new world order gave the hegemonic power greater ability to supersede national sovereignty (p. 44). The United States, therefore, as the reigning hegemon, in Bienefeld's opinion, would be seen as imperialistic in its foreign policy motives. Inimical to the free market tenets of liberal theory, Bienefeld condemned free market ideology, and thought that economies should be politically controlled (p. 47). On the other hand, Silbey (1997) emphasized that globalization was not simply a matter of a shift of jurisdiction from the nation-state to the globe, but rather "a change in how the collective life of individuals were to be governed — a shift from politics to economics — that all land, labor and resources be available for exchange through commodification and pricing" (pp. 216-17). Like William Robinson (1996) and Bienefeld (1994), Silbey (1997) viewed globalization as a form of "postmodern colonialism" that undermined the social justice of individuals and the sovereignty of nations.[34] In this same light, regarding U.S.-China policy, for example, Perez (1995) argued that U.S. trade pressures on China were a method of the U.S. ruling class to dismantle China's state-owned property and to allow the property to fall into the control of U.S. corporations (p. 11).

Wallerstein (1993) described the post-Cold War era as a "black period" for liberalists because the egalitarian promises of global liberalism were not kept. Rather, liberalism created a dominant elite, and excluded a large segment of the world's population from sharing in economic and political beliefs (p. 14). Similarly, Sweezy (1989) predicted the decline of American global power in the 1990s, and in its place, a structure of competing trade and currency blocks, or "competing imperialisms" (p. 15). Accompanying the decline of American imperialism would be, according to Sweezy, the end of imperialism's guiding light: liberal capitalism.[35]

Radical theory was examined from the moral perspective by J. Philip Wogaman (1977). Referring to Karl Marx as the father of socialist thought, Wogaman concluded that Marx rejected any ideological thinking. Economic and social matters, according to Wogaman's interpretation of Marx, were fully scientific and therefore not dependent upon value judgment (p. 19), although, Wogaman qualified, this was not to negate that socialist philosophy did not have moral appeal. Marx's theory of historical materialism was based on a very human concept — that man should not be separated from the fruits of labor — which are the very "life essence" (p. 59). In agreement, Keith Graham (1988) thought that the Marxian quest to transform workers in society was not in itself a moral imperative, but that it was linked closely to morality because of its human concern

(p. 17). Ryan (1988) also examined Marx from a moral point of view and concluded that "Marx both appeared to condemn capitalism as unjust and immoral, and at the same time disparaged all moral assessments as futile and intellectually worthless" (pp. 117-27).

On the other hand, Edel, Flower and O'Connor (1989b) regarded that in radical theory, "no general principles could really be understood apart from the relations of functions — the modes of production and distribution, material changes taking place in technology, the shift in social institutions and class struggle" (pp. 391-93). The writers clarified, however, that morality did exist in radical theory to the extent that whatever morals there were in a society were those of the ruling class — its concept of the good life, obligations, and responsibilities (p. 393). Similarly, Meyers (1991) noted that ethics existed in radical theory only in the context of class struggle, or in efforts to wipe out the bourgeois and their false notions of right and wrong (p. 31). According to the radicalist argument, such moral concerns as human rights abuses, would play no role, or at best, a limited role in U.S. foreign policy.

The strength of the radical paradigm as an explanation for U.S. behavior is that it accounts for actions that may be overlooked by other theoretical approaches. The theory's focus on an emergent post-Cold War international capitalist class, for example, may account for ulterior motives in U.S. foreign policy decisions. With emphasis on the corporation as the carrier of the power of the capitalist class, radical theory may explain U.S. efforts to expand capital markets and corporations throughout the globe.

Radicalism's strength may also be in its ability to explain U.S. foreign economic policy failures. Radical theory, for example, may more easily account for the widening national and global wage gaps between the bourgeois and the proletariat classes.[36] In its principle of a purely equitable and classless society, radicalism may more readily predict and identify economic policy that creates social imbalances within the world system.

However, radicalism's premise that the behavior of capitalist states is solely guided by corporate interests and financial institutions is somewhat myopic. Radicalism neglects to consider such broader international interests as international regimes, international organizations, and above all, a global economic interdependence of nations that results in international cooperation rather than immisseration. As well, the radical version of hegemonic theory neglects to see that states are restrained from acting alone,[37] and therefore, the domination of a single imperialist aggressor may be abated or challenged by another. Moreover, radicalism fails to acknowledge that governments have the capacity, both domestically and collectively, to regulate corporations, and that even under the strictest "free market" mechanism, governments and corporations can and do work in synergy, and that there is, by nature, a check between the public and the private sectors.[38] For example, Huszagh, Huszagh and Hanks (1992) noted that in the United States, there is a two-way interaction between the firm and the government. "Monetary policies are exercised by the Federal Reserve through controls over the money supply, interest rates and reserve requirements. The Congressional and Executive branches control fiscal policy through tax legislation and spending programs" (p. 6). These individual and collective actions, along with free-market policies, the authors argued, can influence industries, and in turn, industries can shape government policy.

Summary

U.S. trade policy toward China is complex. This chapter has considered competing theoretical perspectives which have provided a basis for analysis of the 1994 decision regarding China's human rights practices and MFN. The realist literature consisted of two perspectives: those scholars and practitioners who advocated U.S. economic engagement with states, and those who advocated isolationism. Both realist perspectives were driven by the need to protect U.S. interests from outside threats, such as the threat of a resurgence of communism, or the threat of military aggression. The former realist perspective was based upon the notion that economic engagement with states would prevent states from acting unilaterally in economic decisions.

Alliances among like-minded governments and the support of liberal trade and multilateralism helped to assure the U.S. economic and military hegemony (Haass, 1997, pp. 43-45). The latter realist perspective of isolationism, which represented a much smaller school, was premised on the notion that trade with and investment in "rogue states" could provide the wealth that could fuel a state's military capabilities which, in turn, could potentially threaten the United States. Insofar as morality was concerned, moral considerations, in realist theory, were not an issue and therefore did not drive U.S. foreign policy.

Scholars of political and economic liberalism stressed that U.S. economic engagement with states would enhance the welfare of all, and would therefore hasten the pace of political and human rights reforms in China and elsewhere throughout the world. As opposed to realism, where morality played no role in U.S. foreign policy, morality was a significant factor in policies guided by liberalist principles. U.S. trade with China, for example, was considered to be the moral thing to do because it enhanced the lives of peoples of both nations and introduced the concept of freedom of choice, with the intent that the freedom to choose products in a free-market economy would pave the way for further individual political rights and freedoms. Whether labeled imperialism, neo-imperialism, or neocolonialism, advocates of radical theory viewed the United States as the imperialistic aggressor toward developing countries, and therefore toward China. U.S. monopoly capital and multinational corporations were at the root of the inequitable world order. The inequitable world order created an international capitalist class with the United States as the core capitalist power. Radicals viewed U.S. economic relations with states as avenues of exploitation. Multinational corporations were the culprits in their efforts to dismantle national industries and the self-sufficiency of nations. In the radical view, corporate interests are key to U.S. trade policy. Morality, as in realism, was not a factor in the radical argument.

In the final analysis, no singular school of thought can serve as an explanation for U.S. foreign policy decisions. The restructuring of states and the transnationalization of firms during the post-Cold war era have encouraged many scholars to reassess traditional approaches to the analyses of political and economic events. For example, Rodrik (1997), follower of the neoclassical economic school,[39] criticized those economists who advocated globalization because he believed that globalization did not assure a benefit to all. Globalization, Rodrik argued, had widened the global skill gap causing social tensions between highly skilled groups and unskilled or semi-skilled labor groups.[40]

Rodrik suggested maintaining a balance between the market and society — one that would promote private enterprise without undermining social cohesion (pp. 4, 13). Schlesinger (1997), similarly, did not see the utopian picture of the dedicated liberalist. Though not a self-proclaimed radical, Schlesinger predicted the decline of a U.S. foreign policy driven by laissez-faire ideology because of the problems the market cannot solve. "Unbridled capitalism, with low wages, long hours, and exploited workers, excites social resentment, revives class warfare, and infuses Marxism with new life" (p. 11). Schlesinger may not have been advocating the radical view, but rather an alternative form of humanized capitalism. In further emphasis of the transitional phase of theoretical schools, Ruggie (1997) noted that even Kissinger, "the master practitioner of the realist craft" (p. 92, citing Kissinger, 1994) remarked that "without the Soviet threat, realism by itself cannot suffice to frame U.S. foreign policy — that realism must be coupled with a vision that provided the American public with a sense of hope and possibility that are in their essence, conjectural" (p. 835).

Chapter 2 has provided the theoretical framework which will serve as the foundation for more detailed analysis of the 1994 U.S. decision to delink

China's human rights practices from most-favored-nation status. The following chapter offers an historical perspective of the U.S.-China bilateral trade relationship and will establish an historical linkage between international trade and human rights in U.S. foreign policy.

Endnotes

1   As Stephen D. Cohen emphasizes, "International economic policy by its nature overlaps the discipline of political science. Each tends to approach the broad field of international economic relations with certain preexisting instincts, knowledge and objectiveness. ... Few governments prefer to allow important economic decisions to be made purely by the invisible hand of the free market rather than by political process. In even the most free market oriented country, government macroeconomic monetary and fiscal policies, and regulatory policies, not the invisible hand of the marketplace, are the principal determinants of domestic economic activity". However, Cohen qualified that "external factors, or global economic developments can enhance, alter, or disrupt a chosen domestic economic policy course" (Stephen Cohen, 1988, pp. 23-24).

2   See also Keohane and Nye (1989, p. 11), where Keohane and Nye define power as "the ability of an actor to get others to do something they otherwise might not do (and at an acceptable cost to the actor). Power can also be conceived in terms of control over outcomes".

3   Haass further clarifies that "the real choice facing the United States is not between unilateralism and multilateralism, but between two versions of the latter: the U.S. leadership approach and neo-internationalism. What distinguishes them are matters of substance and style. Neo-internationalism places far more emphasis on harnessing U.S. activism to formal institutions, especially the United Nations and standing regional alliances. U.S. leadership, by contrast, is based more on informal coalitions and arrangements that bring the United States together with other like-minded parties" (p. 57).

4   Hans Morganthau (1967) defined "balance of power" as "a policy, a state of affair, and approximately equal or any distribution of power" (p. 167).

5   Morganthau (1967) explained that "the actual interdependence of nations and the actual political, military and economic dependence of certain nations upon others may make it difficult or impossible for certain nations to pursue independent domestic and foreign policies" (p. 304).

6   John Stremlau identified ten big emerging markets. They included China, India, Indonesia, Brazil, Mexico, Turkey, South Korea, South Africa, Poland, and Argentina. Of these emerging markets, Stremlau identified China as the largest (1994/95, p. 24).

7   An underlying premise of realist theory is that a state must be in constant readiness for war. This concept is rooted in the Hobbesian principle that "Out of civil states, there is always war of every one against every one" (Hobbes, 1994, p. 76).

8   Nye further asserted that "As interdependence grows, stronger transnational ties between the United States and the East Asian economies will make it difficult for East Asians to exclude us [the United States]".

9   Note that the school of economic conservatism runs parallel to the political realist school of isolationism. Andrew Gamble (1996), citing Friedrich von Hayek, observed that the school of conservative economics embraces nationalism, rejects free trade and competition and prefers national to international solutions.

10   Neorealist Kenneth N. Waltz develops the thesis of states' constant threat of war in his 1979 classic, *Theory of International Politics*.

11   Morganthau defines relative power as "a continuing effort to maintain and to increase the power of one's own nation and to keep in check or reduce the power of other nations" (p. 224-27).

12   Realist theory claims that a state must be in constant readiness for war. This concept is rooted in the Hobbesian principle that "Out of civil states, there is always war of every one against every one" (Hobbes, 1994, p. 6).

13   Realist theory, for example, can easily explain the April 7, 1950 national security policy of NSC 68, which continued for three decades. The policy was based on the perceived Soviet threat. "For the authors of NSC 68, American interests could not be defined apart from the threat the Soviet Union posed to them. 'Frustrating the Kremlin design,' as the document so frequently put it, became an end in itself, not a means to a larger end" (Gaddis and Nitze, 1980, p. 167).

14   "The regime challenges the traditional realpolitik ideal of the autonomous, hierarchical state that keeps its options open, but its information and decision-making procedures closed . . . the regime is a bridge to international cooperation in that it opens the flow of information to states" (Keohane, 1984, pp. 258-59).

15   "To the liberal tradition, the key to world order is less the balance of military power than it is the form of economic exchange and balance of fiscal power . . . commercial liberalism proceeds from the belief that open trading systems, less than military might, influence the prospects for peaceful politics. Once a country opens its markets to the world, democracy follows, for as the standard of living rises, so does the thirst for democracy, and democratic states behave less militantly than do closed economic and political systems" (Rosenberg, 1990).

16   Immanuel Kant, philosopher and proponent of human freedom, sets forth the principles of liberalism in his renowned work, *To Perpetual Peace: A Philosophical Sketch* (1983, chaps. 1-3). Kant professed that democracies are less prone to engage in war with one another because the consent of the citizenry is required . . . that there is mutual gain for nations involved in trade and commerce, and that shared commercial interests among nations has a pacifying effect. John Stuart Mill later wrote that "It is commerce which is rendering war obsolete by strengthening and multiplying the personal interests which act in natural opposition to it. And it may be said without exaggeration that the great extent and rapid increase of international trade, in being the principal guarantor of peace in the world, is the great permanent security for the uninterrupted progress of . . . the human race" (Mill, 1848, p. 582).

17   U.S. President Woodrow Wilson, envisioned a universal utopian liberal democracy. As a founding father of liberalism, Wilson outlined his famous idealist agenda in his "Fourteen Points Plan", in January 1918, at the Versailles Peace Conference. That "peace would also be furthered by the removal, in so far as possible, of all economic barriers", was one of the 14 points elaborated in Wilson's plan.

18   Welfare is defined as the quality of life of individuals in society, or a standard of living based on "disposable income", or "that which individuals may spend in accordance with their preferences, over and above income required for the necessities of life" (Edel, Flower, and O'Connor, 1989).

19 Gabriel A. Almond (1991) also explains that "the relation between capitalism and democracy dominates the political theory of the last two centuries. Capitalism is positively linked with democracy, shares its values and culture, and facilitates its development. This case has been made in historical, logical and statistical terms".

20 The meaning of globalization is nebulous and has been subject to debate in both its extent and definition. For the purpose of discussion, two definitions of globalization are provided;
   1. globalization is a "deregulation of financial markets, international mobility of capital, the rise of corporate mergers and acquisitions, integration of business activities worldwide, establishment of integrated operations abroad (including R&D and financing), global sourcing for components, strategic alliances, the rise of information technology, where technology is the primary catalyst, the equalization of global patterns, the diminished role of national governments and parliaments and designs for a new generation of rules and institutions for global governance, a transformation of a state-centered analysis of the integration of world societies into a global political and economic system led by a core power, sociocultural processes as centered on 'One Earth' . . . the 'globalist' movement . . . planetary citizens" (Ruigrok and Van Tulder, 1993, in Boyer and Drache, 1996, p. 66);
   2. globalization is "an increased global mobility of goods, services, capital and employers, and the subsequent increased international integration of markets for goods, services and capital" (Rodrik, 1997, p. 1).

21 As illuminated by George Cho (1995), the theory of laissez faire is that "all participants benefit from specialization and exchange. Often, the term laissez faire is used synonymously with free trade". Free trade is defined as "that trade in which goods can be imported and exported without any barriers in the form of tariffs, physical quotas or any kind of restriction" (p. 125).

22 Ohmae (1991) elaborated this view in his "Declaration of Interdependence Toward the World-2005". Ohmae's "Declaration of Interdependence" parallels the utopian vision of Woodrow Wilson, as in a unified global community united by free-market democracies.

23 Robert O. Keohane defined interdependence as "situations characterized by reciprocal effects among countries or among actors in different countries. Interdependence most simply defined, means *mutual* dependence". Keohane contrasts the meaning of interdependence with the meaning of complex interdependence, the latter being a far broader issue because it involves the entire international arena and a network of multilateral institutions (Keohane and Nye, 1989, 206, 8).

24 As Adam Smith (1994) proclaimed, "The greatest improvement in the productive powers of labour, and the greater part of the skill, dexterity, and judgment with which it is any where directed, or applied, seem to have been the effects of the division of labour". Much of Smith's economic philosophy was based on de Mandeville: "No number of men, when once they enjoy quiet, and no man needs to fear his neighbor, will be long without learning to divide and subdivide their labour" (de Mandeville, 1723, 335).

25 "The moral merit of an agent of goodness of his character does not depend upon the achievement of the intended result. If an agent acts from good will, then he acquires just as much moral credit for his action, whether he fails or succeeds" (Kant, 1970).

26 Rogers makes a distinction with regard to the liberalism of Rawls. "Because Rawls insists that taking rights seriously means taking social equality seriously, he is, indeed, a more radical egalitarian theorist than is generally acknowledged, one considerably to the left of traditional welfare-state liberals". In Rawlsian liberalism, Rogers asserts, equal political and civil liberties overlap with a fair distribution of the wealth (p. 64). For a more precise

argument on this, refer to Rawls (1971, chap. 3), where Rawls speaks of the "original position".

27   The Helsinki Citizens Assembly was formed in 1990 by links between East European dissidents and West European peace activists, after the 1975 Helsinki Accords (Isaac, 1996, p. 71).

28   However, "Richardson vindicates the liberal vision, where he states that major commercial states are trying to collaborate, reflecting that collective management would be necessary for prosperity" (Kegley, 1995b, pp. 249-50).

29   Lenin labeled imperialism the highest stage of capitalism: "Imperialism is capitalism in that stage of development in which the dominance of monopolies and finance capital has established itself, in which the export of capital has acquired pronounced importance, in which the division of the world among international trusts has begun, in which the division of all territories of the globe among the great capitalist powers has been completed" (pp. 107-9). At this stage, Marx predicted the demise of capitalism. "The essential condition for the existence of capitalism is wage labor. The development of modern industry cuts from under its feet the very foundation on which the bourgeoisie produces. What the bourgeoisie therefore produces, above all, are its own grave diggers. Its fall and the victory of the proletariat are equally inevitable" (Marx and Engels, 1994, p. 21).

30   "In place of the old local and national seclusion and self-sufficiency, we have intercourse in every direction, universal interdependence of nations. . . . The bourgeoisie, by the rapid improvement of all instruments of production, by the immensely facilitated means of communication, draws all nations, even the most barbarian, into civilization. It compels all nations, on pain of extinction, to adopt the bourgeois mode of production . . . creating a world after its own image" (Marx and Engels, 1994, pp. 12-13).

31   As Marx conveyed, "The cheap prices of its [the bourgeoisie's] commodities are the heavy artillery with which it batters down all Chinese walls, with which it forces the barbarians' intensely obstinate hatred of foreigners to capitulate" [emphasis added] (Marx and Engels, 1994, p. 13).

32   Robinson explains that Gramsci's hegemony is a "consensus protected by the 'armor of coercion,' and the political superstructures of a coherent social order always combine both coercive and consensual-based elements (whether authoritarian or democratic) . . . also that transitions to polyarchy do not involve eliminating coercive apparatus but subordinating that apparatus to civilian elites" (pp. 628-29).

33   In 1944, Wolfgang Stolpher and Paul Samuelson examined the gains and losses from trade protection. "They showed that in any society, protection benefits — and trade liberalization harms — owners of factors in which that society is poorly endowed, relative to the rest of the world, and conversely, that protection harms — and trade liberalization benefits those owners of factors the given society holds abundantly relative to the rest of the world" (William Robinson, 1996, p. 1122, citing Stolpher and Samuelson, 1944). Rogowski further points out that, in fact, the Stolpher Samuelson theorem is an extension of Heckscher-Olin theorem, which states that "under free trade, countries export products whose manufacture uses locally abundant, and import products whose manufacture uses locally scarce factors intensively" (Rogowski, 1987, p. 1134, note 1).

34   Silbey defined postmodern colonialism as "an achievement of advanced capitalism and technological innovation seeking a world free from restraints on the opportunity to invent and to invest. It is a world in which size and scale in terms of numbers of persons (who can produce), and numbers of outlets (to disseminate and place the products), and capital (to purchase both labor and land) determine the capacity to saturate local cultures" (pp. 219-20).

35 This decline holds true to Marxist-Leninist theory, where Lenin labeled imperialism the highest stage of capitalism. It is at this stage that Lenin predicted the demise of capitalism.

36 As Chomsky (1997) illustrates, "The international class war is reflected in the United States, where real wages have fallen to the level of the mid-1960s. . . . At the international level", Chomsky reported that "protectionist measures of the industrialized countries reduce national income in the South by about twice the amount of official aid to the region — aid that is itself largely export promotion, most of it directed to richer sectors (less needy, but better consumers). These practices, along with the programs dictated by the International Monetary Fund and World Bank, have helped double the gap between rich and poor countries since 1960. Resource transfers from the poor to the rich amounted to more than $400 billion from 1982 to 1990".

37 Morganthau (1967) explained that "the actual interdependence of nations and the actual political, military and economic dependence of certain nations upon others may make it difficult or impossible for certain nations to pursue independent domestic and foreign policies" (p. 304).

38 For further insights, see Dahl (1998). Here, Dahl states that "all democratic countries have not only rejected a centralized command economy as an alternative to a market economy, but have also rejected a strictly free market economy as an alternative to a mixed economy in which market outcomes are substantially modified by government intervention" (p. 279).

39 Rodrik, in explaining his opinion, remarked that "When I mention economists, I am referring to mainstream economists, as represented by neoclassical economists, of which I count myself as one" (pp. 3-7).

40 Rodrik pointed to the asymmetry between two groups that occur as trade and investment expand across national borders. "The first group consists of owners of capital, highly skilled workers and many professionals who are free to take their resources where they are most in demand. The second group consists of unskilled or semiskilled workers and most middle managers (who are not mobile). Thus globalization creates a greater elasticity of demand for the services of individuals because large segments of the working population can be substituted with working groups across borders. This, for example, has increased the skill premium in the United States and has lowered the skill premium in China" (pp. 4, 13).

3 The Evolution of U.S.-China Trade Policy

In the preceding chapter, the literature review placed U.S. foreign policy — in particular, U.S. foreign economic policy — in the broader perspective, discussing scholarly works within the context of traditional schools of thought. But to grasp more fully the 1994 decision to separate most-favored-nation status from human rights, an historical view is necessary. In this chapter, U.S. trade policy toward China and the linkage of trade and human rights are discussed from the perspective of the past, leading up to the year in which the decision was made.

The chapter weaves a net through U.S. presidential administrations and their trade policies toward China, addressing international and domestic events that influenced those policies, in both the United States and China. In discussing the historical linkage of trade and human rights, the chapter explains avenues through which the United States has exercised economic leverage to advance human rights throughout the world. Finally, the chapter provides a synopsis of the MFN/human rights debate and the immediate political events that surrounded the presidential decision to renew China's most-favored-nation trading status without human rights conditions.

Historical Foundations

The United States and China have been engaging in trade, at least on a minimal scale, for centuries. U.S. commercial contacts with China began soon after independence from British rule. Barred from the prosperous "sugar triangle" trade with the British Caribbean islands, merchants of the U.S. eastern seaboard cities found the China trade, particularly tea from Canton, to be a partial replacement for the lost West Indies trade (Burke, 1972, p. 5). As U.S. companies developed, they expanded to new markets in search of new and greater resources. From the early nineteenth century to 1948-49, at the time of China's takeover by the communist party, China was part of this expansion (Wilkins, 1986).

The first U.S. investments in China were found in Canton, in the year 1786, two years after Canton was opened to U.S. trade. U.S. enterprises, mainly from

Boston and New York, took advantage of the opportunity to buy Chinese teas, cloths, and silks in exchange for American furs, specie, and such agricultural products as tobacco, maize, timber, and peanuts (DePauw, 1988, p. 247). By 1870, U.S. firms had invested about seven million in the China trade,[1] reaching the height of investment in 1930 of $129.3 million (U.S. Dept. of Commerce, 1930, p. 26). U.S. businesses continued to operate in China even during the Japanese occupation of Shanghai, from 1937 to the start of World War II. After the war, U.S. entrepreneurs returned to China with hopes to continue business, only to find disastrous conditions (Wilkins, 1986, pp. 275-84). When communism finally triumphed on the Mainland on October 1, 1949 and the People's Republic of China was formed, U.S. export controls were tightened, so that by December 1950, all U.S. shipments to China were banned. The Truman administration had blocked or frozen all U.S. assets that were owned by Chinese nationals, as well as the assets of any U.S. residents in China.[2] Exports to and imports from China were prohibited (Alexander Eckstein, 1971, pp. xxi-xxiii). At the same time, the Chinese communist party had officially taken control of all U.S. property and assets in China.

The total U.S. trade embargo against China actually culminated at the point of China's entry into the Korean War, in late 1950, when China posed a direct threat to the United States because of its military troop support to Korea (Garson, 1971, pp. 6-7). All doors to trade and investment between the United States and China, therefore, closed.[3] The mutual isolation of the two countries was not to be broken until efforts for rapprochement were taken by the Nixon administration. It was in the mid-1960s, however, that a change began to occur in the thinking of U.S. trade policy toward China. In March of 1966, eminent scholars John King Fairbank and Donald S. Zagoria testified before Congress:

> Containment of China alone is a blind alley unless we add policies of constructive competition and international contact. Peiping's rulers shout aggressively out of manifold frustrations. Isolation intensifies their ailment and makes it self perpetuating, and we need to encourage international contact with China on many fronts.[4]

> Our only hope to achieve a stable and tolerable relationship with communist China is to do all we can to promote not a change of the system — which can only be done by War — but a change within the system. The kind of evolution which is already transforming Russia and the East European communist countries will have to come. . . . We can help to hasten its growth.[5]

Domestic policies of the People's Republic of China also precipitated the relaxation of U.S. economic restrictions toward China. In 1960, for example,

China reversed its "lean to one side" policy of a close economic alliance with the Soviet Union (Alexander Eckstein, 1971, p. xxi). The Chinese communist party believed that Soviet communism was not adhering to the basic tenets of communism and therefore declared that "Chinese communism was the only pure form of communism. Mao, not Khrushchev, was the heir to the communist tradition. And Peking [Beijing], not Moscow, should be the rightful center of the communist world" (Congressional Quarterly, Inc., 1980, p. 122).

Future domestic events in China eased tensions between the United States and China. Ten years after the Sino-Soviet break, in April 1970, the *People's Daily*, the *Liberation Daily*, and the theoretical journal *Hongqui,* responded to Brezhnev's invasion of Czechoslovakia. The journals published that "Brezhnev's support of a socialist community based on the excusable grounds of the Brezhnev Doctrine,[6] was nothing more than a synonym for a colonial empire with Russia at the center".[7] The editorials concluded that the Brezhnev doctrine was indeed hegemony. Tensions between China and the Soviet Union were further exacerbated by the growing Ussuri River clashes.[8] To a great extent, then, the U.S.-China rapprochement was inherent in the Sino-Soviet split (Kissinger, 1979, p. 1052).

The Sino-Soviet split was not the only factor that led to warmer relations between the United States and China. Global market forces accelerated the loosening of U.S. isolationist policies toward China. Although the nations of western Europe are democracies and political allies with the United States, they are, at the same time economic competitors (Congressional Quarterly, Inc., 1980, p. 340). While the United States had implemented stringent economic policies toward China, its western allies had not. Australia, Canada, Great Britain, West Germany, and France accounted for approximately three-quarters of China's imports by the mid-1960s. Japan was China's major supplier of wheat and flour. Great Britain and West Germany together accounted for $50 million in Chinese exports (pp. 4-5).[9] China's economic contacts with U.S. western allies weakened the U.S. unilateral trade embargo against China while at the same time giving U.S. business competitors an edge in the China market. Moreover, by the late 1960s, U.S. businesses were looking to avert Japan's restrictive trade policies. By 1969, Japan's exports to the United States far exceeded its imports from the United States (Kissinger, 1979, p. 338).

All of these micro-macro economic and political events triggered a U.S. gravitational pull toward China. By the time Nixon had officially taken office in 1969, international and domestic forces had already been in motion to help forward the Nixon administration's goal of normalizing relations with China.

The first U.S. initiative at opening trade relations with China had taken place in March 1969, when President Nixon's then Assistant for National

Security Affairs, Henry Kissinger,[10] requested that U.S. trade restrictions with Asian communist countries be re-examined. The assessment resulted in a slight relaxation of the U.S. trade embargo against China. The ban on travel by U.S. citizens to China was lifted, and U.S. tourists were permitted to purchase up to US$100.00 worth of Chinese-made noncommercial goods (DePauw, 1981, p. 3). By December 1969, the U.S. government announced that subsidiaries and affiliates of U.S. firms abroad would be authorized to sell nonstrategic goods to communist China and buy communist Chinese products for resale in foreign markets (Congressional Quarterly, Inc., 1980, p. 7).

From this point forward, further trade liberalization developed. In 1971, the selective licensing of U.S. goods for export to the PRC was authorized.[11] Also during this time, the 1971 Peterson Report (1971) of the Nixon Council on International Economic Policy matriculated throughout the White House. The report disclosed America's declining competitiveness and share of the world wealth, and recommended that major attention be given to U.S. commercial policy in order to enhance job creation (Nivola, 1997, p. 235).

Previous to Nixon's memorable trip to China, Kissinger had visited Beijing several times to meet with Premier Zhou En-lai to pave the way for Nixon's meeting. In his pre-trip trade speech of 1971, Nixon remarked:

> China was potentially one of five great economic superpowers and would determine the course of great events in the remainder of the 20th century. . . . The very success of our policy of ending the isolation of Mainland China will mean an immense escalation of their economic challenge not only to us, but to others in the world.[12]

Soon after Nixon's visit to China on February 21, 1972, and the subsequent signing of the Shanghai Communiqué,[13] U.S.-China bilateral trade began to flourish. Beginning with no trade at all, the United States became, by 1983, China's third leading trading partner, and China, the United States' seventh largest trading partner (Qi, 1993, p. 32). Table 3.1 displays the magnitude and growth of U.S.-China bilateral trade. From 1972 to 1980, total U.S.-China trade increased from US$.092 billion in 1972, to $4.7 billion in 1980. After the United States formally recognized the People's Republic of China on January 1, 1979[14] and subsequently withdrew formal recognition of Taiwan,[15] U.S.-China bilateral trade increased dramatically to US$78.6 billion by 1997.

The U.S.-China trade, however, was ultimately solidified by the U.S. conditional restoration of most-favored-nation status to the PRC on February 1, 1980,[16] during the Carter administration.[17] After that, total U.S. trade with China increased from US$4.7 billion in 1980 to US$78.6 billion in 1997. U.S.-China

Table 3.1   U.S.-China Bilateral Trade 1972-1997 (US$billions)

Years	U.S. Exports	U.S. Imports	Total Trade	U.S. Trade Balance
1972	0.06	0.032	0.092	0.028
1974	0.8	0.1	0.9	0.7
1976	0.1	0.2	0.3	-0.1
1978	0.8	0.3	1.1	0.5
1980	3.7	1.0	4.7	2.7
1982	2.9	2.2	5.1	0.7
1984	3.0	3.0	6.0	1.0
1986	3.1	4.7	7.8	-1.6
1988	5.0	8.5	13.5	-3.5
1990	4.8	16.3	21.1	-11.5
1992	7.5	27.4	34.9	-19.9
1994	9.3	41.3	50.6	-32.0
1996	12.0	54.4	66.4	-42.4
1997	12.8	65.8	78.6	-53.0

Note: Total trade = (x + m) trade balance = (x - m).

Source: Direction of Trade Statistics Yearbook (1980, 1985, 1990, 1995, 1996, 1997, 1998).

economic relations grew to include the transfer of some technology as well. In 1980, for example, President Carter approved the U.S. transfer of the new U.S. Landsat photo reconnaissance satellite to China, and facilitated further scientific and technological exchanges between U.S. and Chinese scientists (Congressional Quarterly, Inc., 1980, pp. 260, 263).

Throughout the 1980s, the U.S.-China policy was to encourage a strong and stable China, a China that was independent of the Soviet Union and not vulnerable to Soviet military pressure (Wethington, 1988, pp. 196-98). A combination of economic and strategic concerns formed the rationale behind President Reagan's economic policy toward China. In May 1983, Reagan expanded exports to China to include military products and products made with higher levels of technology.[18] To help carry out his defensive trade strategy, Reagan directed that China be moved from a category P country group, which held strict export restrictions to communist countries, to a category V group, which included most noncommunist countries, thereby allowing a greater flow of high-technology goods to be exported to the PRC (p. 198). "Between October 1983 and September 1984, the U.S. government approved commercial export licenses of defense articles and services valued at about US$72.6 million, practically six times greater than the preceding year" (DePauw, 1981, p. 262). In comparison to total U.S. trade with the China, however, U.S.-China military trade was much less significant (p. 263).

U.S. trade liberalization with China was further opened in April 1984. On the second U.S. presidential visit to China, after Nixon's premiere visit of 1972, President Reagan and Premier Zhao Ziyang signed a joint Nuclear Nonproliferation Pact, and at the same time agreed to open the China market to U.S. industries for participation in a US$20 billion contract for China's nuclear sector projects (*South China Morning Post*; Cheung, 1998, p. 99). Reagan's strategic economic policy brought the United States and China closer together than they had ever been before because the policy served the interests of both nations. The implementation of the Deng modernization reforms of 1982 was heavily dependent on China's ability to acquire the technology and scientific knowledge it had lost during two tumultuous revolutions and centuries of isolation.[19] U.S. exports to China thus helped fuel China's plans to modernize.

Beyond the Cold War-based strategic trade policy of the Reagan administration, U.S. trade policy was economically motivated by comparative cost advantage. The United States enjoyed a relative factor price advantage in physical capital and skilled labor, while possessing a disadvantage in unskilled labor. China, on the other hand, enjoyed a factor price advantage in unskilled labor (Baldwin, 1987). The comparative advantage for both countries further opened the doors to U.S. trade and investment, particularly as it pertained to Chinese labor-intensive goods.

Comparative cost advantage typically resulted in increased U.S. direct investment in China, which generated a growth in China's exports to the United States in the mid-1980s and throughout the decade of the 1990s. More frequently than not, U.S. direct investment in China was targeted toward China's special economic zones (SEZs) where China's firms could import materials and components duty-free from U.S. firms, process them into finished goods, and export them back to the United States.[20] In 1993, for example, at the height of U.S. direct investment in China, China's exports from foreign-funded firms grew 45.4 percent, while China's total exports rose only 8 percent in comparison (Lardy, 1994, p. 112). A comparison of U.S. direct investment in China to U.S. imports from China is demonstrated in Table 3.2.[21] From 1990 to 1997,

Table 3.2   Comparison of U.S. FDI* to China, and U.S. Imports from China 1990-1998 (US$billions and percent)

	U.S. FDI to China	U.S. Imports from China	Total FDI to China	U.S. % of Total FDI to China
1990	0.4	16.3	3.4	11.8
1991	0.3	20.3	4.4	22.7
1992	0.5	27.4	11.0	4.5
1993	2.0	31.2	27.5	7.3
1994	2.5	41.3	33.8	7.4
1995	3.0	48.5	37.5	8.0
1996	3.4	54.4	41.7	8.1
1997	3.2	65.8	45.3	7.0
1998	4.0	71.2	45.5	8.8

*Note: The U.S. Department of Commerce defines U.S. investment abroad as "the ownership or control of one U.S. person of 10% or more of the voting securities of the incorporated foreign business enterprise or an equivalent interest in a unincorporated foreign business enterprise".

Statistics for total and U.S. FDI to China, and 1998 U.S. Import Figure is taken from U.S.-China Business Council (1998); U.S. import figures from 1990 to 1997 are taken from the *Direction of Trade Statistics Yearbook* (various years); percent calculations by the present author.

Source: U.S. Department of Commerce, 1998, p. 793.

U.S. foreign direct investment (FDI) to China increased from US$0.3 billion to $5.0 billion, while during the same time period, U.S. imports from China increased from US$16.3 billion to $65.8 billion.[22] As China's exports to the United States increased, the U.S. bilateral trade deficit with China increased as well (Lardy, 1994, pp. 73-79), which is reflected in the increased concentration of China's labor-intensive manufacturing structure.

Increased trade liberalization along with expanded U.S. technology-intensive and capital goods exports to China resulted in a change of commodity structure in the U.S.-China trade. In 1980, for example, U.S. exports to China consisted mainly of food and industrial supplies and only a small amount of capital goods. By 1985 and into the 1990s, however, U.S. capital goods exports balanced those exports of food and industrial supplies to China (Orr, 1991/92,

p. 49). U.S. imports from China consisted of mainly food and industrial supplies in 1980, for example. However, by 1990, the commodity structure changed to increased U.S. imports of consumer goods from China.

Table 3.3 displays the changing trade structure with selected top commodities exported to and imported from China during the years 1980 to 1998. U.S. exports of wheat declined from US$1,039 million in 1980 to $426 million in 1996. U.S. exports of technology-intensive items such as aircraft/aerospace craft increased from US$155 million in 1980 to $3,585 million in 1998. In addition, U.S. imports of such finished consumer goods as toys, baby carriages, and sporting goods increased from US$3.0 million in 1980 to $11,167 million in 1998. U.S. imports of light industrial goods, such as radio receivers, however, increased steadily, but not as rapidly as imports of toys and garments.

It is noteworthy that during the 1980s, U.S. direct sales to China became increasingly difficult due to tighter controls placed by China on foreign exchange and the Chinese government's promotion of technology acquisition (Brehm, 1988, p. 143). During the period 1982 to 1984, China's foreign exchange was made available under the Deng (sixth) Five-Year Modernization Plan. In 1985, however, China's foreign exchange rapidly depleted.[23] Because of the lack of foreign exchange, China demanded more technology transfer and countertrade as part of U.S. sales.[24]

The strategic economic and political policies of the Bush administration were much like that of the Reagan administration. Like President Reagan, President Bush was motivated by the strategic concerns of the Cold War (Mann, 1999, p. 216). Although Bush imposed a ban on China's high-level contacts with the United States in response to the June 4, 1989 Tiananmen Square pro-democracy massacre, only two weeks after the ban, he resumed contact with China by deploying the Snowcroft mission to Beijing,[25] in efforts to restore the U.S.-China relationship to what it had been previous to 1989.

The motives for the Snowcroft mission were twofold. One motive was premised on China's potential as an economic ally for U.S. exports. The second motive was an effort to restrain the Soviet Union (p. 216). With regard to U.S. trade policy, the 1989 Chinese government's suppression of pro-democracy activists did not arouse any contemplation to revoke China's MFN status. In fact, "each year of his Presidency after the Tiananmen Square massacre, President Bush was able to secure unconditional renewal of China's MFN status despite Congressional opposition" (Orentlicher and Gelatt, 1993, p. 76).

It should be noted, however, that the Bush administration was not totally blind to the mass display of totalitarianism in China, nor to the outrage expressed by U.S. public opinion. Bush did, in fact, respond to the Tiananmen incident by suspending World Bank lending to China (Lardy, 1994, pp. 52-53). China

Table 3.3 U.S.-China Trade Structure, 1980-1998, Selected Commodities (US$millions)

	U.S. Exports to China									
	1980	1982	1984	1986	1988	1990	1992	1994	1996	1998
A	7	16	29	159	161	146	204	329	358	212
B	1,039	1,046	575	6	690	497	273	166	426	N/A
C	152	147	267	96	181	543	629	944	891	1,064
D	155	19	113	295	334	749	2,056	1,911	1,708	3,585
	U.S. Imports from China									
E	39.0	119.0	168.0	225.0	632	1,203	1,728	2,038	2,099	2,328
F	0.3	20.6	130.0	699.0	1,073	2,215	3,860	5,537	8,015	11,167
G	0.3	4.4	22.0	32.4	264	499	829	1,368	1,571	2,328
H	21.8	43.0	48.3	83.8	342	1,477	3,403	5,259	6,392	8,008

A = Specialized Machinery for particular industries, B = Wheat, C = Fertilizers, D = Aircraft and associated equipment, spacecraft vehicles, and parts, E = Outer garments, women, girls coats, capes of textile fabric, F = Baby carriages, toys, games and sporting goods, G = Radio-broadcast receivers, H = Footwear.

Source: U.S. Department of Commerce, "U.S. Foreign Trade Highlights" (1980, 1982, 1984, 1986, 1988, 1990, 1992, 1994, 1996, 1998).

Programs of the Overseas Private Investment Corporation (OPIC)[26] were also halted. The Trade and Development Program (TDP)[27] for China was suspended, and sanctions were imposed on exports of U.S. weapons and munitions (Bush, 1990, p. 13). By 1990, the United States reversed its position and no longer opposed World Bank loans to China (Lardy, 1994, pp. 52-53).

Not until the Clinton administration came to power was there a slight shift in U.S. economic policy toward China relative to the policy of previous administrations since 1972. Clinton came to the presidential campaign platform with economic considerations as the core of his foreign policy agenda. Secretary of State Christopher commented: "President Clinton has placed America's economic strength at the heart of our national security strategy in the post-Cold War world. Our Administration's foreign policy, like our country, stands for open societies as well as open markets. We are convinced that the two are inseparably linked" (Christopher, 1994b).

After the demise of the Soviet bloc, Clinton was free to focus on the build up of U.S. economic strength without having to consider strategic trade policies that were based on the Soviet threat and its ensuing military power strategies. U.S. controls on such technology-intensive exports as computers and telecommunications equipment were further liberalized, as restrictions on COCOM[28] limits were eased (Lardy, 1994, p. 125). The Clinton administration approved for sale to China more advanced computer systems than the United States had previously been exporting, as well as the sale of advanced fiber optic communication systems. And, in 1994 several satellites made by Hughes Aircraft were authorized for sale (p. 124).

At the start of his presidency, President Clinton had focused on commercial diplomacy and free trade without considering human rights issues. Later in office, however, human rights considerations were added to his foreign economic policy agenda. Two distinct and opposing U.S. trade policies resulted, one in 1993, and another in 1994.

In 1993, it was the Clinton policy that human rights and trade were inseparable. "The core of our policy", the President said, "would be a resolute insistence on overall significant progress on human rights if MFN for China was to be renewed once again". The Executive Order was shaped in close consultation with Congress, business leaders, and human rights activists, but was never officially legislated (Christopher, 1994b). On May 28, 1993 President Clinton extended China's MFN for another year, but on the condition that China satisfy certain human rights improvements for renewal in 1994 based on a recommendation by the U.S. Secretary of State (Orentlicher and Gelatt, 1993, p. 79).

Seven types of human rights were identified as measures for MFN renewal in 1994, but only two were distinguished as being absolute requirements. The first mandatory stipulation was that China "will substantially promote the freedom of emigration objectives of the Trade Act of 1974". The second mandatory stipulation was that China comply with the 1992 U.S.-China bilateral trade agreement[29] concerning China's prison labor (p. 79). The other five non-mandatory conditions included:

1. that China take steps to adhere to the Universal Declaration of Human Rights,
2. releasing and providing an acceptable accounting for Chinese citizens imprisoned or detained for the nonviolent expression of their political or religious beliefs,
3. ensuring human treatment of prisoners by allowing access to prisons by international humanitarian and human rights organizations,
4. protecting Tibet's distinctive religious and cultural heritage, and

5. permitting international radio and television broadcasts into China (U.S. Congress, House, 1994 [Shattuck], pp. 44-54).

With regard to these nonmandatory human rights stipulations, "overall significant progress" in these areas was to be determined by the Secretary of State (Clinton, 1993).[30] On May 26, 1994 Clinton reversed his previous economic policy toward China when he made the executive decision to sever the linkage between human rights and MFN.

Linking Trade and Human Rights

Throughout the past decades, the United States has imposed, or at least has threatened to impose, economic sanctions on the basis of countries' human rights practices. Such sanctions have taken the form of cutbacks in either aid (loan disbursements), trade, or direct investment. Traditionally, respect for human rights has been addressed in the form of a country's labor standards, in particular, prison labor. For this reason, the terms human rights and labor (or worker) rights may be used interchangeably.

The U.S. linkage of trade and human rights occurred, for the most part, during the 1970s. Historically, however, the United States first linked trade and human rights more than a century ago through the Tariff Act of 1890, which banned imports of goods manufactured by convict labor (Perez-Lopez, 1988, p. 254). The trade and human rights linkage was further defined in the Treaty of Versailles of 1919, at the Paris Peace Conference (of which the United States was party), which stipulated that all nations "endeavor to secure and maintain fair and humane conditions of labor . . . in all countries in which their commercial and industrial relations extend" (Gadbaw and Medwig, 1996, pp. 142-43). The 1890 Tariff Act was broadened in Section 307 of the 1930 Smoot-Hawley Tariff Act, which increased the restriction of products imported to the United States that were produced by prison labor.[31] In 1945, the United States called for an International Conference on Trade and Employment and established a preparatory committee to develop an agenda. The United States recommended the establishment of an International Trade Organization (ITO), and in March 1948 drafted a document known as the Havana Charter of 1948, the precursor to the ITO (pp. 242-43).

Article 7 of the *Havana Charter* contained provisions for addressing employment and macroeconomic policies, such as the linkage between fair labor standards[32] and trade (Perez-Lopez, 1988, p. 256).

The members recognize that unfair labour conditions, particularly in production for export, create difficulties in international trade, and accordingly, each member shall take whatever action may be appropriate and feasible to eliminate such conditions within its territory.[33]

Although the ITO never came into existence, provisions for labor standards were minimally incorporated into Article XX(e) of the General Agreement on Tariffs and Trade (GATT), "permitting contracting parties to take measures to restrict products of prison labour" (Perez-Lopez, 1988, p. 257). That the United States should address countries labor standards through a multilateral framework, was recommended by the Randall Commission of 1954 (p. 258).

Multilateral approaches to trade and labor rights included U.S. participation in such international conferences and organizations as the International Labor Organization (ILO) and the GATT (p. 258). Eventual U.S. multilateral mechanisms for conditioning economic relations on human rights improvements included the Organization for Economic Cooperation and Development (OECD), the IMF, World Bank, and the United Nations Conference on Trade and Development (UNCTAD). Additionally, the United States has tied human rights issues to domestic financial institutions, such as, for example, the Overseas Private Investment Corporation (OPIC), and the Export-Import Bank (Eximbank).

By the 1970s the United States, to a significantly greater degree than its western allies, began to consider economic measures in the form of sanctions on development assistance or exports[34] in order to pressure countries to respect human rights.[35] In 1973, in response to Kissinger's realpolitik approach to foreign diplomacy and to the disinterest in influencing human rights abroad during the Nixon/Ford years, Congress enacted a series of statutes linking trade and foreign assistance to a country's human rights practices.

One such action on behalf of human rights, taken by the United States, was a call to attention on four minimum international labor standards (MILS) at the September 1973 Tokyo Round of Trade Negotiations (Perez-Lopez, 1988, p. 258). Such U.S. stipulations included, for example, attention to slave or forced labor, child labor, and health and safety practices. The United States received scant support for these human rights concerns, with the exception of a few Scandinavian countries (pp. 258-59).

Additional measures toward the advancement of international human rights standards were initiated in 1974 by the U.S. Subcommittee on International Organizations of the House Committee on Foreign Affairs. Investigative hearings culminated in a 1974 report entitled "Human Rights in the World Community: A Call for U.S. Leadership". The report contained a number of provisions and recommendations for "increasing the priority given to human rights concerns in the United States foreign policy process" (Lillich, 1984, p. 291).

With the passing of the Trade Act of 1974, signed into law on January 3, 1975 by President Gerald R. Ford, the United States instituted its most powerful economic lever to pressure international human rights improvements — that of most-favored-nation status. Attached to the Trade Act of 1974 was the Jackson-Vanik Amendment (Section 402), which stipulated that renewal of a country's MFN status would be contingent upon that country's allowance of its citizens the freedom of emigration.[36] The continuation of MFN status was subject to an annual presidential waiver of the Jackson-Vanik Amendment. The U.S. Congress, however, may override the presidential waiver by a joint resolution of disapproval, which in turn can then be vetoed by the President (U.S. Dept. of State, Bureau of Public Affairs, 1997b). The Amendment, of course, did not apply to China until 1980, at which time the United States restored MFN status to the PRC on a conditional basis.

Under the U.S. Trade Act of 1974, the U.S. Generalized System of Preferences (GSP) was also established. Similar to the GSP under the GATT, the U.S. GSP granted the President to authorize duty-free treatment to certain merchandise imports from developing countries for a ten-year period. The GSP served to create additional leverage to insure that internationally-recognized worker rights were followed (Perez-Lopez, 1988, pp. 266-70). The United States could withdraw or suspend GSP to a beneficiary country if it was determined that the country did not meet internationally recognized worker rights. Section 502(a) of the 1974 Trade Act identified the term "internationally recognized worker rights"[37] to include

> i) the right of association, ii) the right to organize and bargain collectively, iii) prohibition on the use of any form of forced or compulsory labor, iv) minimum age for the employment of children, and v) acceptable conditions of work with respect to minimum wages, hours of work, and occupational safety and health. (pp. 266-70)

In 1985, U.S. allegations of misuse of labor rights were held against Chile, Guatemala, Haiti, Korea, Nicaragua, Paraguay, the Philippines, Romania, Suriname, Taiwan, and Zaire, whereby GSP privileges were threatened to be suspended (pp. 272-73).

Further linkages between trade and human rights were outlined in the 1976 Foreign Assistance Act,[38] which stated that "no economic assistance, such as exports of agricultural commodities, OPIC insurance, or Eximbank lending will be given to a gross human rights violator unless such assistance will directly benefit the needy people in such a country".[39] A case in point is the Eximbank,[40] which in accordance with the Evans Congressional Amendment,[41] prohibited Eximbank financing of exports to the South African apartheid government, unless the buyer adhered to the rights stipulated in the Sullivan[42] Principles.[43]

At about the same time, Congress introduced a series of bills that would prohibit U.S. direct investment in South Africa, only to have them vetoed by the Carter administration. Accordingly, at the objection of the executive branch, Congress enacted a trade embargo against Uganda, in 1978, in protest of the human rights violations of General Amin (Lillich, 1984, p. 301). Thus, the long-standing clash between certain factions of the U.S. legislative branch and the executive branch regarding the application of trade policy to human rights concerns, is evident and ever present.

It was, however, under the Carter administration that human rights in U.S. foreign policy really began to take hold. In his 1978 speech in Paris, to the Palais des Congress, Carter affirmed: "There is one belief above all others that has made us what we are. This is the belief that the rights of the individual inherently stand higher than the claims or demands of the state" (Bitker, 1984, p. 96). Secretary Vance directed the policy planning staff to incorporate a broad human rights policy. Vance thought that economic and social rights should be considered in addition to civil and political rights, because reduction of aid packages could penalize the hungry and poor whose economic and social rights, such as the right to food, shelter, health care and education, deserve to be fulfilled. That a "more humane international economic order" should be established was the reasoning behind the Carter/Vance broad perspective on human rights. As such, economic assistance was to be granted to (noncommunist) repressive regimes with the intent that the assistance would serve as a leverage to improve human rights (Roberta Cohen, 1979, pp. 227-28).

In total, Carter established a human rights bureaucracy by creating the very first Bureau of Humanitarian Affairs, by developing an interagency network to address human rights issues, and by insisting that annual human rights reports on countries receiving U.S. assistance be provided to Congress. However, Carter's usage of economic leverage to pressure human rights improvements in other countries proved to be softer than his rhetoric. Carter, for instance, did not support the imposition of economic sanctions against the South African apartheid government, nor did he support a trade embargo (which was nevertheless enacted by Congress) against the repressive regime of Idi Amin, in Uganda (Lillich, 1984, p. 295). Despite the high priority given to human rights ideals, Carter neither promoted nor discouraged private foreign investment in countries that exhibited human rights violations. Carter's economic policy was hands off toward the trade and investment decisions of U.S. corporations (p. 294).

President Carter's actions were augmented by a reevaluation of U.S. economic policy and the structure of policy formation and implementation in 1979. U.S. exports as a percentage of world trade had fallen from 18 percent in 1960 to 11.2 percent by 1978. European and Japanese firms were increasing their market share in both domestic and foreign U.S. markets. Foreign corporate competition prompted a reorganization of U.S. foreign policy priorities. Because of the United States' declining world trade position, proponents of reorganization argued that "America's foreign economic policy could no longer be subordinated to foreign policy". The commerce department was therefore elevated to primary responsibility for the administration of U.S. trade policy, responsibility which had been previously held by the Department of the Treasury (American Enterprise Institute, 1984, pp. 9-11).

Similar to Carter, Reagan opposed interference with private economic endeavors. Reagan did, however, advocate the use of economic leverage as a cold war weapon against communist countries (Forsythe, 1997, pp. 263-65). In short, Reagan focused his human rights policy on communist human rights violators, whereas "friendly" authoritarian regimes were not subject to U.S. human rights pressures (p. 266). Unlike Carter, who did not coddle authoritarian dictators, Reagan was indeed diplomatically friendly to repressive leaders in Africa and South America (p. 265). No economic sanctions were applied against these countries and their dictators. It was not necessary, therefore, to link the Eximbank or OPIC to international human rights issues, since no credits or insurance were permitted to be given to Soviet countries or allies of Soviet countries (p. 266), the only countries with which Reagan used human rights as a power leverage during the bipolar Cold War structure.

It was the brutality displayed in 1989 in Tiananmen Square, however, that brought the relationship of trade and human rights to the fore of the U.S. congressional agenda. As previously mentioned, aside from temporary cutbacks on OPIC, Eximbank, and some technology exports, only slight economic measures were taken by the White House in response to the oppression of pro-democracy activists in China. The Tiananmen Square incident and the U.S. public response to it, awakened a long and heated Congressional and executive debate over international trade and its influence on human rights.

Although admitting that China fell short of its responsibilities to human rights, President Bush swept through the trade and human rights debate with a policy of comprehensive engagement with China, with most-favored-nation status as the foundation for engagement. Dialogue, not economic sanctions, Bush thought, was the best way to improve human rights in China. This meant "engaging China through democratic, economic and educational institutions" (*CQ Researcher*, 1992, p. 1041).

When Clinton campaigned for president, he admonished Bush's soft stance on China, in particular his renewal of MFN to China without conditions for human rights improvements. Influential to Clinton's criticism of Bush's policy was Winston Lord, Assistant Secretary of State of East Asian and Pacific Affairs under both Bush and Clinton, and U.S. ambassador to China from 1985 to 1989. Lord was a key originator of the "get-tough" policy on human rights in China. As Lord asserted, "We will seek cooperation from China on a wide range of issues. But Americans cannot forget Tiananmen Square" (Mann, 1999, p. 277). Staunch followers of the policy set forth by Winston Lord were Senate Majority Leader George Mitchell and Congresswoman Nancy Pelosi.[44] Both Congressional leaders pressured Clinton to attach human rights stipulations to the 1993 MFN renewal and were the impetus behind Clinton's Executive Order 12850 of May 28, 1993.

To add to the situation, a series of bureaucratic reports alluding to losses in U.S. economic strength were presented in the early half of 1993. In May 1993, for example, the IMF produced a study that concluded that China's economy was four times larger than previously estimated in terms of purchasing power parity.[45] The study placed China as the world's third largest economy, "slightly smaller than Japan, but ahead of Germany" (Rohwer, 1992; Greenhouse, 1993, cited by Mann, 1999, p. 285). The United States Trade Representative (USTR) announced that "China was still using a variety of protectionist measures against U.S. exports, and that the U.S. trade deficit with China for the year 1992 was $18.3 billion, second only to the U.S. deficit with Japan. Moreover, China was not adhering to the 1992 Memorandum of Understanding (MOU)" (Greenhouse, 1992; Morrison, 1993, as cited by Auger, 1995, pp. 1-11). These reports culminated from an investigation on U.S.-China policy that was conducted by an interagency group of mid-level officials from the Departments of State, Agriculture, the Treasury, Commerce, and the USTR. The working group finally recommended that U.S. interests would best be served by cutting the linkage between MFN and human rights (Auger, 1995, pp. 1-11).

Two groups emerged from opposing philosophies. Opponents of unconditional MFN to China argued that economic penalties[46] would pressure the Chinese leadership to improve human rights by using the leverage of lost profits from trade (Auger, 1995, pp. 7-9). They included such groups as Chinese dissidents, the Sierra Club, Human Rights Organizations, Friends of the Earth, Freedom House, Organized Labor, and the Family Research Council (Sutter, 1998, chap. 4). Their views were best summarized by John Shattuck, Assistant Secretary of State for Human Rights and Humanitarian Affairs:

We must not assume that a free market in goods can produce a free market in ideas. Nor can we abandon our responsibility to support human rights around the world. The character of our relationship with China depends significantly on how the Chinese government treats its people. The American people would have it no other way. (1994, pp. 44-54)

Among many Congressional human rights advocates, a "third way" was offered as a compromise.[47] It was proposed that singling out the Chinese state sector for penalties for the disrespect for universal human rights values would avoid undercutting China's dynamic private sector (Bernstein and Dicker, 1994/95, p. 46). On the part of the human rights groups, penalizing only the Chinese state sector served as a conciliatory measure in hopes of appeasing the general tide in Congress toward full delinkage of trade and human rights. However, targeting only China's state enterprises was considered to be unworkable by the Clinton administration, given the growing complexity of China's economy. The definition of a state enterprise was thought to be problematic because of the difficulty in establishing the point where private ended and state began. Many of China's firms were thought to be "quasi-capitalist" (Kanter, 1992, pp. 551-54).[48]

Advocates of unconditional MFN to China argued that increased trade with and investment in China would be a positive force toward respect for human rights in China and that "revoking MFN would only suppress those factions in China who supported the U.S. position on human rights reform" (Auger, 1995, pp. 3-11). Proponents believed that trade with and investment in China would serve as the conduit for human rights reform. They included business coalitions from the United States, China and Hong Kong, independent political and economic analysts, and Clinton advisors.[49] Among the Clinton advisors in favor of delinking China's human rights record from economic exchange were former President Jimmy Carter and former Secretaries of State Henry Kissinger and Cyrus Vance,[50] Assistant Secretary of State for Asian Affairs Winston Lord,[51] former National Security Advisor Zbigniew Brzezinski, Secretary of Commerce Ron Brown, National Security Advisor Anthony Lake, Secretary of the Treasury Lloyd Bentsen and an array of "centrist" Congressional leaders from both Republican and Democratic parties.[52] As James Mann emphasized, with regard to the MFN issue "Clinton was a follower as much as a leader" (1999, p. 313).

In March 1994, John Shattuck and Warren Christopher traveled to China for consultation over the MFN/human rights question. The mainland government deliberately detained some political dissidents to demonstrate its uncompromising position on human rights pressures. Chinese government official Chiang Tse-min informed Christopher that "Some people in the west are not concerned about the interest and well-being of tens of millions of Chinese people, but about those few who attempt to subvert the Chinese government and destabilize China. This is essentially a political issue, a legal issue, rather than a human rights issue" (Zheo, 1994, p. 22). Premier Li Peng advised Christopher that "China and the United States have different perceptions of human rights",[53] and that "China will not accept America's human rights concept" (Seymour, 1994, p. 205). Wu Yi, Beijing's Minister of External Economic Trade, stated that "making MFN status contingent upon human rights is unwise and lacks strategic vision" (p. 205; *People's Daily*, 1994).

Shortly before Secretary of State Christopher's arrival in China, Shattuck met with one of China's most outspoken political dissidents, Wei Jingsheng:

> Shattuck had asked Wei which U.S. policy was more important to improving human rights: i) having the United States apply direct pressure on the Chinese government, or ii) having the United States voice public support for Chinese dissidents? Wei's opinion was that the pressure on the regime was more crucial, because without it, statements of public support for dissidents would never be allowed to enter or be broadcast into China. (Mann, 1999, p. 298)

China's reaction to the 1994 visits by Christopher and Shattuck was disdainful. Jiang Zemin remarked that John Shattuck's meeting with Wei Jingsheng was "ridiculous, and that it showed a lack of sincerity to improve relations with China" (U.S. Congress, House, 1994 [Smith], opening statement). In a special dispatch from Beijing, published in Hong Kong, Jiang Zemin was quoted as saying that "dealing with Mr. Christopher was child's play, and that all Mr. Christopher wanted to do in China was to play tricks". "Since we could not control Christopher", Jiang Zemin said, "we controlled the dissidents" (U.S. Congress, opening statement). On May 23, 1994 Secretary of State Warren Christopher met with President Clinton to discuss the human rights conditions contained in the Executive Order 12850 of May 1993. Christopher reported that China had met the first two mandatory conditions, which were: 1) progress on emigration, and 2) compliance with the prison labor agreement stipulated in the Jackson-Vanik Amendment. The other five human rights stipulations, Christopher reported, had not been met. Christopher left the final decision to renew China's MFN status to President Clinton (Auger, 1995; Mann, 1999, p. 299).

On May 26, 1994, President Clinton announced that the end of the usefulness of the 1993 policy on China had been reached, and that in the future there would be no link between China's human rights record and most-favored-nation status. As the President stated, "Pursuant to the requirements of the Jackson-Vanik Amendment, only freedom of emigration would be considered in subsequent decisions on the MFN waiver" (Auger, 1995; Mann, 1999, p. 299). U.S. House Majority Leader Richard Gephardt and House Majority Whip David Bonior responded to the decision by introducing legislation that proposed the very sanctions Clinton chose not to impose.

After Clinton reversed his 1993 policy, he increasingly transferred human rights responsibilities to U.S. corporations. In 1994 President Clinton established a new human rights strategy, one in which U.S. corporations would help to advance the cause of human rights in China and elsewhere, through voluntary codes of conduct.[54] The President also stated that he would seek to multilateralize efforts to improve human rights in China through such mechanisms as the United Nations and nongovernmental organizations (Dumbaugh, 1994, p. 5).

The United States-China Act of 1994 (H.R. 4590), introduced in the Congress by Representatives Nancy Polosi, David Bonoir, and Richard Gephardt, asked that U.S. businesses in China adopt the following commitments:

- To follow internationally recognized human rights principles;
- To adopt nondiscriminatory employment practices;
- Not to knowingly use prison labor;
- To recognize the rights of workers to organize and bargain collectively;
- To discourage mandatory political indoctrination in the workplace (Dumbaugh, 1994, p. 5).

However, even before Clinton's promotion of human rights through the private sector, several U.S. corporations had already responded to international human rights abuses. One such company was Reebok International, which adopted a set of human rights principles in 1990, to be utilized in operations overseas, including business operations in China (Orentlicher and Gelatt, 1993, p. 108). The Reebok principles exhibited in Table 3.4 underscore such basic democratic tenets as freedom of assembly and association.

Other U.S. corporations adopted similar codes of ethical conduct. In 1992, Levi Strauss & Co., for example, withdrew from China when it was discovered through corporate avenues that its suppliers were utilizing prison labor. At the same time, Levi Strauss ceased all direct foreign investment in China, pending on the improvement of human rights conditions, and also withdrew from Myanmar when its military regime silenced a human rights movement. Timberland Corporation also bans business relations with countries that violate basic human rights (Borrus and Barnatham, 1992, pp. 51-52, as cited by Compa and Darrecarrere, 1996, p. 190). A 1996 survey conducted by the U.S. Department of Labor of 42 major U.S. apparel manufacturers, department stores, and mass merchandisers, as measured by 1995 annual sales, found that 36 firms had

Table 3.4   Reebok International Human Rights Policy, 1990

1. Reebok will not operate under martial law conditions or allow any military presence on its premises.

2. Reebok encourages free association and assembly among its employees.

3. Reebok will seek to ensure that opportunities for advancement are based on initiative, leadership, and contributions to the business, not political beliefs.

4. Reebok will seek to prevent compulsory political indoctrination programs from taking place on its premises.

5. Reebok reaffirms that it deplores the use of force against human rights.

Source: Orentlicher and Gelatt, 1993, p. 108.

adopted some form of human rights policy (U.S. Dept. of Labor, 1996; Forcese, 1997, pp. 21-22). Table 3.5 displays the breakdown for firms by labor or human rights. The largest percentage of those firms (78%) prohibited child labor, and the next largest percentage (73%) prohibited forced labor. Freedom of association, the right to organize and bargain collectively, and fair wages were among the lowest percentages, at 5%, 5%, and 22%, respectively. In another survey, roughly 10% of U.S. multinationals had overseas guidelines on human rights.[55] "Human rights codes of conduct are becoming increasingly popular among U.S. firms, particularly those firms selling consumer products. At the same time, these codes suffer from several shortcomings, particularly in the area of monitoring and enforcement" (Forcese, 1997, p. 30).

Summary

U.S. economic policy toward China has changed very little since the late 1960s. Minor changes in the motivation behind trade policy toward China did exist, however, between Cold War and post-Cold War presidents. The impetus for opening trade with China during the Cold War years was not only to expand markets for U.S. products, but also to weaken Sovietism by befriending its communist ally. The most staunch advocate of U.S.-China trade induced by the Soviet threat was, of course, President Reagan, who had taken Kissinger's realpolitik approach toward China to its greatest degree. With the end of the Cold

Table 3.5   U.S. Department of Labor Survey Results

Labor Right	Number / % of Firms	
Freedom of Association	2	5%
Right to Organize and Bargain Collectively	2	5%
Prohibition of Forced Labor	27	73%
Prohibition of Child Labor	29	78%
Nondiscrimination in Employment	19	51%
Safe and Healthful Work Environment	22	59%
Fair Wages	8	22%
Working Hours and Overtime	12	59%

Sources: Forcese, 1997, p. 21; U.S. Dept. of Labor, 1996.

War, and with it the Soviet threat, Clinton was free to focus on economic issues, which became the centerpiece of his campaign platform.

The single thread that was indicative of U.S. presidential administrations since 1972 was that all administrations condoned the opening of trade with China and took steps, through legislation and diplomacy, to increase trade with and investment in China. Presidents Nixon, Ford, Carter, Bush, Reagan, and Clinton all followed a similar pattern of trade liberalization.

Despite questionable human rights practices in countries with which the United States has engaged in aid, trade, or direct investment, the most outspoken human rights advocate, President Carter, did not use economic sanctions as a leverage to improve human rights. By 1994, the Clinton administration combined both public and private sectors in recommending that U.S. corporations voluntarily provide measures to assure that internationally recognized human rights are not violated in countries where U.S. business is conducted.

The trade and human rights linkage is not new to U.S. foreign policy. More than one hundred years ago, with the passing of the U.S. Tariff Act of 1890, trade and human rights were inextricably linked. Economic and political strategies may have altered slightly during the past decades, but overall, the U.S. trade policy toward China, and the linkage of trade and human rights has been consistent throughout history.

Even after the 1994 decision, however, the relationship between trade and human rights continued to be a major issue of contention among U.S. policymakers. By assigning much of the moral and social responsibility to U.S. corporations, the linkage between economic and social considerations has remained a vital issue. The prospect of China's entry into the World Trade Organization has not yet lessened the debacle of trade and human rights in U.S. foreign policy.

The following chapter will discuss the U.S. 1994 decision in detail, and will place each of the first three stated hypotheses into a competing theoretical argument, offering further insights into the motivations behind the 1994 U.S. decision to end the connection between China's human rights practices and MFN.

Endnotes

1   Among the major corporations in Canton and Shanghai by the 1870s, 1880s, and 1890s were American Tobacco, Columbia Phonographs, General Electric, International Harvester, Sherwin Williams, Singer Sewing Machine, Parke Davis, and Standard Oil. See Wilkins (1986), pp. 263-66.

2   John R. Garson (1971, pp. 7, 24-25) clarifies that the U.S. trade embargo on China proceeds from the president's authority under the Export Control Act of 1949 and the Trading with the Enemy Act of 1917. The Trading with the Enemy Act was passed six months after the U.S. entry into World War I to prevent American sources from being used to aid the enemy and to create a fund from which American creditors of enemy aliens could be paid. The act prohibited unlicensed foreign trade and authorized the seizure of enemy-owned property in the United States, as well as regulation by the president of transactions of foreign exchange.

3   It is noteworthy that during the 1950s and 1960s, figures for international trade revealed that the United States had a comparatively low ratio of foreign trade to domestic economic activity. The U.S. ratio of total trade turnover $(x + m/gdp)$ was below 10 percent. Thus in terms of total domestic activity, foreign trade was not a major sector of the U.S. economy. However, because of its absolute size, U.S. trade accounted for approximately 15 percent of the total world trade during the late 1950s. For further explanation, refer to Cohen, Dernberger, and Garson (1971), p. 185.

4   John King Fairbank, director of the East Asian Research Center, Harvard University, March 10, 1966: "The hearings were triggered by the expansion of the Vietnam War and fear that the Chinese might intervene, as they had in Korea. The witnesses included virtually all of the most prestigious China scholars in the United States. Although divided on the Vietnam War itself, they were almost unanimous in their opinions that although the United States should try to 'contain' China, the policy of isolation should be admitted to have failed and be dropped. In turn, it was argued that the United States should step up cultural, educational, and technical contacts with the PRC" (Congressional Quarterly, Inc., 1980, p. 161).

5   Donald S. Zagoria, professor of Government at Columbia University, March 21, 1966 (Congressional Quarterly, Inc., 1980, 161).

6   The Brezhnev Doctrine, which was declared on September 16, 1968, also known as "The Doctrine of Limited Sovereignty," stated that the world socialist community had a right to intervene when socialism came under attack in a fraternal socialist country, and denied that

this had in any way violated Czechoslovakia's "real sovereignty" (Congressional Quarterly, Inc., 1980, p. 181).

7   Also, as explained by the Chinese leadership in the journal *Hongqui,* China's purpose in opening ties with the United States was to "distinguish between the primary enemy (the Soviet Union) and the secondary enemy (the United States), allying itself with the secondary enemy in order to form a united front against Moscow" (Congressional Quarterly, Inc., 1980, p. 200).

8   The Ussuri river consists of a 4,000 mile stretch of border between the Soviet Union and China. At a point in the river about 250 miles from Vladivostok is the tiny island of Damansjky, about a third of a square mile. In March 1969, Chinese troops fired on a Russian frontier patrol group, killing 23 and wounding 14 Russians in 20 minutes (Kissinger, 1979, p. 166).

9   Among the 49 countries which recognized the communist Chinese regime (while the United States did not) were Denmark, Finland, France, Great Britain, the Netherlands, Norway, Sweden, and West Germany. France was the first western European nation to recognize the PRC, in 1950. The aforementioned countries later began contact.

10   Henry Kissinger was appointed Assistant for National Security Affairs under President Nixon from 1969-73. From 1973 to 1977, Kissinger served as Secretary of State under President Nixon and President Gerald R. Ford (Kissinger, 1979, p. xxi).

11   Such U.S. goods that were authorized for export to the PRC included "farm, fishery and forestry products, tobacco, fertilizers and chemicals, coal, rubber and textiles, some metals, agricultural, industrial and office equipment, household appliances, some electrical appliances, consumer goods, road building and construction equipment and some relatively unsophisticated computers" (Congressional Quarterly, Inc., 1980, p. 8).

12   Richard M. Nixon, speech to Midwestern News Media executives attending a briefing on domestic policy in Kansas City, Missouri, July 6, 1971 (Congressional Quarterly, Inc., 1980, p. 332).

13   The Shanghai Communiqué, issued in Shanghai on February 27, 1972 was a joint U.S.-China agreement that established U.S. diplomatic relations with the PRC and subsequent trade relations between the two countries. An excerpt from the agreement is that "both sides view bilateral trade as another area from which mutual benefit can be derived, and agreed that economic relations based on equality and mutual benefit are in the interest of the peoples of two countries. They agree to facilitate the progressive development of trade between the two countries" (Congressional Quarterly, Inc., 1980, p. 323).

14   In 1979, President Carter looked to U.S. business for help in gaining congressional approval of the 1979 U.S.-China trade agreement. Business lobbyists included the National Council for U.S.-China Trade which represented the banking, construction, transportation, and other industries that were eager to enter the China market. Such U.S. corporations as Coca-Cola, Bethlehem Steel, and Pan American Airways were among the early entrants to the China market (Congressional Quarterly, Inc., 1980, pp. 68-70).

15   The United States and the People's Republic of China announced in a joint Communiqué in Shanghai on December 15, 1978 that they would formally recognize each other on January 1, 1979, and exchange ambassadors and establish embassies on March 1. At this time it was also announced that Deng Xiaoping, the Chinese vice premier would visit Washington. It was agreed by the two parties that the United States would withdraw recognition of Taiwan and would terminate its mutual defense treaty with that nation by the end of 1979 (Congressional Quarterly, Inc., 1980, p. 39).

16   Conditions for MFN were first stipulated in the U.S. Trade Act of 1974. The conditions included: i) the conclusion of a bilateral trade agreement that included trade reciprocity, and ii) compliance with the Jackson-Vanik Amendment, which was attached to the 1974 U.S. Trade Act. The Amendment stipulated that MFN can be extended to nonmarket economies only if its citizens are permitted the freedom of emigration. The continuation of MFN was contingent on a presidential waiver of the Jackson-Vanik Amendment on a yearly basis. Since the 1980 U.S. granting of MFN to China, however, such further conditions were added as China's progress on an array of human rights conditions, the ceasing of China's nuclear arms sales to third countries and piracy of U.S. copyrights.

17   President Carter remarked that "Conclusion of this agreement is the most important step we can take to provide greater economic benefits to both countries from this relationship" (DePauw, 1981, p. 4).

18   Such exports included greater quantities of advanced machinery and instruments, aircraft, locomotives and avionics equipment.

19   In 1982, Deng Xiaoping introduced to the Twelfth CCP Party Congress a series of market reforms with a goal to take China out of the status of a developing country by the year 2000. Deng's four modernizations include the development of: i) agriculture, ii) science and technology, iii) industry, and iv) the military (Baum, 1994, p. 341).

20   As Lardy (1994, pp. 112-13) clarifies, "[T]he value of these exports is the sum of the value of the imported components and the processing fee. International marketing is handled by the foreign firm that supplies the materials and components".

21   FDI Figures are Actual Amount Utilized, as opposed to Actual Amount Contracted by corporations. "Invariably a proportion of pledged investment is never actually absorbed because deals fall apart. However, because there is a lag between the time contracts are pledged and when the capital is actually contributed (utilized), some capital not absorbed in the year of the signing will be absorbed in later years" (Pearson, 1997, p. 167).

22   U.S. import figures from China were utilized rather than China's export figures to the United States because of the "discrepancies in bilateral trade statistics as reported by China and its trading partners, particularly with industrial countries. Trade with these countries is classified by China as trade with Hong Kong if it passes through Hong Kong ports" (*Direction of Trade Statistics Yearbook*, 1997, p. 159). This method of statistical reporting remains consistent even after Hong Kong's 1997 reunification with China due to the fact that the 1984 Sino-British Joint Declaration stipulates that Hong Kong will retain its existing economic system for 50 years after 1997.

23   "U.S. firms frequently cite China's foreign exchange controls and non-convertibility of the renminbi as the most significant non-tariff barrier to trade and investment" (U.S. Department of State, 1992, p. 78).

24   Brehm (1988, pp. 149-51) defines countertrade (*duixiao maoyi*) as "Various trade arrangements that contain a requirement to purchase products as a condition of sale. Among the various types of countertrade include: i) barter (*yihuo maoyi*) : a one time exchange of products that does not involve cash; ii) compensation trade (*buchang maoyi*): an agreement to sell technology and/or machinery and equipment and to accept full or partial payment in the form of goods manufactured with the equipment; iii) counterpurchase (*fangou mai*): involves the same principle as balanced trade between the buyer and seller, but the Chinese side will offer goods that are not related to or manufactured by the items purchased from the foreign side".

25　The Snowcroft Mission, comprised of National Security Advisor Brent Snowcroft, Deputy Secretary of State Lawrence Eagleburger and Secretary of State Baker, was created by Bush and was, at the time, a mission conducted secretly to try to "continue the U.S. security cooperation with China against the Soviet Union". Two missions to China were carried out, one in 1989, and the other in 1990 (Mann, 1999, p. 208).

26　OPIC (Overseas Private Investment Corporation) is a U.S. government agency that facilitates the participation of U.S. private capital and skills in the economic and social development of developing countries. It provides insurance against political risk for U.S. companies investing abroad by providing loan and loan guarantees for specific investment projects.

27　The U.S. Trade and Development Program (TDP) is a government program that serves to fund feasibility studies by U.S. companies on major projects in countries that facilitate U.S. exports.

28　"U.S. exports to China, as well as exports from other major Western industrialized countries have been subject to not only domestic export controls but also to a multilateral approval process known as COCOM (Coordinating Committee for Multilateral Export Controls). COCOM is an arrangement which includes the United States, its European allies, and Japan for the purpose of reviewing technology and commodity transfers to controlled destinations, principally the (former) Soviet Union and China" (Wethington, 1988, p. 196). COCOM controls have become increasingly relaxed throughout the decades in order to assist the progress of trade and investment liberalization.

29　A Memorandum of Understanding (MOU) in regard to prison labor in China was agreed upon by the United States and China in 1992. The agreement facilitates U.S. inspections of Chinese prisons with the intent to establish the origin of Chinese exports to the United States that are produced with prison labor. In the event China refuses inspection of its prisons, U.S. customs may prevent the importation of Chinese goods suspected of being produced with prison labor (U.S. Department of State, Bureau of Public Affairs, 1997a).

30　The ambiguous terminology of the phrase "overall significant progress" fueled further debate.

31　"In addition to manufactured products, goods which were mined or produced by prison labor were also prohibited from being exported to the United States. The prohibition also extended to goods produced by forced or indentured labor under penal sanctions. However, an exemption of the ban was provided for goods produced by forced labor if such goods were not produced in the United States in sufficient quantities" (Perez-Lopez, 1988, p. 254).

32　It is interesting to consider the position of T.N. Srinivasan, who argues that "the diversity in labor standards among countries is not only legitimate, but also does not detract from the case for free trade. In other words, such diversity, like diversity in tastes, technology and factor endowments, is a source for gainful trade based on comparative advantage" (Srinivasan, 1998, p. 233). The neoclassical argument put forth here contradicts the ideology of U.S. sanctions based on violations of U.S. (and international) norms for labor standards or "sub-standard" wages of foreign countries.

33　U.S. Dept. of State, Pub. No. 3206, Havana Charter for an International Trade Organization (1948), p. 32, in Perez-Lopez (1988, p. 256). The author points out that "a proposal introduced at Havana by the United States calling for the condemnation of prison labor elicited no support [from other countries], therefore Art. 7 of the Havana Charter was silent on the issue" (p. 257).

34　In 1969, for instance, the Export Administration Act was passed. The act gave the Department of Commerce, with input from the departments of State and Treasury, the authority to administer export controls on the license to businesses to sell various products for human rights purposes (Lillich, 1984, p. 301).

35   "More and more members of Congress see trade and aid as part of a continuum of tools to affect performance on human rights" (Vogelgesang, 1978, p. 819, cited in Lillich, 1984, p. 296).

36   The Jackson-Vanik Amendment was originally meant to allow for the emigration of Jews from communist bloc countries.

37   Gadbaw and Medwig offer a point to contemplate in regard to internationally-recognized human rights. That is "the vast majority of workers in developing countries do not enjoy the labor standards listed under the U.S. Trade Act. Simply because the economies are too poor. If the choice is between subsistence needs and 'decent' work hours, the work days will be very long. Or, if the choice is between child labor on the family farm or a smaller harvest, children will work long and hard in the fields. In other words, conditions that many labor/ human rights advocates point to as 'abuses' may really be less a function of [U.S.]policy failure than the unavoidably harsh conditions of life in a developing economy" (Gadbaw and Medwig, 1996, pp. 144-45, citing Fields, 1990).

38   "The Foreign Assistance Act of 1976 defines internationally recognized human rights in civil and political terms, in particular, the act specifies the denial of the right to life, systematic use of torture and prolonged detention without trial, as human rights abuses" (Roberta Cohen, 1979, p. 227).

39   Foreign Assistance Act of 1961, Public Law 94-161 (Lillich, 1984, pp. 295-96).

40   The Eximbank (Export Import Bank) is a U.S. government agency that lends low interest loans to foreign or developing countries that wish to engage in trade with the United States.

41   The Export-Import Bank Act of 1945 provides that human rights factors are one of only four nonfinancial or noneconomic reasons that the president can rely upon when ordering the Eximbank to deny applications for credit, as cited by Lillich (1984, p. 298).

42   "Former civil rights leader and General Motors Board Member, Rev. Leon Sullivan, first introduced his voluntary codes of conduct for corporations operating in South Africa, in 1977. He continually updated them, until he eventually abandoned them agreeing with critics that they were ineffective. In 1992, a final version of the Sullivan Principles was adopted. The 1992 Sullivan Principles include: Principle 1) Nonsegregation of the races in all eating, comfort, locker room, and work facilities; Principle 2) Equal and fair employment practices for all employees; Principle 3) Equal pay for all employees doing equal or comparable work for the same period of time; Principle 4) Initiation and development of training programs that will prepare blacks, coloureds, and asians in substantial numbers for supervisory, administrative, clerical, and technical jobs; Principle 5) Increasing the number of blacks, coloureds, and asians in management and supervisory positions; Principle 6) Improving the quality of employees' lives outside the work environment in such areas as housing, transportation, schooling, recreation, and health facilities; Principle 7) Working to eliminate laws and customs that impede social, economic, and political justice" (Corporate Watch, n.d.). "This approach was replicated in the 'MacBride Principles,' a code of conduct issued in 1984 by the Irish Statesman, Sean MacBride, to influence the activities of U.S. companies conducting business in Northern Ireland. The code focuses on nondiscrimination and affirmative action programs to overcome antipathy between the Protestant majority and the Roman Catholic minority in the British-ruled territory" (Gadbaw and Medwig, 1996, p. 185).

43   The Export-Import Bank Act of 1945 was amended in 1977 "to discourage exports to countries not observing human rights". Public Law 95-143, 16 Oct. 1977, as cited by Bitker, 1984, p. 95.

44   Joining them were Congressmen David Bonior, Pat Buchanan, Dan Burton, Richard Gephardt, Bernie Sanders, and Senator Alfonse D'Amato, among others.

45   "PPP exists between two currencies when changes in the exchange rate reflect only relative changes in the price levels of the two countries" (Gregory and Ruffin, 1989, p. 402).

46   "The revocation of MFN would mean the abrogation of the 1980 U.S.-China Agreement on which the entire structure of the economic relationship is based. It would also mean that duty rates on imports from China would rise to the rates established in the 1930s under the Smoot-Hawley Tariff Act. Tariff rates for Chinese goods would rise from about 6-8% to as high as 40 to 50%. Since MFN is extended on a reciprocal basis, China would respond by blocking access to U.S. goods and putting U.S. investment at stake" (American Electronics Association, 1996).

47   The Peace/Pelosi Bill, H.R. 5318, 4-26, was introduced to Congress in June of 1992, as an alternative solution to the two extremes of total delinkage of human rights and trade, or total granting of MFN to China. The bill called for increasing tariffs on imports produced by state-owned enterprises in the PRC as an appropriate response to China's violations of internationally-accepted norms in human rights, nuclear proliferation, and distortion of trade (U.S. Congress, House, 1992).

48   Kanter further explains "The silk industry is illustrative in this regard. The degree of 'state' control of silk production and marketing increases as the product moves up the production chain into cloth fabrication, but the basic raw material, the silk cocoon, is produced by individual farm families and collectives, while finished silk garments are produced by joint ventures and wholly owned foreign enterprises. These quasi-capitalist farm enterprises and joint ventures would be harmed as much, if not more, by MFN revocation, as the state silk industry".

49   As Auger points out, "The Chinese government exerted pressure on the United States to end conditional MFN status by awarding over US$1 billion in contracts to U.S. corporations in April 1993, and at the same time by warning the U.S. that economic competitors of the U.S., especially those business competitors in Japan and western Europe would eagerly snap up any contracts that the U.S. lost" (Auger, 1995, p. 5).

50   Former Secretary of State Henry Kissinger and former Secretary of State Cyrus Vance wrote letters to President Clinton advising him to "sever the ties between trade and human rights in the case of China" (Neier, 1994, p. 1).

51   Since Lord was the originator of the "get-tough stance" on human rights in China, this represented a complete reversal of opinion. In mid-July 1993, "Lord argued in a classified paper that the [U.S.-China] relationship was on a downward spiral and urged an entirely new strategy of intensive engagement with Beijing in which incentives would substitute for threats" (Sciolino, 1994, p. A8).

52   These centrist leaders included "Senators Dole (R), Boren (D), Kerry (D), Baucus (D), Bradley (D) and Johnston (D), and Representatives Foley (D), Hamilton (D), Gibbons (D), Matsui (D), McDermott (D), Ackerman (D) and Leach (R)". See Lampton, 1994, p. 606.

53   Article 51 of the Chinese Constitution states: "The exercise by citizens — of their freedoms and rights may not infringe upon the interests of the state, or society and the collective". Therefore, the State mandates and withholds individual rights. Of all the various human rights, the "right to development has the strongest vote of approval among China's leaders" (Seymour, 1994, p. 205). As Giles further explains, in China, human rights are not seen as individual, but rather collective, to live for others — for the collective good, instead of living for oneself (Giles, 1970, xi).

54   A business code of conduct "is a statement of principles a business agrees to abide by voluntarily over the course of its operations. Corporate codes of conduct have become relatively commonplace in the United States. Surveys in the late 1980s suggest that, at that time, as many as 77% of large U.S. corporations had some sort of corporate code of conduct" (Forcese, 1997, p. 14).

55   "This Boston-based pollster focused on major U.S. retailers and brand name goods manufacturers" (Simon Billenness, Franklin Research and Development, personal communication of February 1997 by Craig Forcese. Forcese, 1997, p. 20).

4 Delinking Trade and Human Rights

The previous chapter advanced that there had been relatively little change, historically, in the U.S.-China trade and economic policy of past U.S. presidential administrations since 1972. The linkage of trade and human rights was shown to be evident for over a century in U.S. foreign economic policymaking. In principle, respect for individual human rights was a consistent part of U.S. ideology when engaging in economic relations with countries. Respective or irrespective of human rights, it was concluded that the U.S. policy of economic engagement with China had been historically consistent since 1972. The significance of the 1994 executive decision, however, was that the decision and public decree of the separation of trade and human rights meant that MFN, clearly the single most powerful U.S. economic lever, officially and legally, could no longer be used as a vehicle, in terms of either threat or action to improve human rights in China.[1]

To review, the purpose of this study is to establish a relationship between the economic interdependence and the moral responsibilities of nations by examining and analyzing the U.S.-China case of the 1994 decision by the Clinton administration to separate China's human rights practices from most-favored-nation status. By investigating the U.S.-China bilateral relationship, this research will attempt to provide insights into explanations for the motivations of U.S. government leaders who were involved in the 1994 U.S. decision, while gaining a greater understanding into the broader relationship between market forces and ethical principles.

This chapter examines the U.S.-China case in detail by applying competing theoretical paradigms in order to discern more thoroughly the motives for the 1994 U.S. decision. The chapter is divided into three major sections. Each section focuses on one of the three stated hypotheses presented in the first chapter. Following each section is a critical evaluation of the theoretical argument put forth.

National Interests

As indicated in chapter 1, the first hypothesis, premised on realism, was that the U.S. intent to sustain and increase power in the Asian region influenced the 1994 decision to separate China's human rights record from most-favored-nation status. The realist argument espouses that "the primary obligation of every state — the goal to which all other objectives shall be subordinated — is to promote the national interest, defined as the acquisition of power" (Keohane and Nye, 1989, p. 11; Kegley, 1995b, pp. 4-5). The economic policies of nations are therefore judged primarily from the point of view of their contribution to national power (Morganthau, 1967, p. 2).

According to the tenets of realism, the superior economic capabilities of a state can be used as direct leverage over the "outside world".[2] National security[3] interests were the impetus behind U.S.-China policy. U.S. economic strength at home and abroad, particularly in the Asian-Pacific region, would be enhanced and expanded by fully engaging China.[4] Therefore, it was in the U.S. interest to grant most-favored-nation status to China without attaching human rights conditions — conditions that were viewed by proponents of unconditional trade to impede the process of trade liberalization and diplomatic relations between the two countries.

First, there were international macroeconomic conditions that influenced the U.S. national interest in forming closer economic ties with China. Starting in 1991, there was a slowdown in the growth of the world economy. The Japanese high-growth "bubble economy" of the 1980s had burst. At the same time, western European nations were experiencing sluggish GDP growth rates together with high unemployment. Table 4.1 reflects that in the developed countries and in the world, GDP growth rates dropped considerably in 1991. In particular, in 1991 both the United States and the United Kingdom experienced negative growth rates of -1.2 percent and -2.2 percent respectively, while the total world growth rate declined from 4.3 percent in 1988 to 0.1 percent in 1992. The demise of the Soviet Union and the socioeconomic complications of a newly-reunified Germany intensified the economic stagnation in western Europe.

The slowdown in the world economy in 1991 affected the growth rate of the volume of total U.S. exports to the world, which increased 83 percent from 1986 to 1991, but then decreased considerably to a 9 percent growth rate between 1991 and 1994. The decrease in the U.S. volume of exports, in turn, negatively affected the growth rate of U.S. jobs, particularly jobs in the high-technology industries. From 1991 to 1994, the decline in the growth rate of jobs was concentrated in three high-technology industry groups: 1) electronic

Table 4.1   A Comparison of Gross Domestic Product (GDP) Growth Rates in Real Terms of Major Developed Countries/Regions of the World 1988-1992* (annual change in percent)

	1988	1989	1990	1991	1992
World	4.3	3.3	2.3	0.1	1.1
Developed Countries	4.3	3.3	2.4	0.6	1.7
Japan	6.2	4.7	5.2	4.4	2.0
United States	3.9	2.5	0.8	-1.2	1.9
European Union	4.0	3.5	3.8	0.8	1.4
Germany*	3.7	3.8	4.5	0.9	1.8
United Kingdom	4.3	2.3	1.0	-2.2	-0.8
France	4.5	4.1	2.2	1.2	2.2

*Note: Data through 1990 apply to West Germany only. Data for 1992 were estimates.

Source: International Monetary Fund, 1993.

components, 2) computing equipment, and 3) aircraft engines, parts, and equipment (Davis, 1996, p. 12).

Between 1991 and 1994, U.S. jobs in the high-technology sectors supported by goods exports decreased by 138,000. The greater part of the job decrease was in the aircraft industry, which experienced a 34 percent lower volume of jobs in 1994 than in 1991 (p. 13). In recent years, the U.S. commercial aircraft industry had supplied 95 percent of China's total aircraft purchases (Prybyla, 1993, p. 13). Table 4.2 demonstrates that of the total U.S. high-technology exports, the aircraft industry represented to the United States the highest value amount in exports to China, totaling $2.2 billion for the year 1993. In terms of all U.S. high-technology industries, the U.S. aircraft industry represented the second largest employer supported by goods exports, creating nearly 250,000 U.S. jobs (including aircraft parts and missile engines) in 1994, first only to the computing equipment industry, which accounted for 128,000 jobs supported by exports, as indicated in Table 4.3.

While the United States, European, and Japanese economies were stagnating, China was experiencing an average GDP growth rate of 12.3 percent between 1991 and 1993, and 13.7 percent by 1993 (World Bank, 1995, p. 78). Figure 4.1 indicates China's rapid economic ascendancy, where the absolute

Table 4.2   Top Ten U.S. Exports to and Imports from China During the Year 1993 (US$million)

Industry	Value Amount
Top Ten Exports to China	
Aircraft and associated equipment	2,229
Motor vehicles	616
Telecommunications equipment	603
Precision instruments	323
Specialized machinery	314
Fertilizers	293
Wheat	274
Oil	242
Data processing equipment	167
Heating and cooling equipment	160
Top Ten Imports from China	
Footwear	4,520
Baby carriages, toys, games, sporting goods	4,459
Women's and girl's coats/capes, etc. (textile)	2,222
Other articles of apparel	1,599
Trunks, suitcases, vanity cases, briefcases	1,321
Mens/boys' coats, jackets (textile)	1,126
Articles of plastic	969
Telecommunications equipment	917
Radio broadcast receivers	914
Misc. articles, candles, umbrellas	912

Source: Congressional Quarterly, 1994, p. 318.

Table 4.3   Ten High-Technology[a] Individual Industries with the Highest Number of U.S. Jobs Supported Directly and Indirectly[b] by Goods Exports in 1994 (000s of jobs in decreasing rank)

Industry	Number of Jobs
Computing equipment	128.9
Aircraft	111.7
Solid state semiconductors	93.2
Other electronic components	83.9
Other aircraft parts & equip.	73.7
Other non-elec. measuring inst.	59.3
Aircraft & missile engines	55.7
Medical instruments	33.5
Industrial inorganic chemicals	32.0
Telephone & telegraph eq.	28.2

[a] There are ten industrial groups that are defined as "high-technology" industries by the U.S. Department of Commerce in terms of the 1987 SIC (Standard Industrial Classification of the United States) DOC-3 definition. They are: 1) Industrial inorganic chemicals; 2) Plastic materials & synthetic resins, rubbers, & fibers; 3) Drugs & medicines; 4) Ordinance & accessories; 5) Engines, turbines, & parts; 6) Office, computing & electronic components; 7) Communication equip. & electronic components; 8) Aircraft & parts; 9) Guided missiles & spacecraft; 10) Professional & scientific instruments.

[b] U.S. jobs supported directly and indirectly include jobs upstream in the production process and jobs downstream in the production process. Upstream jobs (production-oriented) include: Research and Development, Design, Purchasing, Manufacturing. Downstream jobs (to move the product through the market) include: Marketing, Selling, Distribution, and Service.

Sources: Yip, 1992, p. 105; Davis, 1996, pp. 14, 38.

GDP increased from US$391.1 billion, in 1985 to $630 billion, in 1994. China represented to the United States a fertile and growing economy for exports, imports, and investment. The sluggish economic growth of the U.S. domestic economy would be reversed by opening the China market through the

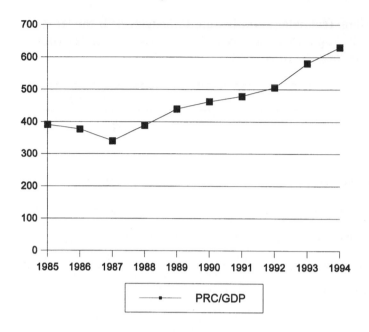

Figure 4.1   China/Real GDP 1985-1994 (US$billion)

Sources: International Financial Statistics, 1996; *Europa World Yearbook*, 1994; *Asian Development Outlook*, 1993.

permanent granting of MFN, thereby increasing the U.S. competitive position in the Asian-Pacific region, and in the global economy. In his first presidential debate, Clinton emphasized the importance of U.S. economic security: "In order to keep America the strongest nation in the world, we need some continuity and change. We have to face the fact that in this world, economic security is a whole lot of national security" ("Campaign '92", 1991, p. A16). The importance of the United States' economic security was exemplified in Clinton's new "economic model". Clinton created the National Economic Council (NEC), patterned after the National Security Council (NSC), dating back to the Truman administration (Rosenbaum, 1994, p. A1).[5] "While pledging to continue to pressure Beijing on human rights, Clinton couched his change of heart in economic and geopolitical terms, citing U.S. interest in profiting from Asia's economic boom and thwarting North Korea's nuclear weapons program" (Daniel Williams, 1994, p. A1).

In 1994, after the formation of the North American Free Trade Agreement, Clinton sought to liberalize trans-Pacific trade. As Clinton remarked:

By taking the courageous steps of opening trade in our own hemisphere, we have the economic, the political and the moral standing to make the case that ought to be done throughout the world, that America is serious about lowering trade barriers and promoting growth in our country and throughout the globe. (Schoenberger and Helm, 1993, pp. A1, A3)

Human rights considerations became increasingly subordinated to concerns for U.S. economic expansion in the Asian region. In April 1994, one month before the decision to end the ties between human rights and trade, an informal debate had taken place in the White House between the president and his top aides. When National Security Advisor Anthony Lake recommended some partial sanctions the United States might have imposed on China in the event of human rights violations, he was interrupted by Secretary of Commerce Ron Brown who asserted, "This is not what we ought to be talking about". Secretary Brown challenged the moral superiority of those worrying about human rights in China more than economic growth in the United States. He further articulated, during the course of the meeting, "Look at some of these inner cities; take a ride over to Anacostia [a section of Washington, D.C.]. What about their human rights?" Madeleine Albright, then U.S. ambassador to the United Nations, replied: "How can you be so insensitive to human rights in China?" (Greenberger and Frisby, 1994, p. A18).

Secretary Brown assured the American Chamber of Commerce that politics would no longer be a detriment to foreign competitors in the China market (Kaye, 1994, pp. 16-17). Brown wanted to "tilt the field" in favor of U.S. businesses, even if it meant a revival of low-cost credits to help U.S. firms compete with European and Japanese interests in China. A prevailing factor that had influenced the 1994 decision was the growing U.S. trade deficit with China, which was thought by U.S. officials to impede U.S. domestic and international economic strength by its negative effect on U.S. producers, consumers, and workers.

Table 4.4 displays that in 1994 the U.S. trade deficit with China was US$-32 billion, the second highest after the trade deficit with Japan, at $-65.7 billion. U.S. officials accused China of having a mercantilist trade regime, imposing high tariff rates and protectionist policies on U.S. goods and investment, thereby contributing to the skewed U.S.-China trade relationship. As shown in Figure 4.2, the United States experienced a rapidly growing trade deficit with China beginning in the year 1986, at US$-1.6 billion and increasing to $-32 billion by 1994. By 1994, U.S. imports from China, amounting to $41.3 billion, far exceeded U.S. exports to China, at $9.3 billion. The eminent regard for U.S. power and hegemony on the Asian continent through the attainment of superior

Table 4.4   Comparison of U.S. Trade Balance with Selected Asian Nations During the Year 1994 (US$billion)

	U.S. Exports	U.S. Imports	Balance (x - m)
Japan	53.4	119.1	-65.7
China	9.3	41.3	-32.0
Hong Kong	11.4	9.7	1.7
South Korea	18.0	19.7	-1.7
Taiwan	17.1	26.7	-9.6
Singapore	13.0	15.3	-2.3

Source: U.S. Department of Commerce, "United States Foreign Trade Highlights", 1994.

Figure 4.2   U.S. Trade Balance with China 1972-1997 (US$billion)

Sources: Direction of Trade Statistics, various years.

economic capabilities was articulated in the discourse of U.S. government officials and analysts. In February 1994, for example, three months before the executive decision was made to end the connection between trade and human rights, Arnold Kanter, Under Secretary for Political Affairs, emphasized a U.S.-China economic policy that was driven by U.S. national interests, specifically the maintenance and enlargement of the U.S. position as a global economic power. Kanter testified before the U.S. Senate: "This committee knows better than anyone that the economic future of the United States depends upon the strong, competitive position of American firms in all regions of the world" (U.S. Congress, Senate, 1992 [Kanter], p. 16).

The U.S. interest for power in the Asian region was illustrated through public statements that were articulated in the Congress concerning China's threat as a rising superpower in the Asian region.[6] For example, in a conversation before the House between Congressman Gary Ackerman of New York and former U.S. ambassador to China, James Lilley, Ackerman expressed concern for China's economic leverage over North Korea.

Congressman Ackerman: If China were not fully engaged on an economic basis with North Korea, would it cease to have influence on that government?

Mr. Lilley: My sense is that when you use leverage like this, it is not a zero sum game. It is a game of what we call China's "wearing the small shoes", pinching slow water torture, pushing your target in a certain direction, moving somebody, let's say, 20 degrees in one direction.

Congressman Ackerman: This is Asian Philosophy?

Mr. Lilley: "Wearing small shoes" is a Chinese expression. But they feel that what the Chinese are trying to do is walk a line between using their leverage to get certain advantages which are in their interest, namely to enhance their position in the world, to get good trading relationships with the South, and keep the buffer zone in North Korea. (U.S. Congress, House, 1993 [Ackerman], pp. 10-12; U.S. Congress, House, 1993 [Lilley], pp. 10-12)

And, in another question addressed to Mr. Lilley by Congressman Smith:

Congressman Smith: Is it a long-term goal on the part of the Chinese in terms of hegemony?

Mr. Lilley: When you deal with China, you are dealing with contradictions. Look at the history of their support for insurgency in southeast Asia. They were pouring money into all kinds of insurgencies while they maintained friendly relations with the governments involved. The answer was, we have friendship with governments but we support the international proletarian movement. . . . We cannot isolate China. For 5,000 years they lived under authoritarian rule. We must engage them. It is too easy to go back to authoritarian rule and isolationism for China. (U.S. Congress, House, 1993 [Smith], p. 44; U.S. Congress, House, 1993 [Lilley], pp. 10-12)

Thomas W. Robinson, president of the American Asian Research Enterprises, further articulated the threat of China as a global power: "China will never again be a weak country. It is becoming, in fact, a global power, eventually a superpower. Growing Chinese power can be ignored for a few years or more, but eventually China will project its power even more and in every regard" (U.S. Congress, House, 1993 [Robinson], p. 89). And in another example: Senator Larry Pressler to Ambassador Lord: "Regarding India, in December, an Indian official told me of the Chinese intent on regional dominance. Is this concern justified?" (U.S. Congress, Senate, 1994 [Pressler], p. 27).

Some U.S. policymakers thought that withdrawing or conditioning China's MFN on the basis of China's human rights conditions, would mean a loss of competitiveness for U.S. firms in the China market. Loss of competitiveness would also mean a loss of U.S. national power because of a weakened private sector. "Japan, Taiwan and the EU would supplant the United States and it would take the United States years to regain its current position as China's major western trading partner" (U.S. Congress, Senate, 1992 [Wolf], p. 19). Former U.S. Secretaries of State Henry Kissinger and Cyrus Vance publicly commended the 1994 Clinton decision for this reason:

> President Clinton made a difficult but correct decision. America's broader interests in Asia require a reasonable relationship with the region's emerging superpower. European, Japanese and other businessmen would have rushed to fill the resulting vacuum. America would have been isolated. (Kissinger and Vance, 1994, p. A19)

In many respects, the U.S. national interest did drive the U.S. economic policy of delinkage in 1994. Withdrawing or conditioning MFN would have been a call for disaster to U.S. workers, consumers, and employers. For U.S. workers, it might have meant the loss of jobs. Of the 250,000 total jobs supported by U.S. aircraft exports to foreign markets, a percentage of those jobs that depend on the China market for sales and profits would have been at risk.

Moreover, U.S. aircraft exports, of which the United States enjoyed a monopoly in the China market, may, for example, have been lost to foreign competitors, such as, for instance, the European Airbus consortium (Rowen, 1994, p. H1).

U.S. jobs would also have been maintained and increased in the agricultural sector through unconditional MFN to China. U.S. fertilizers and wheat accounted for US$567 million in 1993 (see above Table 4.2). U.S. farmers could have potentially lost millions in commodities sold to China annually and would also have lost the opportunity of future food and fiber sales to one of the most populous countries in the world (Kleckner, 1997). For U.S. manufacturers and importers of consumer goods, conditioning or revoking MFN would have led to billions of dollars in lost retail goods in the event that China retaliated with higher tariffs and other types of trade sanctions on finished goods. By the early 1990s, China supplied 48 percent of the toys in the U.S. market, 14 percent of imported garments, and 15 percent of the footwear sold in the United States. The markup on prices would have negatively affected middle- and lower-income Americans who would have been compelled to pay higher prices for consumer goods produced in China because of higher import tariffs. Cheaper prices for consumers would create an increased demand for goods in the U.S. market. The increased demand for finished goods would in turn generate an increase in U.S. jobs in the importing and retailing sectors of the economy (U.S. Congress, House, 1992 [Moscow], p. 42).

Table 4.5 indicates the tariff rates with and without MFN on major U.S. imports from China. As shown, U.S. import tariffs on Chinese goods would have risen substantially had MFN been revoked. Footwear would increase from 6 percent to 35 percent. Various garments would increase from 6 percent to 60 percent, and toys from 6.8 percent to 70 percent.

Were U.S.-China trade restrictions to have been removed and MFN to have been granted unconditionally, U.S. exports would have risen, in part because of China's demand for high-technology goods, goods in which the United States holds a comparative advantage. China's demand and a more open market for high-technology and capital-intensive goods would serve to heighten the demand for skilled human capital in the U.S. labor market.[7] China's demand for high-technology and capital-intensive goods would increase U.S. demand for jobs in high-technology industries, both directly and indirectly, in the service support industries. U.S. jobs in the high-technology industries that had been declining between 1991 and 1994 would then begin to rise.

U.S. interests in future revenue streams generated by China's increasingly prosperous market could be capitalized on by U.S. firms (Prybyla, 1993, pp. 11-12). U.S. firms, in their desire to be first to gain competitive market share in China, either through FDI or exports, saw great future profits from China's

Table 4.5   Comparison of Tariff Rates with and without MFN on Major U.S. Imports from China

Product	MFN Tariff	Non-MFN Tariff
Footwear (uppers over 90% plastic)	6.0%	35.0%
Sweaters, shorts, & vests	6.0%	60.0%
Toys, garments, baby carriages, etc.	6.8%	70.0%
Luggage (outer surface man-made fibers)	20.8%	65.0%
Luggage (outer surface ramie, jute)	6.5%	40.0%
Gloves, Mittens (leather)	3.5%	45.0%
Leather Belts	5.3%	35.0%
Cordless Phones	6.0%	35.0%
Christmas-Tree Lights	8.0%	50.0%

Source: U.S. Congress, House, 1994 [Fashion Accessories Shippers Association], p. 147.

potentially immense and growing consumer market. In total, U.S. firms, skilled workers, and consumers would benefit by further opening of the China market through unconditional MFN. The granting of unconditional MFN to China would create a growing and healthy U.S. domestic economy. A healthy domestic economy would then ensure and increase the U.S. national security which would be further enhanced by a strong U.S. presence in the Asian-Pacific region. Finally, it was in the U.S. national interest not to revoke or condition human rights on trade because of the ripple affect it would cause in the Asian region. A significant amount of U.S. trade with and investment in China is dependent on Hong Kong and Taiwan, which are heavily invested in China, and serve as economic segues to and from the Mainland for U.S. investors, importers, and exporters.

Not only, therefore, would China have been affected by trade sanctions, but so would the entire trilateral economic relationship of Hong Kong, Taiwan, and China. Impediments to trade in the Asian region would not have been in the best interests of the United States because they would have deterred economic and diplomatic relations.[8] Politically, revocation of MFN to China would have only weakened the U.S. influence on the policies and practices of the Chinese government by isolating China from U.S. commercial contacts. "If trade was disrupted, cooperation on other issues would probably have disintegrated" (Daniel Williams, 1994, p. A28).[9]

Critique

That the national interest was the driving force behind U.S. policy displayed some shortcomings. To begin, U.S. policymakers who denounced the Chinese regime for supporting mercantilist trade practices may not have considered China's total world trade. On the whole, trade statistics reflected that China was not a surplus country. Between the years 1980 and 1994, inclusive, China had been a net deficit country with the exception of only five years out of the fifteen total years, as shown in Figure 4.3. In 1993, China had been running a negative trade balance with the world at $-12.2 billion. With more imports than exports, China's total world trade pattern revealed that it was not engaging in mercantilist practices.

The unfavorable U.S. trade balance with China that U.S. policymakers frequently cited in policy debates, was (and is) in part due to direct foreign investment through U.S. firms. Much of China's exports accrue from foreign money investment going back to the United States. As earlier mentioned in chapter 3, in 1993, when U.S. inflows to China increased to $2.0 billion, China's exports to the United States increased by 9 percent from the previous year (see Table 3.2). By the early 1990s, almost half of China's exports were processed or assembled and contained 80 percent foreign intermediate or final parts. From these processed exports, China earns only 20 cents on the dollar (Sung, 1991, p. 301).

In U.S. trade data, however, China is calculated as having earned the full dollar. This calculation in effect misrepresents China's actual export earnings. U.S. direct foreign investment does not enter into official U.S. trade data reports even though a significant portion of U.S.-China trade occurs through FDI avenues. The nationalist argument faulting China for the U.S. trade deficit evidenced some deficiencies. One was the role of Hong Kong as entrepôt. In 1990, for example, two thirds of China's exports to the United States were first being sold to Hong Kong and then re-exported to the U.S. Indirect sales of U.S. goods through Hong Kong are not counted in U.S. official data, so that U.S. exports to China appear somewhat less than in reality.

Table 4.6 indicates the adjusted and unadjusted trade balance before and after accounting for re-exports through Hong Kong for both the United States and China. For the year 1993, for example, U.S. data show a bilateral trade balance of US$-29.5 billion, while China's data show a bilateral balance, for the

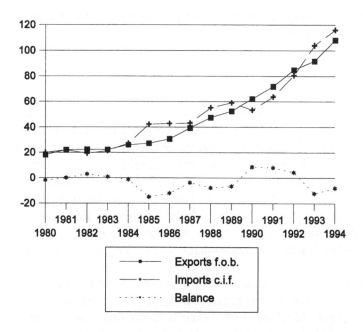

Figure 4.3　China/Total World Trade 1980-1994 (US$billion)

Sources: China Statistical Abstract, 1998.

same year, of $-7.5 billion. After adjusting for China's re-exports through Hong Kong, however, the trade balance figures became closer in number, at $-25.8 billion, according to U.S. data., and $-29.1 billion, according to China's data. Additionally, U.S. economic policymakers who disparaged China for unfair trade advantages may have overlooked that China's trade surplus with the United States may be cyclical, rather than a "contrived neobullionist phenomenon", which will adjust itself through increased Chinese imports as China develops its vast infrastructure and technology upgrading program, and when the Chinese demand for quality consumer goods increases (Prybyla, 1993, pp. 11-12).

Beyond the problem of differing trade calculation methods and cyclical patterns, obstacles to U.S. exports to China may have been self-imposed. For example, the United States places restrictions on exporting technologies to China. If these restrictions were removed, U.S. exports would substantially increase because of China's demand for technology and capital goods. Additionally, the nationalist argument that U.S. jobs would have been lost by sanctioning trade on human rights, was deficient. The China trade, for example,

Table 4.6 U.S.-China Trade Balances Adjusted for Re-exports (U.S. and Chinese data, US$billion)

	Official US-China trade balance (US data)	Official US-China trade balance (Chinese data)	Fung and Lau estimate of US-China trade balance after adjusting for re-exports (US data)	Fung and Lau estimate of US-China trade balance after adjusting for re-exports (Chinese data)
1989	-6.2	+3.5	-4.9	-3.7
1990	-10.4	+1.4	-9.1	-7.8
1991	-12.7	+1.8	-11.0	-9.9
1992	-18.3	+0.3	-15.9	-15.4
1993	-22.8	-6.3	-19.5	-24.9
1994	-29.5	-7.5	-25.8	-29.1
1995	-33.8	-8.6	-28.9	-31.2

Sources: Fung and Lau, 1998, p. 36; General Administration of Customs of the People's Republic of China, various years; Hong Kong Census and Statistics Department, various years; U.S. Department of Commerce, "U.S. Foreign Trade Highlights", various years.

did not affect U.S. jobs at aggregate levels, but only jobs in certain key industry sectors.[10] True, 250,000 U.S. jobs may have been dependent on total U.S. exports of aircraft and aircraft parts. But only a small percentage of those jobs were dependent specifically on the China market. For example, Figure 4.4 demonstrates that the total U.S. jobs dependent on goods exports to China for the year 1994 amounted to 138,000 jobs.

Of those 138,000 jobs, 106,000 jobs were dependent on manufactured exports to China (Davis, 1996, pp. 34-37).[11] Still, of those 106,000 jobs, the aircraft industry — the largest U.S. exporter to China in terms of value amount — would have accounted for an even smaller percentage of those 106,000 jobs.[12] Figure 4.5 indicates that only 13.5 percent of U.S. jobs were in the high-technology manufacturing sector in 1994, of which the aerospace and defense industries would be included. The greater part of U.S. jobs supported by goods exports were in non-high-tech manufactures (35.1%), and services (40%) for the year 1994. For the most part, U.S. jobs generated by exports to foreign markets

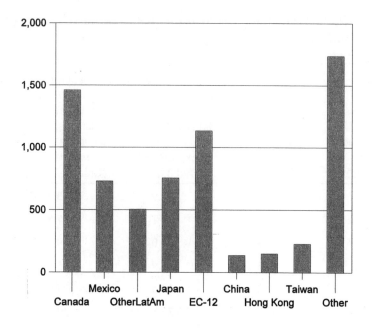

Figure 4.4 U.S. Jobs Supported by Goods Exports to Key Foreign Markets in 1994 (in 000s)

Source: Davis, 1996, p. 16.

in 1994, as Figure 4.4 illustrates, were dependent on the foreign markets of Canada (1,460,000 jobs), the EU (1,133,000 jobs), and Mexico (729,000 jobs).

Moreover, as demonstrated in Figure 4.6, between the years 1986 and 1994 the largest increase in U.S. jobs dependent on foreign export markets was to the Mexican market, with an increase of 479,000 jobs. The China market represented the least increase in U.S. jobs supported by key foreign markets, amounting to a 74,000 job increase. In total, U.S. jobs that were supported by goods exports to China represented very little in the total U.S. labor market. The impact that revoking or conditioning China's MFN would have on U.S. jobs would only be in key industry sectors, but not in aggregate employment.

In this respect, the nationalist position, espousing that the United States would lose thousands or hundreds of thousands of jobs by conditioning trade on human rights, was exaggerated. In further weakness of the nationalist argument, that U.S. consumers would have been compelled to pay higher prices if MFN were to have been revoked, may not have been totally exact. As the economist

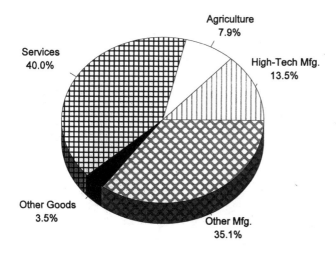

Figure 4.5   Share of Jobs Supported by Key Industry Sectors by Goods Exports in 1994 (in %)

Source: Davis, 1996, p. 9.

Jagdish Bhagwati clarified, "The costs to the U.S. economy were much exaggerated by advocates of unconditional MFN to China. If MFN to China were to be denied, U.S. retail prices would have risen only temporarily, until American companies began manufacturing in other low-wage countries, such as India, Indonesia, Malaysia, or the untapped African continent" (Jagdish Bhagwati, quoted in Berlau, 1997, pp. 16-20). Lastly, the nationalist policy position that China — as a rising superpower — would be a potential threat to U.S. security interests, revealed some deficiencies. The China market, for instance, may not have been as large as the proponents of unconditional MFN had claimed it to be. To begin, China had been a continuing net debtor nation. China had consistently increased its external borrowing to facilitate the transition from a command to a market economy, and therefore has increased its foreign debt. Figure 4.7 demonstrates that China's external debt grew from US$16.7 billion in 1985 to $69.3 billion by 1992 (Asian Development Bank, 1993; *International Financial Statistics*, 1997). By 1996, China's external debt had increased to $129 billion,

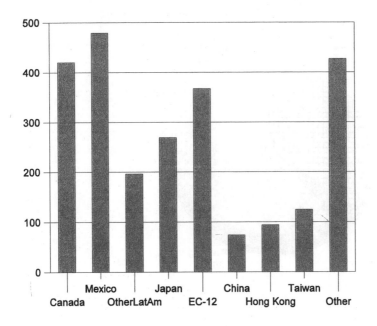

Figure 4.6   Increase in U.S. Jobs Supported by Goods Exports to Key Foreign Markets 1986-1994 (in 000s)

Source: Davis, 1996, p. 16.

ranking it as the fourth highest foreign debtor nation in the world, after Brazil, Mexico, and Indonesia, consecutively (*Economist*, 1999d, p. 36).

Unlike many of the commonly-held conceptions, "China is not like Japan, which held a chronic global surplus. China is more like Mexico and Indonesia or Korea which through their early decades of development borrowed capital from the rest of the world and ran global trade deficits" (U.S. Congress, House, 1994 [Bergsten], p. 241). Moreover, the 30 to 40 million absolute poor in rural areas in China continue to live on the margin of subsistence. Many poor rely on China's grain relief system, which provides minimal grain provisions. Peasants are required to pay high fees for basic services,[13] and also high taxes to provincial and local governments at the same time the government is giving them IOUs as payment for their grain. There had also been reports that if parents couldn't pay, their children were prohibited from attending school. As central and local government funds decreased in the process of market reform in China, the financial burdens transferred to the peasants, the largest segment of China's

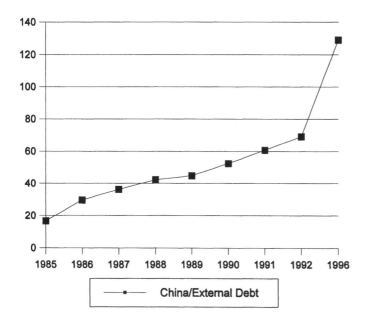

Figure 4.7 China/External Debt 1985-1996 (US$billion)

Sources: Economist, 1999d; World Debt Tables, 1996, 1997.

population, who could ill afford it. As Figure 4.8 illustrates, the rural population of China comprises over 70 percent of the population. One quarter of the rural workers are now wage earners, yet still lack the labor insurance coverage that is offered to urban workers (World Bank, 1996, pp. 78-80).

Aside from the problem of rural poverty, there is an increasing "floating population" of migrant workers in China who represent a growing poverty group. In 1993, for example, there were 60 million roaming Chinese workers without social safety nets, largely due to China's transition from a plan to a market economy (pp. 78-80). The income disparities between the coastal region and the hinterland have been widening, and only a small segment of the population have been able to profit and benefit from the economic growth (U.S. Congress, House, 1993 [Binyan], pp. 113-19). It had been pointed out, as well, that the IMF report that was submitted to the executive branch in 1993 overestimated the per capita income of China, which was estimated to be about US$340.00 by the World Bank (U.S. Congress, House, 1994 [Bergsten], pp. 238-45),[14] whereas the IMF report estimated nearly three or four times as much. "That still gives China a total economy of US$1 trillion, which would put it in the top five or six

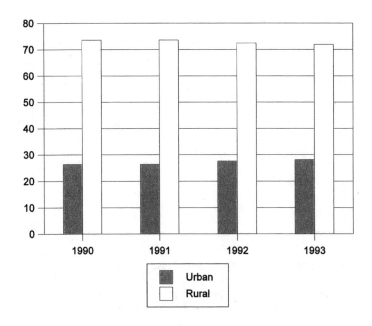

Figure 4.8   Urban/Rural Split in China Population (%)

Source: Consumer Asia 1996, 1996.

in the world. But it is nothing like the second or third largest economy" (U.S. Congress, House, 1994 [Bergsten], p. 240). As Bergsten further commented:

> China is not going to be as big as the United States in economic terms for at least half a century or maybe more, and it is not going to have anything like the per capita income of the United States, even if they grow twice as fast as we do for another couple of centuries. This is only to say that China, though big, is still a poor country. It is a developing country. Its per capita income is low, and we have to think of it in those terms rather than thinking of it as a big, new economic superpower on the order of the United States or Japan. (p. 239)

The U.S. hegemonic position in the Asian-Pacific region was indeed a critical variable in the 1994 decision, as evidenced in the rhetoric of U.S. leaders. The realist argument did, in part, account for the 1994 policy decision. Given the weaknesses uncovered in the realist argument, however, the U.S. national interest was only partially able to account for the motives behind the 1994 Clinton administration decision to delink China's human rights practices from trade. U.S. economic engagement with China, premised on the threat of China's emergence as an economic hegemon in the Asian region, is weakened, given China's internal structural economic and political impediments, and the realities of the vast and transient global marketplace where corporations and capital are footloose, and where workers can be substituted within and across borders.

Humanitarian Values

The second hypothesis, premised on liberalism, was that the U.S. intent to improve the respect for human rights in China through economic engagement influenced the 1994 decision to separate China's human rights record from most-favored-nation status. To review, followers of the liberal school of thought envisage that the peace and prosperity of nations would be advanced by the removal of economic barriers. U.S. trade with China, therefore, is viewed as a catalyst for democracy and the alleviation of political repression in China. U.S. corporations, by way of their products (that would enable individual choice), management techniques, and production practices, would serve as pathways to democracy and human rights reform in China by reaching beyond government constraints, directly to the people (Clark, 1916, pp. 209-29; Bernstein and Dicker, 1994/95, pp. 43-47; Garten, 1997, p. 71). It was President Clinton who argued in 1994 that human rights in China would best be improved through economic engagement, or that corporations would help democratize China. As the president stated:

> To those who argue that in view of China's human rights abuses, we should revoke MFN status, let me ask you the same question that I have asked myself; will we do more to advance the cause of human rights if China is isolated or if our nations are engaged in a growing web of political and economic cooperation and contacts? (President William J. Clinton, quoted in Thomas Friedman, 1994, p. A1)

Many positive social and economic reforms had taken place in China since 1989. For example, "more VCRs and satellite dishes were available, stores were filled with television sets, Beijing was marked with construction cranes, and facsimile machines were available to send word of political arrests in Beijing across the nation" (Senator John Kerry of Massachusetts, quoted in Greenberger and Frisby, 1994, p. A18). The years preceding the 1994 decision, from 1990 to 1993, bring out that China's standard of living had risen, as measured by key consumer durables.

Table 4.7 indicates that consumption of such consumer goods as bicycles, sewing machines, color TV sets, and washing machines had risen steadily in

Table 4.7   China's Standard of Living as Measured by Consumer Durables
(items per 100 households)

	1990	1991	1992	1993
Urban				
Bicycles	188.6	158.5	190.5	197.2
Motor Cycles	n/a	n/a	2.8	3.5
Sewing Machines	70.1	66.4	65.9	66.6
Color TV Sets	59.0	68.4	74.9	79.5
Monochrome TV Sets	52.4	43.9	37.7	35.9
Electric Fans	135.5	143.5	146.0	151.6
Washing Machines	78.4	80.6	83.4	86.4
Refrigerators	42.3	48.7	52.6	56.7
Rural				
Bicycles	118.3	121.6	125.7	133.4
Motor Cycles	0.9	1.1	1.4	2.1
Sewing Machines	55.2	55.8	57.3	61.3
Color TV Sets	4.7	6.4	8.1	10.9
Monochrome TV Sets	39.7	47.5	52.4	58.3
Electric Fans	41.4	53.3	60.1	71.8
Washing Machines	9.1	11.0	12.2	13.8
Refrigerators	1.2	1.6	2.2	3.1

Source: Consumer Asia 1996, 1996.

both rural and urban geographical areas. It was further expressed in the U.S. Congress that China was approaching its "fourth revolution", meaning that there had been systematic change in the standard of living of the Chinese people, that patterns of information flow were increasing, and that political and economic decentralization was taking place (U.S. Congress, Senate, 1994 [Gong], p. 51). Section 402 of the Trade Act of 1974, noted earlier in chapter 3, was the Jackson-Vanik Amendment. The amendment stipulated that the renewal of a country's MFN status would be contingent upon that country's allowance of its citizens the freedom of emigration. In his June 2, 1994 communiqué to Congress, Clinton had affirmed to China's foreign minister, Qian Qichen, in keeping with the promise to Secretary of State Christopher, to "resolve all pending emigration ('blocked passport') cases the United States government pressed upon them for the pending year [1993]" (Clinton, 1994).

The president continued to assure, in his communication to the Congress, that some of the individuals who were released from prison were relatives of prominent dissidents, some of whom held government jobs in China with access to politically sensitive information. The principal barrier to the departure of ordinary Chinese, the president concluded, was the inability to secure a visa, and that record numbers of U.S. visas were issued worldwide to tourists and business visitors from China, an approximate 90 percent increase over the previous year (1993) (Clinton, 1994).

President Clinton's position in 1994, that ending the connection between MFN renewal and human rights would further the cause of human rights in China, was supported by major U.S. government executives. Under Secretary of State for Political Affairs Arnold Kanter affirmed that "the renewal of MFN without conditions continues to influence those policies that permit tens of thousands of Chinese every year to choose to leave China permanently and to travel abroad and gain exposure to the outside world" (U.S. Congress, House, 1992 [Kanter], p. 30). Kanter further claimed that the economic growth that China has experienced since the implementation of economic reforms and economic engagement with the United States has improved the lives of ordinary Chinese by increasing household incomes through the expansion of agricultural and industrial production. China's economic growth had given Chinese citizens newly found freedom over their lives: "Since 1978, there has been a dramatic change. Chinese are free to travel domestically, purchase foreign-made consumer goods and wear Western or traditional dress. Non-governmental-controlled media are available in China today than ever before, including cable TV in parts of China, satellite dishes and American TV programs" (p. 33).

The second human rights stipulation specified in Clinton's 1993 Executive Order was a mandatory condition for MFN renewal in 1994. This mandatory condition was that China comply with the 1992 U.S.-China bilateral Agreement on Prison Labor.[15] Winston Lord, Assistant Secretary for East Asian and Pacific Affairs, reported in February 1994 that the Chinese indicated a willingness to cooperate with respect to meeting the agreements of the 1992 Memorandum of Understanding regarding China's prison labor, and that China had acquiesced to additional visits of prisons requested by the U.S. Customs (U.S. Congress, House, 1994 [Lord], p. 76).

Secretary Lord recognized that although there had been areas of "slippage" in some areas of human rights stipulated in the 1993 Executive Order, there had been some progress. "Some dissidents had been released from jail prior to completion of their term, either unconditionally or on medical leave" (p. 76). China had also provided an initial response and readiness to discuss the possibility of the release of a list of prisoners Assistant Secretary Shattuck had provided to them in October of 1993. China had discussed with the International Red Cross the possibility of visits to prisons and suggested further human rights dialogue (p. 76).

U.S. government leaders who advocated the granting of unconditional MFN to China believed that only through the use of capitalist tools could freedom and human rights reforms take place in China, because "free commercial contacts change the way people interact with each other" (U.S. Congress, House, 1994 [Kolbe], p. 26). Private enterprise would be the catalyst for societal change in China. U.S. corporations in China, for example, have insisted that they be given the right to interview and to choose their own employees, as opposed to receiving government assignees. Free and unhindered interviews by U.S. corporations changed the relationship between the government and the university labor market because students were given a choice of working for a U.S. company or working for a state-owned enterprise to which they might otherwise be automatically assigned (pp. 26-28). U.S. government and business leaders who advocated unconditional MFN to China felt that trade sanctions and liberty were incompatible. Conditioning or revoking China's MFN would only harm those factions in China who were encouraging political reform. U.S. leaders who held this opinion believed that economic sanctions "were really a 'feel good' approach to promoting human rights without any chance of being effective" (Bartlett, 1985, p. 10, cited in Dorn, 1996, p. 79). Sanctions would only antagonize the Chinese government and further radicalize those officials already in power. According to the opinions of some U.S. policy analysts and business executives, human rights concerns did influence the 1994 U.S. policy decision to delink trade and MFN. They believed that trade and corporate engagement with China would produce a rising middle class in China that would insist on democratic social and political values.

Critique

The liberalist argument that human rights was the driving force behind the 1994 trade policy decision revealed some weaknesses. Many U.S. policymakers, human rights groups, and public citizens believed that MFN should be contingent upon human rights improvements in China. Concerns had mounted in Congress for the numerous reports of continued repression in China. In a poll taken in December 1993 by NBC News and the *Wall Street Journal*, Americans across the country were asked their opinions on U.S. trade with China. Nearly 29 percent said "we should maintain good trade relations with China, despite disagreements we might have with its human rights policies", whereas 65 percent of the respondents endorsed the statement "we should demand that China improve its human rights policies if China wants to continue to enjoy its current trade status with the United States" (Bowman, 1994, p. 150).

On March 1, 1994, 276 members of the House signed a letter to Secretary of State Warren Christopher demanding that China meet its human rights conditions (Beher, 1994, p. A28). Human rights advocates inside and outside of government expressed that overall significant progress in China's human rights had not been met in accordance with the 1993 Executive Order. It was argued that despite the U.S. yearly renewal of MFN to China since 1980, the human rights situation (particularly since the 1989 Tiananmen democracy movement) had only worsened. U.S. officials, human rights advocates, and public citizens articulated that MFN should be conditioned on the improvement of China's human rights practices. They supported the past presidential policies of attaching human rights conditions to the U.S. yearly renewal of MFN to China. A major international human rights group, Human Rights Watch/Asia had expressed this sentiment: "We believe that the continuing attention to MFN for China is crucial for maintaining pressure on the Chinese Government and the need has never been greater" (U.S. Congress, House, 1992 [Jendrzejczyk], p. 92).

Human rights advocates agreed that U.S. engagement and corporate involvement, through a voluntary code of conduct based on the model of the Sullivan Principles, could play a positive role in bringing about human rights reform and societal change in China, but that corporate initiative, alone, was not enough. It was expressed, however, that no other measure would substitute for MFN in terms of its power as a bargaining tool to pressure China to respect basic human rights. Moreover, the delinkage of MFN and human rights was thought by major human rights groups to hinder the safety of dissidents and reformers in China and damage the credibility of U.S. policy on human rights issues across the globe (U.S. Congress, Senate, 1994 [Jendrzejczyk], pp. 78-79).

Specifically, in 1993 and 1994 some liberal factions in the U.S. government believed that MFN should be conditioned on China's progress on all seven human rights items addressed in the 1993 Executive Order issued by the president. Human rights stipulations in all seven categories, specified in the 1993 Executive Order, had not improved enough (or at all), according to many opinions articulated in government. Senator Feingold articulated to Secretary Lord:

I lend my support to the administration's past emphasis on linkage, particularly in Asia, where we have very real economic and human rights concerns. And I urge you, Secretary Lord, not to subsume human rights to other concerns. I think it is second to nothing, and what America stands for. And we would be abdicating our role as a superpower if we were to shy away from that concern. (U.S. Congress, Senate, 1994 [Feingold], p. 8)

Representative Neil Abercrombie reiterated Senator Feingold's value-based position:

It has been said that [human rights] is an internal matter for China and that our in-sistence on human rights improvements constitutes interference in China's internal affairs. This line of argument turns the truth on its head. The decision whether to grant or withhold MFN status is an internal affair of the United States. We are ob-liged to frame our national policies in terms of the Constitution, which forms the basis of our national government, and the United Nations Declaration of Human Rights, to which we are a signatory. (U.S. Congress, House, 1994 [Abercrombie], pp. 38-41)

Amnesty International USA, a leading international human rights NGO, ex-pressed the opinion that humanitarian values did not drive U.S. policy choice on China. Immediately after the Clinton decision was made, for instance, the in-fluential NGO alluded to the inconsistency in U.S. human rights policy regar-ding China. As stated by Amnesty International before Congress in July of 1994, "It remains unclear today what constitutes the administration's human rights policy toward China and Tibet" (U.S. Congress, House, 1994 [Jones], p. 171). While Amnesty International did not take a position on linkage, the organization stated:

In renewing MFN trade status to China, President Clinton announced certain actions that would be part of a human rights policy, including increased support for Non-Governmental Organizations (NGOs) in China, increased radio broadcasts into China, and working with businesses to establish a voluntary code of conduct. While we welcome efforts by offices and individuals of the U.S. government to develop such human rights initiatives, many have not yet been attained, and in no way can they be regarded as constituting a human rights policy. Furthermore, these efforts taken collectively do not assure the significant position that human rights deserves in overall U.S. policy. (p. 172)

Thus, the nature of the policy-making process vis-à-vis China, in 1994, was such that there were different actors involved, and those actors reflected a wide range of opinion on how human rights in China should be approached. Some actors wanted to continue to liberalize trade between the two countries and delink MFN and human rights, while other actors wanted to maintain the linkage, or felt that the United States did not take human rights seriously enough in its policy making. In short, there was not a unified liberal view on how to improve human rights in China. Even among human rights groups, there had not been a consensus on how to instill human rights in U.S. foreign policy. The human rights group Asia Watch, for example, clearly expressed that MFN should be conditioned on China's human rights practices, whereas Amnesty International did not take a stance on the policy issue of linkage at all. Because of these discrepancies within the liberal argument, the desire to advance human rights in China through increased trade did not entirely shape U.S. foreign policy choice in 1994.

Corporate Influence

The radical paradigm formed the underlying premise for the third hypothesis, which was that U.S. corporations influenced the 1994 decision to end the relationship between China's human rights record and MFN status. This economically-determinist perspective suggests that corporations maintain a considerable amount of influence on U.S. foreign economic policy. In this case, China is considered to be the main geographical target of the corporate expansionist agenda, backed by monopoly capitalists.

In the years preceding the 1994 decision, U.S. corporations became more vocal in the public arena in expressing their views on U.S.-China policy. The growing appearance of business lobbying groups in Congress gave evidence of the increasing attempts by business groups to influence the 1994 policy decision. Business lobbyists pointing to the losses of jobs and profits that would result if MFN were to be revoked became increasingly present and vocal on Capitol Hill. Business and agricultural groups argued that the increase in tariff rates that both the United States and China would apply if MFN were to be revoked would harm U.S. exporters, importers, and consumers. The National Retail Federation (NRF), for instance, claimed that there were an "estimated 170,000 jobs[16] created by exports to China, that Chinese imports helped to sustain 2.4 million jobs in the service sector, and that revoking MFN would cost American families $300 a year in higher prices of such popular Chinese imports as toys" (Berlau, 1997, pp. 15-16). Similarly, before 1990 farmers had been largely absent from the U.S. Congressional scene. By 1991, however, the National Association of Wheat Growers was one of the major business groups that lobbied for unconditional MFN (Lee, 1991, p. A5).

Chief executive officers of major U.S. corporations involved in trade and commerce with China spoke privately with Clinton's cabinet secretaries about the potential jobs and profits that would be lost if MFN to China were to be withdrawn (Awanohara, 1993, p. 156). A vast array of statistics, statements, and overstatements were thrown in the public arena, together with private contributions to U.S. political parties and officials on behalf of the MFN and human rights delinkage.

In February 1994, three months before the decision was made, U.S. business lobbyists and coalitions came to the forefront of the Congressional agenda to plead their cases for the termination of the linkage of MFN and China's human rights practices.[17]

What solidified many thousands of small firms to large multinationals, however, was the Business Coalition for U.S.-China Trade. Formed in 1991, the coalition was created to support the position of President Bush, that MFN be extended to China without conditions (Sutter, 1998, p. 57, citing Stone, 1991). The coalition began with over 75 major trading groups and by 1994 had grown to include over 800 corporations and trade associations. The goal of the Business Coalition was to speak with a single voice to influence Congress and the executive branch to permanently delink MFN and human rights.[18]

The hypothesis that U.S. corporations influenced the 1994 policy to end the relationship between human rights and MFN did show some validity. Many business lobbyists in 1994 represented key industries and corporations that were specifically engaged in the China trade as importers, exporters, or manufacturers in China. A prime example was the U.S. Aerospace Industries Association,[19] which had written a letter to President Clinton on May 13, 1994, asking for the extension of most-favored-nation trading status and a "halt to the linkage of human rights with trade" (*Defense Daily*, 1994, p. 265). Table 4.8 lists the U.S. corporate aerospace and defense signatories, whose sales to China collectively represented $2.2 billion in 1993 (see Table 4.2). Fear of profit and market loss was certainly a motive for the writing of the letter.

Concerns of loss of market share to foreign business groups were even more pressing to such U.S. aircraft manufacturers as Boeing and McDonnell Douglas, which had maintained a "monopoly on China's purchases of foreign aircraft, accounting for 76 percent of all Chinese purchases" (U.S. Congress, House, 1993 [Anderson], p. 97). In a testimony to Congress by Boeing/McDonnell Douglas Corporation, for example, it was articulated:

> Boeing and McDonnell Douglas are currently well positioned in the Chinese market, but Airbus — as well as Russians — are waiting to quickly take advantage if the relationship between the United States and China deteriorates. Already, [European] Airbus took 50 percent of new orders last year. . . . As the nation's largest

Table 4.8   U.S. Aerospace and Defense Firms: Signatories of the May 13, 1994 Letter to President Clinton Asking for the Delinkage of Human Rights and MFN

U.S. Aerospace and Defense Corporate Signatories
Aerojet
Boeing
Hughes Aircraft
Harris
Lockheed
Martin Marietta
McDonnell Douglas
Northrop
Rockwell
Sundstrand
Teledyne
Textron
United Technologies
Westinghouse

Source: Defense Daily, 1994, p. 265.

exporter, with more than 60 percent of revenues from non-U.S. customers, Boeing is one of many American companies whose future clearly depends on access to global markets. (U.S. Congress, House, 1994 [Boeing/McDonnell Douglas, Inc.], p. 304)

In addition to the aerospace industry, the Leather Apparel Association Industry, comprised of 125 companies involved in the manufacture, importation, and retailing of leather apparel products voiced their dependency on cheap Chinese labor and quantity of labor output. They expressed that "clearly no other location in Asia, other than China", could "produce the quantities necessary at the price points and quality essential to success in the U.S. market" (U.S. Congress, House, 1994 [Leather Apparel Association], p. 313). The Toy

Manufacturers of America (TMA), top importers of finished goods that are produced in China (which amounted to $4.4 billion in 1993) (see Table 4.2), expressed that if "U.S. producers and importers cannot take advantage of the China market, foreign competitors from Japan, Germany and elsewhere will have free reign in the quickest growing market in the world" (U.S. Congress, House, 1994 [Miller], p. 322).

Other business interests also expressed their opinions in the China/MFN and human rights debate. For example, the U.S. agricultural industry was represented by the Fertilizer Institute (TFI). The institute contended that "China buys 80 percent of its fertilizer from the U.S., approximately 16 percent of total U.S. fertilizer exports" (U.S. Congress, House, 1994 [Fertilizer Institute], pp. 308-9).[20] The application trade of sanctions would have meant a loss of those exports to China. Statements expressed by U.S. business lobbyists indicated that competition existed among cross-national corporate groups for economic control of the China market.

U.S. businesses were determined to influence U.S. government leaders to the point of utilizing inflated statements and economically unsound arguments. One such example was uncovered, during a Congressional session, by Representative Tom Lantos in his questioning of Donald Anderson, president of the United States-China Business Council. Anderson had stated that "withdrawing or conditioning MFN would mean a loss of $8 billion in U.S. exports" (U.S. Congress, House, 1993 [Anderson], p. 10). Representative Lantos questioned this assertion:

> *Representative Lantos:* You mean that what you are saying is that withdrawing or conditioning MFN would mean $8 billion in lost exports . . . the size of our total exports [to China]?
>
> *Mr. Anderson:* No sir, that is an over-statement.
>
> *Mr. Lantos:* It is a lie, Mr. Anderson. It has no relationship to reality. You ought to be ashamed of yourself. You prepared this statement on behalf of the United States-China Business Council and in the opening paragraph that is not tangentially related to the truth. As a matter of fact, I predict to you . . . that despite the fact there will be a conditioning of MFN to China, there will be an increase in American exports to China next year and the year after and the following year. Because China is a growing economy and they desperately need the things it buys from us. (U.S. Congress, House, 1993 [Lantos], pp. 21-22; [Anderson], p. 21)

Attempts by corporations to influence the 1994 decision constituted more than simply public rhetoric. Before Clinton signed the Executive Order of 1993 granting the extension of MFN status to China for another year, he received a letter signed by 298 companies and 37 trade associations requesting that conditions not be attached. During the same time, 50 companies gave soft money contributions, averaging about $30,000, to the Democratic National Committee (Kruger and Lewis, 1993, p. C3).

In anticipation of further Congressional debates on MFN conditionalities, U.S. corporations involved in commercial relations with China also gave soft money contributions to both Democratic and Republican parties in attempts to influence the extension of MFN in 1995. Table 4.9 demonstrates that total corporate contributions to both parties amounted to approximately $6.6 million.

Critique

There were some shortcomings to the claim that corporate influence was the principle motive for the 1994 decision. U.S. corporate interests were not the sole influence on the formulation of U.S.-China policy in 1994. As noted above, U.S. national interests were critical to the decision. A strong U.S. private sector and corporate growth in the China market would serve to increase the national welfare and create a strong U.S. economic presence in the Asian region. For this reason, the 1994 decision was supported by key U.S. officials. As former president Bush asserted in 1990, "the United States has a long-term stake in maintaining and developing its economic relationship with China" (Bush, 1990). As well, former Secretary of State Eagleburger confirmed that Americans benefit from the inexpensive imports they receive from China (U.S. Congress, House, 1991 [Eagleburger], pp. 70-72). These views were also expressed by President Clinton in statements that were made earlier in office, on the reasoning for the delinkage.[21]

An alternative weakness to the radical argument was that there had not been a unified corporate position. Not all corporations advocated MFN and human rights delinkage. One such major and influential rival of delinkage was the American Textiles Manufacturers Institute (ATMI), collectively accounting for over 80 percent of total textile mill activity in the United States, and ranging in size from "small family-owned enterprises to publicly-owned billion dollar corporations with several thousand workers" (U.S. Congress, House, 1994 [Bremer], p. 251). The Institute's Director of International Trade expressed it thus:

Table 4.9 Political Contributions of Selected U.S. Companies who Lobbied to Extend MFN Status for China for the Year 1995 (US$thousands)

Company	To Democrats	To Republicans	Amount
United Parcel Service	370,729	641,240	1,011,969
AT&T	309,963	596,470	906,433
Lockheed Martin	161,100	343,850	504,950
Northrop	142,650	333,050	477,200
Bell South	137,100	332,317	469,917
Ameritech	125,542	324,123	450,665
Federal Express	133,000	306,225	440,500
Philip Morris	118,750	321,225	440,475
Union Pacific	45,300	339,518	384,818
General Electric	115,350	223,500	339,350
WMX Technologies	82,500	250,200	332,950
General Motors	101,009	205,588	308,597
CSX	59,750	228,850	291,350
JP Morgan & Co.	104,500	181,500	286,000
Nations Bank	144,700	159,300	273,500
Totals:	1,872,943	4,786,956	6,659,899

Sources: Danitz, 1997, pp. 22-24; Center for Responsive Politics, Washington, D.C.

ATMI believes that most-favored-nation status for China should not be renewed beyond its scheduled expiration on July 3 of this year and that there are compelling reasons for it not to be renewed. From ATMI's perspective, a decision whether or not to continue China's MFN status should be equally conditioned on China's conduct as a trading partner. In this regard, the record is clear. It is an understatement to say that China's conduct has been deplorable. To say that it has been resolutely criminal would be more to the point and more in accordance with the facts. . .

Whether it be false declarations to the U.S. Customs Service for the purpose of evading tariffs, mislabeling of merchandise, or transshipping through third countries in order to evade bilateral quota agreements, there is not a single type of customs fraud that the Government of China and its agents have not engaged in repeatedly during the past several years. (p. 248)

In addition to the sentiments expressed by corporations opposing or condoning U.S. trade with China, there were also groups within U.S. society that expressed the traditional American values of free trade. Representative Jim Leach, for example, expressed that historically, several key points have stood out in U.S. foreign policy. "One, we stood for the open door, and that implies opening China to the West. In addition, for a number of years, very progressive elements in American society pressed for political and economic normalization [with China]" (U.S. Congress, House, 1992 [Leach], p. 90).

That freer bilateral trade with China would hasten political and human rights reforms in China represented many of the traditional American values that linked free trade to peace and democracy. Because of the inconsistencies expressed in corporate opinion and the influence of opinions beyond the corporate sector, the radical argument that corporations influenced the 1994 decision did not hold sufficient explanatory power.

Summary

This chapter tested each of three hypotheses within the context of competing theoretical paradigms. The first hypothesis was that the U.S. intent to sustain and increase power in the Asian region influenced the 1994 decision to separate China's human rights record from MFN. The U.S. national interest, defined as the "acquisition of power" (Kegley, 1995b, pp. 4-5) was evident in the rhetoric of U.S. government leaders. U.S. economic engagement with China was thought to be a means to influence the actions and policies of the Chinese regime in order to gain influence in the Asian region. This threat-driven policy was apparent in the concern among U.S. officials for China's potential to become a hegemon in the Asian region.

The nationalist argument displayed some drawbacks, however. There was evidence that U.S. policymakers overestimated China's economic wealth and power. In world aggregate figures, China was not in a position to assume hegemony in the Asian region. China was, in fact, surmounting internal structural impediments that were precipitated by economic transition and the movement of populations into major cities. China, on the whole, had incurred a trade deficit with the world that was worsened by a large national external debt.

Also, when looking at aggregate levels, it was determined that China was not a major source for U.S. jobs in 1994 when compared to other foreign markets. Additionally, for U.S. producers, it was found that conditioning MFN on China's human rights record would not prevent profits and success in the long term. The low-cost labor of China could be easily substituted in other countries, which could then offer U.S. consumers the same affordable products as were manufactured in China. The U.S. national interest, therefore, could not fully be accepted as a motive for the decision by the Clinton administration.

The second hypothesis, that the U.S. intent to improve the respect for human rights in China was the motive for the decision was, in some respects, confirmed. That economic freedom gained through contact and exchange with U.S. corporations would pave the way to human rights reform in China was the opinion of many U.S. government officials and human rights groups during the time of the decision. To a certain extent, the argument was valid. Some human rights reforms were evident in China. A number of Chinese political dissidents, particularly dissidents who were on the U.S. list of "known" political prisoners, were released, according to both U.S. and Chinese officials, and many Chinese were permitted to emigrate in accordance with the Jackson-Vanik Amendment.

Notwithstanding, it was also realized in the argument that U.S.-China bilateral agreements on human rights were not being met by China, nor were the rights stipulated in the Universal Declaration. For the few prisoners who were released, many more were imprisoned for their political beliefs, or for behavior that was judged by the state to be in subversion of the state. It was also discerned that China's prison conditions were inhuman, that torture was practiced, and that no fair system of justice was evident.

Moreover, the evidence suggested that the entirety of the 1992 Memorandum of Understanding between the United States and China, with regard to prison labor, was not being adhered to by the Chinese government. Many prisons that operated as factories were found to be under the auspice of China's "reform through labor" program, where products were destined for both domestic and foreign markets. Additionally, it was disclosed that the major human rights condition for the 1994 renewal, which was the condition of emigration provided for in the Jackson-Vanik Amendment, had not been obliged. It was discovered that political dissidents and their families were forbidden to emigrate or were deterred from emigrating through bureaucratic methods.

Because of the inherent weaknesses of the liberalist-based hypothesis, the U.S. intent to improve respect for human rights in China could not be fully accepted as the motivation for the 1994 decision.

The third proposed hypothesis was that the influence of U.S. corporations was the motive for the 1994 decision. The findings suggest that U.S. corporate executives did indeed attempt to influence U.S. officials in the congressional and executive branches of government. Testimonies by lobbying groups on behalf of U.S. corporations engaged in trade with and investment in China had mounted during the years preceding the 1994 policy decision. U.S. corporate leaders believed that conditioning or withdrawing China's trade on the basis of human rights concerns would prevent firms from gaining and maintaining market share and leadership in China, and that foreign competitors would seize the opportunity of lost U.S. business.

Although there were significant attempts by U.S. corporations to convince U.S. governmental leaders to vote for the delinkage of MFN and human rights, a major weakness of the radical argument was that there was no unified corporate position. Many U.S. corporations believed that MFN and China's human rights record should continue to be linked because of China's unfair trade practices and forced labor conditions. There was also evidence for delinkage beyond the U.S. corporate influence. U.S. national interests exhibited a strong positive influence on the policy of 1994. Economic power and influence in the Asian region was found to be in the interest of the U.S. government leadership.

U.S. economic gains from trade with and investment in China would help to build a stronger United States, both at home and abroad. Security interests were also at stake. China's position as a rising regional hegemon in Asia, conflict on the Korean peninsula, and the political and economic instability in Cambodia and the nations of the South China Sea, were major U.S. security concerns. In light of these findings, the third hypothesis, that corporations were the sole influence on the U.S. decision to separate MFN and China's human rights practices, proved to be too narrow a formulation.

In conclusion, each theoretically-based proposition was limited in explaining the motives for the decision to separate trade and China's human rights practices in 1994. In the following chapter, therefore, an alternative hypothesis is proposed that considers elements of the first three hypothesis while introducing further complexities that factored into the 1994 decision to end the association between China's human rights practices and trade.

Endnotes

1   "In U.S. international economic policymaking, the *threat* of a congressional action can affect the substance of executive branch policy and its international negotiating efforts" (Stephen Cohen, 1988, p. 109).

2   Klaus Knorr (1977, pp. 99-101) defines leverage as "one actor using a lever to gain advantage over another actor. National economic capabilities that afford international leverage can be used for four distinct purposes. The first is coercion. A can withhold or threaten to withhold something of value to B in order to make B comply with some specified form of behavior. The second purpose is to extract monopoly profit from market control over a highly valued product. Thus, A announces to all states that they can buy a particular commodity only at high prices substantially exceeding marginal production costs. Third is to have direct impact on another state's economic security, welfare, and capabilities without any attempt at compelling it to behave in a specified way. The desired impact can be harmful or beneficial. A may withhold certain commodities, financial aid, or his market from B in order to weaken him economically or in some other way. Thus, in times of military conflict [such as the United States action with the former Soviet Union], A may refuse to export to B certain goods that are expected to enhance B's military capabilities. On the other hand, A may give financial aid or other economic valuables to B in order to strengthen him economically or in some other way. The fourth purpose is being pursued when a government gives economic valuables to another country in order to gain a position of general influence over it. For example, beginning in 1956, the Soviet Union gave economic aid to Egypt and other Arab countries to achieve influence over them. Similarly, the United States has extended aid to Latin American countries in order to maintain or increase its regional influence". Knorr further explains that "the four purposes of using economic leverage are, of course, analytical distinctions. In the real world, some of these purposes may be combined in a particular policy" [emphasis added].

3   "The term 'national security' needs to have its definition broadened to include economic strength and stability along with military strength and deterrence. A strong domestic economic base is therefore a critical prerequisite, at least for a democracy, for assuming superpower status" (Stephen Cohen, 1988, p. 27).

4   As Richard Haass (1997) contended, "the support of liberal trade and multilateralism helped to assure the U.S. military and economic hegemonic position" (pp. 43-45).

5   Clinton's economic team included Lloyd Bentsen (Secretary of the Treasury), Leon Panetta (Budget Director), Laura Tyson (Chairwoman of the Council of Economic Advisers), Ron Brown (Secretary of Commerce), and Jerry Rubin, who headed a new coordinating structure called the National Economic Council.

6   As Senator Charles S. Robb of Virginia stated, "I would submit that it is in our national strategic interest to engage mainland China now and in the future, notwithstanding the breadth and scope of disagreements that may arise between our two countries. Not doing so risks, if not in the short term, a major rupture in relations in the long term with the most powerful nation in East Asia at the very time the so-called Pacific Century approaches. . . . In crafting an approach on China's MFN status these next few weeks, I would encourage the administration to keep in mind our larger priorities" (U.S. Congress, Senate, 1994 [Robb], p. 2).

7   Deputy U.S. Trade Representative Charlene Barshefsky stated: "We have a historic opportunity to expand our trade relations with China and to help create hundreds of thousands of high-wage jobs here in the United States through increased export. We have a great stake,

not only from a global strategic perspective, but also from a domestic perspective in opening China's markets and ensuring that China plays by the rules" (U.S. Congress, House, 1994 [Barshefsky], p. 103).

8   This position was forcefully advanced by U.S. ambassador to China, Winston Lord: "The President and others in the administration have emphasized on several occasions the importance of a stable and prosperous China for U.S. interests. . . . Open societies do not attack each other, therefore, you have a more secure Asia, a more secure world" (U.S. Congress, Senate, 1994 [Lord], pp. 6, 25).

9   Also in 1991, China's Vice Foreign Minister Liu Huaqiu was quoted as saying "if most-favored-nation status is revoked or the United States attaches conditions [to the extension], this will exert a very serious influence on U.S.-China relations", that there would be an "unprecedented decline in trade, a heavy blow to the 1,300 U.S.-Chinese joint ventures and wholly owned U.S. companies operating here . . . serious restrictions on all exchanges and contacts and a major retrogression in the political relations between the two nations" (Oberdorfer and Sun, 1991, p. A18).

10   These industries included aerospace exporters, agricultural producers, telecommunications, and construction industries. Also see Table 4.2.

11   Export related jobs figures (full-time equivalent civilian U.S. jobs, including self-employed) were arrived at by "multiplying the export-related output of each industry by the appropriate ratio for the FTE jobs per unit of output for that industry for the year being estimated".

12   It was quoted that 40,000 U.S. jobs were dependent on exports of aircraft, parts, and components to China (U.S. Congress, House, 1993 [Anderson].

13   By 1998, "Chinese economists put the ratio of urban to rural income at 12 to 1. Urban per capita disposable income for the year 1998 was $656, while rural per capita net income was $261" (U.S. Dept. of State, 2000, China sec.).

14   The $1,000 per capita 1990 estimate was that of Dwight H. Perkins (1992). Robert Summers and Alan W. Heston (1991, p. 352) estimated China's per capita income in 1990 to be $2,598. The World Bank estimate was $370.00 (World Bank, 1992; Lardy, 1994, p. 15).

15   This agreement was a Memorandum of Understanding (MOU of 1992) which facilitates U.S. inspections of Chinese prisons with the intent to establish the origin of Chinese exports to the United States that are produced with prison labor. In the event China refuses inspection of its prisons, U.S. Customs may prevent the importation of Chinese goods suspected of being produced with prison labor (U.S. Department of State, Bureau of Public Affairs, 1997a).

16   Estimates of job losses claimed by various corporations, in lieu of MFN revocation, were anywhere from 130,000 to 250,000. These numbers were not consistent.

17   Among the many U.S. corporations that testified in favor of delinkage were the American Chamber of Commerce in Hong Kong, the Emergency Committee for American Trade, the American Association of Exporters and Importers, Mattel, Inc., the Fashion Accessories Shippers Association, Inc., the National Retail Federation (NRF), the U.S. Association of Importers of Textiles and Apparel, Kamm & Associates, Ltd., the U.S.-China Business Council, the Washington State-China Relations Council, McDonnell Douglas Corp., and the Fertilizer Institute (U.S. Congress, House, 1994 [various, see above], pp. 163, 170, 180, 188, 243, 248, 254).

18   Sutter, 1998, pp. 44-46, citing Calman Cohen, chair of the Business coalition for U.S.-China Trade and President of the Emergency Committee for American Trade (ECAT). Interview by Tricia N. Cortez, March 6, 1996, in Cortez, 1996.

19   "On some issues, the technology industry will ride to the rescue of business as a whole". "America's Business Lobby: Who Speaks for Main Street?" *Economist*, 1999b, pp. 75-76.
20   It was stated that China purchases its remaining needs from Morocco, Jordan, and Europe.
21   Note presidential candidate William Clinton's statement during the first presidential campaign, in 1991: "[E]conomic security is a whole lot of national security". "Campaign '92", 1991, p. A16.

5 Transnational Influences

Chapter 4 presented and tested alternative hypotheses within the context of competing theoretical perspectives. These included the theoretical perspectives of realism, liberalism, and radicalism. It was concluded that because of theoretical deficiencies in the drive for policy choice, each hypothesis alone could not serve as an explanation for the decision to separate trade and human rights. Chapter 5 will summarize and synthesize the major findings from the previous hypotheses and proceed to introduce a fourth alternative hypothesis that may more fully clarify the policy motives for the 1994 U.S. decision on MFN and China's human rights practices.

Hypotheses as Partial Truisms

The first hypothesis, the U.S. intent to sustain and increase power in the Asian region, was true, partly, as an influential factor in the 1994 decision. It was determined that it was in the U.S. interest to increase economic engagement with China in order to gain greater access to the China market. A competitive U.S. economic presence in China would enhance the U.S. influence in the Asian region and increase the economic strength of the U.S. economy at home through job creation in the technological, importing, and service sectors of the economy. China's demand for capital and technological goods would serve to expand U.S. exports and create a demand for skilled labor in the U.S. market. The nationalist position claimed that the economic strength and competitiveness of the U.S. private sector would have been weakened by the relationship of MFN and human rights. For example, it was in the U.S. interest to protect its agribusiness sector, which complained of the future loss of food and fiber sales to the world's most populous market.

The U.S. interest in protecting its domestic aerospace industry was a contributory factor to the decision to delink trade and human rights in 1994. Some U.S. officials were sympathetic to the cause of aircraft and space producers. They argued before Congress that foreign competition would mean a loss of U.S. sales, should China turn to foreign aircraft producers for purchases, such as the European Airbus consortium, in the event the United States conditioned trade on China's human rights record.

Moreover, it was argued in congressional debates that the denial of MFN, or trade sanctions in any form, would have damaged the U.S. political ability to influence the Chinese regime by isolating China from U.S. commercial contacts. The U.S. revocation of MFN to China would have been a risk to U.S. consumer welfare, as well. Increased tariffs on Chinese imports as a result of China's expected retaliation would have caused a rise in the prices of consumer goods. U.S. consumers had come to rely on such affordable finished goods as toys where, for example, 48 percent of the toys in the U.S. market were imported from China (U.S. Congress, House, 1992 [Moscow], p. 42).

Further observations, however, suggest that this realist-based assumption could only partially be accepted due to inherent flaws in the argument. It was discerned, for example, that U.S. officials had overestimated China's relative trade advantage. Total trade figures revealed that between the years 1980 and 1994, China incurred a trade deficit with the world, with the exception of only five years out of the total fifteen. In 1993, China's total trade balance amounted to US$-12.2 billion (*China Statistical Abstract*, 1998). The U.S. nationalist rhetoric condemning China for unfair trade advantages was partly due to different calculation methods of trade flows between the two countries. In one investigation of the measurement of U.S.-China trade flows, it was found that after adjusting for U.S. re-exports through Hong Kong, the bilateral balance dropped in U.S. official trade data from $-29.5 billion to $-25.8 billion in 1993 (Fung and Lau, 1998, p. 36; General Administration of Customs of the People's Republic of China, various years; Hong Kong Censes and Statistics Department, various years; U.S. Department of Commerce, "U.S. Foreign Trade Highlights", various years).

Moreover, the threat of China's economic wealth to the U.S. national security that was articulated in the Congress was determined to be exaggerated. Empirical evidence showed that China's external debt had grown from US$16.7 billion in 1985 to $69.3 billion by 1992 (Asian Development Bank, 1993; *International Financial Statistics*, 1996). Additionally, the estimated increased per capita income, even when measured by purchasing power parity, was eclipsed by China's increasing poverty population surviving on the margin of subsistence. Further flaws in the nationalist argument pertained to threats to the welfare of U.S. consumers. Although consumer prices on goods imported from China would have risen, they would have risen only temporarily, according to some experts, until such new and viable production and import markets as India, Malaysia, Indonesia, or Africa were discovered (Jagdish Bhagwati, quoted by Berlau, 1997, p. 16).

The second proposition, premised on liberal theory, was that the U.S. intent to improve the respect for human rights in China through economic engagement influenced the 1994 decision. Many U.S. policymakers in both legislative branches of Congress felt that deepened economic engagement with China would pave the way to individual freedoms and human rights reform by creating a rising middle class that would insist on democratic values. These U.S. leaders thought that by further isolating China from U.S. economic and political contacts, progress on China's human rights reforms would be deterred.

Not all groups within the U.S. polity, however, agreed that economic engagement with China would advance the cause of human rights. Some U.S. leaders and groups expressed that the best way to advance human rights in China was to maintain the linkage of conditionality between MFN and human rights, serving to pressure the Chinese regime to politically liberalize. These leaders questioned the morality of a U.S. foreign policy of economic engagement with a government that clearly violated the basic American values of individual freedom and the 1948 Universal Declaration.

Human rights groups such as Amnesty International USA questioned the notion that humanitarian values drove the Clinton policy to delink MFN and China's human rights in 1994. Moreover, it had been the U.S. public opinion at the time that MFN should be conditioned on human rights improvements in China (Bowman, 1994, p. 150). Because of these discrepancies of opinion, the value-based liberal argument of the intent to improve respect for human rights in China held only partial weight as an influence on the U.S. decision to no longer condition MFN on China's human rights record.

The third proposition, that U.S. corporations influenced the U.S. policy choice on China, had proven to be flawed. In the years directly preceding the decision, U.S. corporations had become increasingly prominent in the Congress and had increased their contacts with the executive branch. Hired lobbyists representing a plethora of business groups argued in favor of delinkage for various corporate interests. Between 1991 and 1994, for example, the Business Coalition for U.S.-China trade had grown from 167 members to 800 members, becoming a unified voice in the crusade for unconditional U.S. trade with China (Sutter, 1998, p. 64).

Political contributions of business interest groups to congressional political parties advocating for the continuation of MFN for China amounted to nearly $7 million (Danitz, 1997, pp. 22-24). Financial contributions and written and verbal testaments to U.S. policymakers on Capitol Hill came from such corporate interest groups as the aerospace and electronics industry, that had held both present and future ambitions in the China market. Additional major business interest groups, such as the American Association of Exporters and Importers, the National Retail Federation (NRF), and the American Chamber of Commerce, were also outspoken on behalf of MFN renewal to China without the imposition of human rights conditions. Loss of market entry, future profits, and market competitiveness were given as major reasons for their position.

A major weakness of the radical argument was that there had not been a unified corporate position. Some corporations wished to maintain the linkage of trade and human rights because of China's unfair trade practices, such as the use of forced labor in production, which created competitive market and price advantages that could not be matched on the U.S. side. Moreover, corporate interests were not alone in their desire to influence U.S. foreign policy toward China in 1994.[1] Broader U.S. political interests had been at stake. It was in the broader U.S. national interest to maintain and strengthen the private sector through increased penetration and liberalization of foreign markets, including the emerging market of China. Centrist leaders in both Democratic and Republican parties expressed that economic engagement with China was in the best interest of the United States.

Deepened economic relations with China would not only secure U.S. economic advantages, but would also enhance the capacity for U.S. diplomatic and political contacts with China's leaders, thus serving as a means for greater U.S. influence in China and on the Asian continent. U.S. corporate interests and the U.S. nationalist interest were one and the same in 1994. Further, it was articulated in the liberalist-based argument that increased corporate engagement with China would advance the cause of human rights in China through direct linkages to the Chinese citizenry. Corporations, with their own set of rules and standards, would be able to bypass China's vast bureaucratic hiring procedures. Because of the lack of a unified corporate position, as well as the influence of interests outside of the corporate sector, the third corporate-based proposition was unable to fully explain the reasoning for delinkage. This was affirmed by Peter Tarnoff, U.S. Under Secretary of Political Affairs:

> While it is certainly the case that this administration has ranked the defense of American business and commercial business right up there at the top of our national agenda, we have never intended — the President and the Secretary of State have been quite explicit about this — to make our business, and commercial business, paramount. (U.S. Congress, House, 1997 [Tarnoff], p. 23)

In total, each hypothesis could not be fully accepted as causation for the 1994 policy decision. Neither alone nor in combination did they hold sufficient explanatory power for the motives of the 1994 decision to end the connection between MFN and China's human rights transgressions. Apart from U.S. policy motives to sustain and increase power in the Asian region, or for altruistic motives to improve the respect for human rights in China, or for motives of U.S.

corporate interests, external environmental factors also played a role in the decision to delink. Increased economic interdependence through multiple transnational linkages and channels came into play in the 1994 U.S. decision. These transnational channels include linkages through multinational corporations,[2] global linkages through international organizations, and cross-national alliances between businesses and governments.

> The emergence of a truly global economy and the dawning of the information revolution have combined to create a set of truly transnational actors. These actors are weaving a dense web of ties, blurring familiar distinctions between foreign affairs and domestic affairs and calling into question traditional assumptions about national identity and interests. (Stanley Foundation, 1995, pp. 5, 16-17)

Complex Interdependence

The intricate network of transnational actors that affected the 1994 decision on U.S.-China policy is labeled, in this study, as "complex interdependence". To review, complex interdependence is defined as "a situation among a number of countries in which multiple channels of contact connect societies, where states do not monopolize these contacts" (Keohane and Nye, 1989, pp. 24-25). With relation to the events surrounding the 1994 decision, these multiple channels of contact include transnational corporate linkages, multilateral governmental linkages, and transnational formal and informal ties between government and business elites. In lieu of these environmental factors, a fourth alternative hypothesis is proposed, which is that U.S. national interests, U.S. interests in advancing the progress of human rights in China, U.S. corporate interests, and complex interdependence motivated the 1994 decision. The fourth or alternative hypothesis draws upon elements of previous approaches but places U.S. foreign policy in the context of complex interdependence.

Transnational Corporate Linkages

While the third hypothesis focused on U.S. corporations in the domestic sense, a transnational linkage is now established, centering on the interdependencies of multinational firms. The trend toward the global privatization of public assets, which has often been referred to as part of the globalization process, has brought the role of the multinational corporation into the global limelight. The recent western-led growth strategy of most developing and transitional countries[3] has been to follow a market-oriented structure where the emphasis has been placed on growth through the private sector, patterned similarly after the economic growth experience of Japan and the Asian newly-industrialized countries (NICs) (International Monetary Fund, 1992, p. 3).

The increased privatization of global public assets had increased the intensity of cross-border corporate linkages and therefore the interdependencies of nations. These broader cross-border and cross-cultural transnational business and commercial activities were a major influence on the reasoning behind the delinkage of human rights and MFN in 1994. These commercial cross-border linkages had developed through various modes of contact which included intrafirm and interfirm trade and foreign direct investment.

It has been pointed out that firms engage in intrafirm trade for two reasons: first, because it is more efficient to conduct business within firms, and second, transnational firms "internalize intermediate-product markets across borders through intra-firm trade" (Dunning, 1993, as cited in Chen and Wong, 1997, p. 90). This network formation consists of a "corporate strategy designed to internationalize the activities that are designed to integrate production both vertically and horizontally" (p. 90). In 1993/94, intrafirm sales by U.S. firms in the electronics industry were between 87 percent and 100 percent in China, Malaysia, and Thailand, where a major part of assembly operations of finished goods for export are located (Yue and Dobson, 1997, p. 262).

Foreign direct investments in China and other emerging markets have taken the form of wholly-owned enterprises, joint ventures, cooperative ventures, or offshore projects (Yan, 2000, p. 22).[4] "The joint venture, however, remains one of the key strategic arrangements in international management" (p. 25). "Research has shown that foreign investment companies invest in the China market to use the high profits obtained there to invest and compete in other parts of the world, particularly in the Asia-Pacific region" (p. 30). In China, for example, Hewlett Packard corporation not only serves the Chinese market, but also looks to integrate with the entire Asia-Pacific market (p. 30).

To U.S. corporations, the joint venture is often the mode of entry into foreign markets. International corporate alliances offer a more cost-effective and rapid way to achieve output than by building plants or making acquisitions (Samli, Kaynak, and Sharif, 1996, p. 26). In emerging markets such as China, for example, "the multinational corporation actively seeks possible joint ventures in order to take advantage of emerging opportunities, to reduce risk and to deal with strong nationalism in countries like China" (Yan, 2000, p. 30). For China and other developing and emerging economies, the joint venture can create certain advantages which include the acquisition of local knowledge, marketing and management procedures, and technology transfer (p. 25). In

China, joint ventures have been formed mostly in the industrial sector, the favored market-entry mode by the Chinese government (p. 23).

These types of transcorporate linkages, or mutual dependence between firms, are reflected in Table 5.1, which illustrates the U.S.-China network of two major U.S. multinational corporations in China: AT&T and Motorola. By 1995, U.S.-China joint ventures had been formed with both corporations, increasing the economic integration between the two country's firms through such value-added activities as research and development, materials production, assembly manufacturing, marketing and sales, and services.[5] Joint ventures are of particular importance to China because they are the mode by which the greatest amount of foreign direct investment occurs. In 1993, for example, 54.2 percent of foreign direct investment to China had been invested through joint ventures (Wang, 1993, p. 10, cited in Funabashi, Oksenberg, and Weiss, 1994, p. 37).

In addition to the increasing number of intrafirm linkages, interfirm trade had increased as well, creating further cross-border linkages through multinational corporations. U.S. MNCs had become linked to local firms in developing economies, for instance, by placing orders with indigenous suppliers for materials or components. The expanded activities of supplying firms create ancillary firms involved in transport and distribution activities between foreign and domestic enterprises (Dicken, 1998, p. 6). These international production linkages between manufacturing, agriculture, and service sectors create employment generation, further deepening the economic integration between countries through corporate ties and economic development.[6]

By the mid-1990s, the United States pushed for further entry of its financial institutions into China by requesting establishment of offices in cities outside Shanghai and Beijing and by pressing for further engagement in China's local currency business and underwriting deals (Shuman, 1995, p. 23). Aside from these bilateral and transnational U.S. business and commercial linkages, there had also been a growing number of overseas Chinese who managed and owned corporations (about 55 million worldwide). These mid-size Chinese-owned multinationals had become a new and powerful economic influence through linkages to China and the Asian region. "The overseas Chinese have accounted for 80 percent of all foreign investment in China, making this powerful group the driving force behind the nation's explosive economic growth" (Drucker, 1994, p. A14). Many overseas Chinese multinationals reside in the United States, Canada, Europe, and Australia. Any sanctions imposed on China by the United States would have impeded transnational bilateral and multilateral business activities and the growing network of linkages resulting from them.

Table 5.1 Mapping the U.S.-China Network: AT&T and Motorola in China: Value-Added Activities

Products	Research and Development	Raw materials-components production	Assembly/ manufacturing	Marketing and Sales	Services
			AT&T		
facilities, switches, computers, telecommunication systems, direct-call service	1995, technology transfer contract with Ministry of Electronics Industry for processing and design of semiconductor IC 1993, R&D [a] facility	1995, JV [b] to upgrade switch-manufacturing operations 1993, opened switch JV 1982, refused switch JV 1979, refused switch JV	1995, nine JVs in marketing wireless systems, long-distance service, computer products, and networks 1994, JV with government and Megga Telecom for manufacture and distribution of Telecom products 1992, AT&T fibre-optic cable JV 1985, fibre-optics JV	1995, network infrastructure equipment (Guangdong) 1994, JV to manufacture and sell consumer products 1994, digital-transmission system (Shenzhen) 1994, high-speed telecommunications-transmission equipment 1994, transmission-and network-management equipment (Beijing) 1993, telecommunications supplier	1994, US direct call service

Table 5.1 (continued)

Products	Research and Development	Raw materials-components production	Assembly/manufacturing	Marketing and Sales	Services
			MOTOROLA		
Cellular phones, semiconductors, pagers, consumer electronics products	1995, JV to develop intelligent machine maintenance tools 1994, Beijing Catch JV to design mobile telecommunication network	1993, low-end pager	1995, expansion of cellular phone and chip assembly facility 1995, Panda JV to produce pagers, computers, and other telecommunications equipment	1995, analogue cellular equipment 1994, opened mobile telephone production line 1994, large-capacity phone system in Shanghai	1994, headquarters in Beijing to handle sales, marketing, and engineering

[a] R&D: Research and Development
[b] JV: Joint Venture

Source: Dobson, 1997a, pp. 230, 236.

Although U.S. direct foreign investment in China in early 1994 had only begun to take root — amounting to a mere US$2.4 billion in actual amount utilized (*China Statistical Year Book,* 1995) — it was future expectations of U.S. business in the China market and opportunities for increased U.S.-China transnational corporate linkages that spurred U.S. decision makers to drop human rights conditions from MFN renewal in 1994. Although present and future anticipations of U.S.-China multinational corporate ties were a highly significant influence on U.S. decision makers in 1994, there were also additional transnational linkages that proved to be of critical significance to the framing of U.S. policy on trade and human rights.

Multilateral Institutional Linkages

In addition to U.S. linkages through multinational corporations, there were also multilateral institutional linkages that had affected the U.S. 1994 decision to end the association between trade and human rights. U.S. multilateral linkages to such major international governmental organizations as the World Trade Organization and the United Nations had influenced the opinions of U.S. decision makers. In 1994, global trade and investment activities became solidified and controlled under the authority of the WTO. The new WTO exercised a degree of power that had been previously denied due to its former existence as a "provisional organization".[7]

The culmination of the Uruguay Round (UR) agreements, signed in Marrakesh, Morocco in April 1994 by 124 countries, formed the legal and institutional framework for new global trading rules in goods and services and market access commitments. The World Trade Organization, carried over from the GATT, represented the end of seven years of bargaining negotiations that began in 1986 in Punta del Este, Uruguay (Schott, 1994, p. 3). The timing of the completion of the Uruguay Round was most auspicious. It occurred only one month before the U.S. decision was made to end the relationship between trade and China's human rights record. Peter Sutherland, the director-general of the GATT, warned the United States that "it ran the risk of jeopardizing a $500 billion boost to global income if Congress failed to ratify the Uruguay trade deal by the end of the year" (Elliot, 1994, p. 1).

It was, in addition to the previously discussed causal factors, the influence of the WTO that affected the U.S. decision in 1994. "The WTO, like its predecessor, was founded on liberal principles" (Marc Williams, 1999, p. 153). The theory of comparative advantage and factor endowments was the underlying pulse of the new WTO. Free trade, from the perspective of the WTO, was superior to no trade because the gains from trade outweighed the disadvantages (Krugman, 1986, p. 153). The global welfare gains resulting from the Uruguay Round negotiations are presented in Figure 5.1. As shown, gains were to be made by most of the world's trading nations as measured by percent change in real GDP.

The greatest welfare gains, based on projected outcomes to the year 2005, were to be found in the Asian region, where the ASEAN countries showed a 2.5 percent increase in growth as a result of Uruguay Round trade liberalization pact. China experienced a 1.5 percent increase in GDP growth, South Asia, a 1.4 percent growth increase, and the newly-industrialized economies (NIEs), 0.8 percent projected GDP growth increase. Projected benefits to the Asian region far surpassed world gains, which were only 0.4 percent. Much of the high growth in the Asian region was due to the ten-year phase-out of the Multi-Fiber Arrangement (MFA), which had placed substantial quotas on imports of textiles from developing countries to developed countries through bilateral agreements (Schott, 1994, p. 11). Because most textiles and apparel were exported from countries of the Southeast Asian region, the phase-out of the MFA opened possibilities for greater economic gains to Asia through increased exports of apparel and (though to a lesser extent) increased imports of textiles (Yang, 1995, pp. 503-6).

Although most of the world's countries were expected to experience positive welfare effects from the Uruguay Round agreement,[8] the least gains in welfare were projected for Latin America (0.2 percent), North America (0.1 percent), and Australia (0.2 percent).[9] Table 5.2 provides a more detailed projection of welfare gains to the United States from the Uruguay Round. U.S. gains through the UR legislation were expected to be manifested in increased imports, exports, and consumer welfare. Total welfare gains to the United States were projected to increase from $8.8 million in 1994 to $31 million by 1999 (Schott, 1994, p. 31).

During and after the formation of the WTO, it was maintained by many groups across the globe that the scope of the Uruguay Round favored the multilateral trading system as superior to national policymaking in this "new world liberal order" (Marc Williams, 1999, pp. 155-58). Admittedly, the WTO strengthened multilateralism, and at the very least, was viewed as a complement to national policies. In 1994, almost every nation in the world supported the new multilateral institutional framework for trade and trade-related policies.

The prospect of increased global economic integration brought about by a new world trade authority was supported by leaders from the north, south, east, and west. "President Clinton spoke for many of the world's leaders when he told the United Nations General Assembly that 'a strong GATT agreement will

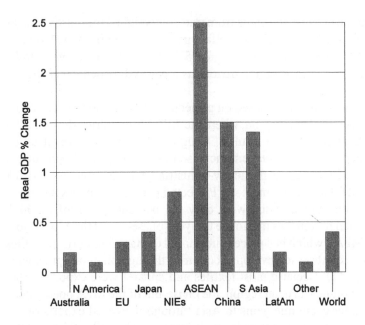

Figure 5.1   Global Welfare Effects of the Uruguay Round Trade Liberalization as Projected to the Year 2005 (%)

Source: Yang, 1995, p. 507.

create millions of jobs worldwide.' Virtually every other world leader had expressed similar sentiments" (Sutherland, 1993, p. A20).

The move toward globalization, the U.S. support of it, and gains from it averted U.S. leaders in the executive branch and centrist leaders in Congress from forming a policy that would deter the process of economic liberalization, and hence WTO objectives.[10] Governors of all fifty U.S. states endorsed the new world trade agreement in 1994, and urged Congress to approve it as quickly as possible ("50 Governors for Trade Pact," 1994, p. D5). President Clinton received a letter from 446 economists urging Congress to ratify the Uruguay Round agreement as soon as possible (*Public Papers of the Presidents of the United States*, 1995b, p. 1432). Further endorsements came from former presidents, secretaries of state, secretaries of the treasury, and U.S. trade representatives (*Public Papers of the Presidents of the United States* [Clinton], 1995a, p. 1638). As Peter Sutherland, former director-general of the GATT put it: "If GATT fails, we all lose" (Sutherland, 1993, p. A20).

Table 5.2 Projected U.S. Gains from Uruguay Round Tariff Liberalization 1995-1999 (US$million unless otherwise noted)

	U.S. GDP (billions of dollars)[a]	U.S. demand for imports before UR cuts[b]	World demand for U.S. exports before UR cuts[b]	Increase in U.S. imports due to UR[c]	Increase in U.S. exports due to UR[c]	To U.S. consumers from import liberalization[d]	To U.S. producers from foreign import liberalization	Gov't net tariff revenue loss	Total welfare gains
		671,020	507,534	18,018	33,153	9,253	8,626	9,025	8,853
95	6,753	671,020	507,534	3,604	6,631	1,851	1,726	1,805	1,771
96	6,888	711,281	537,988	6,640	14,057	3,923	3,657	3,827	3,754
97	7,028	753,958	570,265	12,147	22,351	6,238	5,815	6,084	5,969
98	7,166	799,195	604,481	17,168	31,589	8,816	8,219	8,599	8,438
99	7,310	847,147	640,750	22,747	41,855	11,681	10,890	11,394	11,177
				63,304	116,482	32,508	30,306	31,708	31,106

[a] U.S. GDP for 1995 is estimated by adjusting actual 1993 GDP for growth in 1994 and 1995 as projected by the OECD (United Nations, OECD, 1993); for 1996 through 1999 an annual growth rate of 2 percent is assumed.

[b] In the absence of Uruguay Round liberalization, imports and exports are both assumed to grow at an annual rate of 6 percent.

[c] The increase in the levels of imports and exports due to Uruguay Round cuts, and the corresponding welfare gains, are assumed to accrue in equal increments over five years, subject to an annual growth rate of 6 percent, starting in 1995.

[d] Increases in U.S. import levels due to import liberalization partly replace U.S. domestic production and partly reflect a net increase in total consumption. The U.S. consumer surplus gains therefore include some loss from liberalization to U.S. producers of import-competing products.

Source: Schott, 1994, p. 31.

Many global groups and coalitions supported the cause of multilateral trade liberalization under the WTO. The Cairns group, for example, a group of 14 countries, sought to liberalize agricultural trade through the WTO mechanism.[11] For these smaller countries, the successful conclusion to the Uruguay Round meant greater access to markets that had previously been available only to the world's bigger economic players (Foster, 1993, p. 7).

In addition to global economic gains from liberalized trade and investment, deepened global economic integration was thought to bring security gains to the world. As Peter Sutherland (1993) further articulated: "It would be cruel irony if following the collapse of the Iron Curtain the U.S. and the EC were unable to keep in place a secure and effective trading system" (p. A20). U.S. Secretary of State Warren Christopher affirmed the opinion of Sutherland in his statement that "Security in the post-Cold War world depends as much on strong economies as on strong arsenals. Advancing transatlantic security requires us to focus not only on renewing the NATO alliance, but also on successfully concluding the GATT negotiations" ("Secretary Christopher's Remarks", 1994, p. 81). The WTO was viewed as a safeguard against the possibilities of regional protectionism that would threaten global security:

> Economic blocs either remain open within the multilateral trading system — if that system is alive and healthy — or they turn inward and become fortresses. If it is the latter, then the prospects for long-term growth and job creation are, even inside the fortress, doomed. And if the response to a failed round is regionalism, where will Russia fit in? Where will the rest of Eastern and Central Europe or China be? To whom do the countries of Africa look? And can the nations of Latin America expect to be welcomed with open arms by members of a protectionist NAFTA? We are talking here about most of humanity. (Sutherland, 1993, p. A20)

The WTO rule-making body was viewed, in addition to facilitating free trade, as a means to prevent the U.S. and USSR confrontation that had plagued the world for nearly fifty years (Chartier, 1998, pp. 275-76). Therefore, beyond state-centered, corporate-centered, or seemingly altruistic interests that may have affected the 1994 decision, global welfare and security interests also influenced the decision. Multipolarity under the aegis of the WTO was thought to be a better guarantee for global security than had been the previous bipolar Cold War arrangement.

With the acceptance of economic liberalization by most nations of the world, "global" interests were thought to be best served by the integration of China into the international marketplace and the global political community. Unilateral government-imposed barriers to China's economic integration with the world, such as U.S. trade sanctions based on China's human rights transgressions, were not viewed by world leaders as being in the best interests of the new multilateralism and global cooperation. To close a potential market such as China would have been counterproductive to the rule of GATT free trade (Schott, 1994, p. 31).

Moreover, China held a "powerful and politically sympathetic constituency for sustaining its general course and influencing developments" through linkages to multilateral institutions. In 1980, Beijing had expressed, once again, an interest in becoming a member of the GATT.[12] Formal negotiations between China and GATT officials began in 1987, and China had since established increasingly stronger relations with them. Chinese trade officials had presented to the GATT steps that had been taken to decentralize the economy as part of its case for accession (Boardman, 1994, pp. 143-44). By 1994, China had gained the support of the GATT because of extensive diplomatic lobbying with GATT officials, backed by her rapidly-growing global economic presence. China used her economic leverage successfully to work through the GATT bureaucracy to offer her vast market to the world. At the eighteenth meeting of the working party in Geneva studying China's entry into the GATT, Long Yongtu, leader of the Chinese delegation, made it clear that "a world trade organization without China would lack comprehensiveness and would be an imperfect multilateral trade system" (Matsumoto, 1994, p. 5). More than the United States, however, which had taken a confrontational stance with China until the 1994 delinkage, the EU had unremittingly taken a positive position on China that consistently stressed cooperative efforts to bring the country into the multilateral trading system of the GATT (Eglin, 1997, p. 495). The EU's support for China served to strengthen China's political clout in the GATT.

Consistent with the traditions of the International Bank for Reconstruction and Development (IBRD) practices, there had also been a close connection between China, the World Bank, and IMF officials who had been advising China on the selection of modernization projects and macroeconomic policies (Boardman, 1994, p. 142). Leaders from multilateral trade and financial institutions did not wish to see China isolated by U.S. unilaterally-imposed trade sanctions. More problematic was that the imposition of U.S. trade sanctions on China would have entailed political consequences for the United States. Had the United States taken steps to push China into further isolation in 1994, the United States would have isolated itself from the international community. Isolating China would have been counterproductive to the GATT procedures and the framing of the new WTO.[13] U.S. political and economic linkages to multilateral institutions, therefore, further encouraged President Clinton to end the relationship between China's human rights practices and MFN, contrary to the ideals that had been expressed in the 1993 Executive Order.

Aside from multilateral trade and financial linkages that had affected the 1994 decision, the role of the United Nations was also a key component. The United Nations serves as a multilateral forum for discourse and grievances on human rights violations around the world. U.N. decisions, activities or in-activities with regard to human rights issues affect the manner in which human rights violations are handled within the global community of citizens. The main body dealing with human rights issues in the United Nations is the Commission on Human Rights, established by the United Nations Economic and Social Council (ECOSOC) in 1946 (Kent, 1999, p. 53).[14] The Commission serves as a "legitimator of norms and protector of individuals and groups" (p. 53). The U.N. human rights regime has formed part of the complex web of interdependence opposing the centrifugal forces of global change, ethnic tribalism, and political atomization that had been unfolding in the postmodern era (p. 186).

Between 1993 and 1996, however, there had been a weakening of the human rights regime within the United Nations. The U.N.'s lack of success in peacekeeping missions in Haiti, Bosnia, and Somalia had taken its toll on the organization. The U.N. human rights center in Geneva received 500,000 complaints of human rights abuses during the first half of 1993. Human rights advocates complained that the center merely delivered a "slap on the wrist" to these worldwide abuses. The U.N. human rights regime, in addition to being politically weak, had also been financially weak. In 1993, the U.N. spent only about $11 million, or less than one percent of its budget, on human rights work (Mouat, 1993, p. 2).

The small amount invested in global human rights priorities did not nearly meet the vast needs and responsibilities confronted by the U.N. during the post-Soviet era, when ethnic strife and the fight for new nationalities and identities were taking its toll on human lives. While the U.N. had weakened its human rights stance and credibility in the world, China's increased economic bargaining position as a formidable world trading power added leverage to her unyielding posture on the relativism of human rights, the reinstatement of the principles of state sovereignty, and the self-determination of states in U.N. human rights forums (Kent, 1999, p. 248).

Conceived by Jan Martensen, U.N. Under Secretary General for Human Rights, and with considerable support from Germany, the seed of the Vienna Conference was planted in 1988. The Conference mandate (1990 UNGA) was to "take stock of accomplishments in human rights, assess remaining obstacles in implementing the Universal Declaration, consider ways to make U.N. human rights mechanisms more effective, and ensure adequate resources to the task"

(U.S. Congress, House, 1993 [Committee on Foreign Affairs], p. 62). By 1990, the General Assembly adopted the resolution to hold the conference which convened in June 1993 (Kent, 1999, p. 162). Prior to the U.N. World Human Rights Conference in Vienna, there had been several meetings of preparatory groups, the Bangkok conference being the major pre-Vienna conference human rights initiative.

The Bangkok conference, held in April 1993, consisted of a group of 49 Asian and Middle Eastern governments (p. 165). Intra-regional divisions on the definition of human rights were found among the Asian nations at the Bangkok meeting. The countries of Japan, Thailand, Nepal, South Korea, and the Philippines had a more relaxed, westernized view of human rights, whereas China, Indonesia, Iran, Iraq, Malaysia, North Korea, and Burma had taken a more hard-line position (pp. 165-66). Although the final Bangkok Declaration reaffirmed states' commitments to the universality of human rights and the Universal Declaration, the Declaration also mentioned the principles of state sovereignty and non-interference, though not as a prior right, as had been the position of China (p. 167).

China's rigidity on human rights issues was publicly expressed only a few days before the U.N. World Human Rights Conference in Vienna. In alluding to the human rights objectives of the forthcoming U.N. Human Rights Conference in Vienna, China's Vice Minister of Foreign Affairs, Liu Huaqiu, commented: "The conference should reflect different political systems, economic and social as well as historical, religious and cultural differences of countries".[15] Chinese leaders lobbied hard to forward their position on human rights among Asian countries and to the rest of the world. In the final Vienna Declaration, the principles that China had insisted upon, such as the role of historical conditions, the right to development, and the importance of state sovereignty were mentioned, but were not granted the prominence of the universality of human rights, and civil and political rights, enumerated in U.N. doctrine.[16]

Although no single nation, including China, had been able to influence the outcome of the Vienna Human Rights Conference in 1993 and the reinstatement of the universality of human rights expressed in the Universal Declaration of Human Rights,[17] what was of crucial significance was China's ability to influence the U.N. human rights regime. China's influence on U.N. human rights activities had been most apparent since 1989:

> In the 1989 U.N. Sub-Commission and when the draft resolution criticizing its human rights conditions was first introduced, China's inordinately aggressive lobbying tactics prompted the experts to adopt a resolution requiring a secret ballot for all country specific resolutions. China opposed this procedural innovation in

1989 and continues to oppose it. China has consistently argued against the right of the Sub-Commission to engage in political debate and attack states through country-specific resolution. (Kent, 1998, pp. 6-7)

Further attempts by China to manipulate U.N. human rights procedures were taken through the tabling of a procedural no-action motion, thereby preventing the issue of its human rights practices from being brought to vote (p. 7).[18] Although the principles of the universality of human rights were emphasized in the final Vienna Declaration, there were practical signs that the U.N.'s capability to censure and act upon China's internal affairs on human rights had been weakened. Although outwardly China complied with the rest of the world in the final determination on decisions on human rights, internally the Chinese government continued to implement its own version of humans rights practices. For example, directly after the 1994 decision had been made, China quickly rounded up thousands of political dissidents and subjected them to crimes against the state, torture, and life-time imprisonment. Some were never to be seen again (Kaye, 1994, p. 18).

China's increased economic and political leverage in the WTO, the IMF, and the World Bank was a causal variable in the U.S. 1994 decision. Further contributing to the U.S. decision on China, there was a heightened global trade "euphoria" in 1994 as a result of the final formation and solidification of the World Trade Organization. The triumph of trade liberalization overshadowed the activities and actions of the U.N. human rights regime. The goal of most of the world's nations in 1994 was to promote the process of globalization through increased trade and investment liberalization. Therefore, the imposition of trade sanctions in any form, by any country, was not part of the international mind set or "global" public opinion during the time the Clinton decision on China was finalized. Few countries wanted to upset the new liberalized world order.

Transnational Elite Alliances

In addition to the complex web of interactions of states, international organizations, and regimes, international elite alliances also swayed the 1994 decision. These elite alliances had taken place between governments, and between governments and multinational corporations, both intra-regionally and extra-regionally.[19] Much of the reasoning for these alliances was driven by ideology as well as by economic considerations. With regard to ideology, the (non-Japan) Asian region, despite minor differences of opinion in the practice of human rights, shared a similar authoritarian value system. By 1991, a Sino-ASEAN alignment[20] had been formed to oppose the post-Cold War international human rights campaign.[21]

> At the 24th ASEAN Ministerial Meeting (AMM) in Kuala Lumpur in 1991, an ASEAN consensus on human rights was formulated. Interestingly, it was remarkably similar to China's human rights theory. Both China and ASEAN emphasize that the standards vary from one country to another because of differences in cultural traditions and the level of economic development . . . that in developing countries the rights to economic subsistence and development should take precedence over political and civil rights and that the application of human rights should not violate national sovereignty and should not be linked to economic cooperation. (Jie Chen, 1998, pp. 9-10)

In order to further solidify the Sino-ASEAN alignment, Chinese Premier Li Peng had visited the ASEAN region several times in the early 1990s to improve the cohesiveness of China and the Asian region (pp. 9-10). As a result of Asian solidarity, Asian nations successfully arrested the U.S. demand for a specific reference to labor standards in the final Uruguay Round agreement in Marakesh (Islam, 1994, p. 82). It was, in part, Asian solidarity on human rights ideology that strengthened its resistance to western values, and thus weakened the U.S. 1993 position of linking MFN and China's human rights record.

In addition to a shared authoritarian ideological history, Asia had become increasingly economically interdependent. Table 5.3 demonstrates an intra-regional and U.S. comparison of capital inflows to China. As displayed, the greater part of these financial inflows to China had come from the Asian region. Total Asian and U.S. inflows to China amounted to about US$40 billion, most of which had come from Hong Kong and Singapore, $20.3 billion and $11.7 billion, respectively. The greater part of Hong Kong's investment was concentrated in Guangdong, where an estimated two to three million Chinese worked for Hong Kong firms (Jones, King, and Klein, 1992, p. 14). The U.S. percentage of total U.S. and Asian inflows was a much less significant 6 percent.

Asian integration is further evidenced by the degree of trade intensity in the Asian region. Tables 5.4 and 5.5 illustrate the degree of trade intensity among Asian nations. Table 5.4, for example, presents the trade intensity of office and computing machinery for Southeast Asia, Japan, the United States, and Europe for the year 1992. As exhibited, in looking at China, the highest degree of trade intensity for this product group is between China and the ASEAN-8, at a coefficient of 7.35, reflecting China's close economic integration with the Asian (non-Japan) region. Similarly, for textile and garments, shown in Table 5.5, the trade intensity coefficient was largest with regard to the intensity of trade

Table 5.3   Comparison of Foreign Capital Inflows into China from Selected Asian Countries for the Year 1994 (US$billion)

Country/Investor	Inflow to China
Hong Kong and Macao	20.3
Japan	2.0
Singapore	11.7
Taiwan	3.3
(United States)	2.4
Total Inflows to China	40.0
U.S. Percentage of Total Inflow	6%

Source: China Statistical Year Book, 1995, pp. 556-57.

between China and the rest of the Asian (non-Japan) region, at 2.92. Figures in both tables illustrate the intensity of China's integration within the Asian region.

Because of these economic interdependencies, Asian elites in government and business used their political and economic clout to influence U.S. foreign policy across the Pacific. A major forum of global elite influence was the Asia Pacific Economic Cooperation (APEC), a government-to-government group of 21 countries both within and outside of the Asian region engaged in dialogue concerning Asian and global economic security interests.[22] In 1994, in Bogor, Indonesia, APEC world leaders convened to discuss the economic future of the Asian region and the opening of the exchange of goods and services.

The Bogor Declaration, devised by APEC leaders, envisioned an open global trading system and sustainable economic growth for the Asian region.[23] Prior to the 1994 Bogor meeting in Indonesia, however, there had been evidence of the increasing influence of the Asian region on global affairs. For example, Mexico's Secretary of Foreign Relations Fernando Solana Morales had "aggressively pursued expanded economic ties with Asia, hoping to join APEC even before NAFTA negotiations got off the ground" (Schoenberger and Helm, 1993, p. A13).

In addition to Asian regional unity on human rights ideology, there had also been Asian regional unity with regard to strategic economic interests. It was in the best interest of the elites of Asia, in 1994, to keep the region open to world trade and investment. The denial by the United States of MFN to China would

Table 5.4 Office and Computing Machinery (ISIC 3825)[a] Trade-Intensity[b] Coefficients for Eight East Asian Economies, 1992

	Japan	United States	Europe	ASEAN-8[c]
China[d]	0.63	1.04	0.55	7.35
Hong Kong	1.62	1.02	0.58	4.48
Indonesia	0.19	0.19	0.42	12.13
Malaysia	1.36	1.21	0.51	6.95
Philippines	1.02	0.58	0.77	7.74
Singapore	0.80	1.72	0.98	1.84
Taiwan	0.46	1.60	1.30	1.23
Thailand	2.74	1.19	0.50	6.38

[a] ISIC: International Standard Industrial Classification.

[b] The authors Wendy Dobson and Chia Siow Yue define trade intensity as a measure of the trade between pairs or groups of countries relative to their shares of world trade. The intensity index (I_{ij} is calculated as follows:

$$I_{ij} = \frac{X_{ij} / X_i}{M_j / (M_w - M_i)}$$

where X_{ij} is country i's exports to country j; X_i is country i's exports; M_j is country j's exports; M_w is world imports; and M_i is country i's imports.

[c] In this study, the ASEAN-8 include those eastern Asian economies of China (Guangdong province), Hong Kong, Indonesia, Malaysia, the Philippines, Singapore, Taiwan, and Thailand.

[d] China, in this instance, is Guangdong province.

Source: Dobson, 1997b, p. 22.

have affected the economic stability of the entire Asian region because it had become economically interdependent. In Hong Kong, for example, it was estimated that the U.S. denial of MFN to China would have cost the British Colony US$ "$24 billion in lost trade, and up to three percentage points off a current 5.5 percent economic growth rate". In the words of one Ministerial leader, Lee Kuan Yew, of Singapore: "U.S. trade sanctions could destabilize the region and drive up Pentagon costs". Similarly, Hong Kong's Governor Christopher Patten stated, "We are all concerned with human rights abuses, but we have never believed the solution is in limiting trade. Opening up markets is the best way to

Table 5.5   Textile and Garments (ISIC 321 and 322)[a] Trade-Intensity[b] Coefficients for Eight East Asian Economies, 1992

	Japan	United States	Europe	ASEAN-8[c]
China[d]	2.07	0.83	0.58	2.92
Hong Kong[e]	0.31	1.44	0.73	0.24
Indonesia	1.01	0.99	1.29	2.38
Malaysia	0.73	2.02	1.38	1.51
Philippines	0.63	2.88	1.14	0.72
Singapore	0.22	1.58	0.83	1.65
Taiwan	0.93	1.42	0.37	3.29
Thailand	1.35	1.21	1.08	0.67

[a] ISIC: International Standard Industrial Classification.

[b] The authors Wendy Dobson and Chia Siow Yue define trade intensity as a measure of the trade between pairs or groups of countries relative to their shares of world trade. The intensity index is calculated in the same manner as in Table 5.4.

[c] In this study, the ASEAN-8 include those eastern Asian economies of China (Guangdong province), Hong Kong, Indonesia, Malaysia, the Philippines, Singapore, Taiwan, and Thailand.

[d] China, in this instance, is Guangdong province.

[e] "Of Hong Kong's apparel, 93% was also imported from the ASEAN region in 1992, of which 89 percent came from China. The United States and the European Community (EC) were the most important export markets, whereas the importance of the Japanese market for re-exports had been increasing".

Source: Dobson, 1997b, pp. 23, 90.

open up minds". Prime Minister Tsutomu Hata of Japan "praised the U.S. decision as important for the continued economic development of the Asia-Pacific region" (Branigin, 1994, p. A8).

Elite alliances advocating unconditional MFN to China had also been formed in the United States. In 1993, for example, the prestigious Council on Foreign Relations met in Washington to advocate the end of the MFN/human rights linkage concerning China. Among the attendees were such renowned U.S. diplomats as Henry Kissinger, Cyrus Vance, and Lawrence Eagleburger, who had previously been engaged in diplomatic contacts with leaders in Beijing (Awanohara, 1994b, p. 25). Cross-national business to government alliances had also been formed to further influence the decision. Immediately before the 1994 decision by Clinton was made, Chinese Vice Premier Zou Jiahua was visiting such U.S. corporations as AT&T with prospects of a billion telephone lines to be bought by the Chinese government. The Vice Premier also informed U.S. oil companies of China's exploration plans and U.S. transportation and construction companies of objectives to build a minimum of $600 billion of road, bridges and construction projects (Schoenberger and Helm, p. 1993, A1).

U.S.-Asian business to government linkages had also been formed through U.S. government agencies. John Huang, for example, an official at the U.S. Commerce Department, had also been a top executive for the Lippo Group, "a multi-billion dollar Indonesian conglomerate with extensive dealings in China". The Riady family, who owned the multinational, reportedly had asked the Clinton administration in 1994 to hire Huang because of their interest in U.S. policy toward China ("Did China Try to Influence Elections?" 1997, p. 972). It was this complex network of regional and global elite alliances, both in business and in government, that was a direct causal variable in the formation of the 1994 U.S. decision to no longer condition China's human rights record on MFN status.

Summary

This chapter has introduced a fourth causal variable as an explanation for the 1994 decision. I have argued that complex interdependence influenced the U.S. shift in China policy from 1993 to 1994. The previously discussed independent variables of U.S. national interests, U.S. humanistic interests, and U.S. corporate interests were unable to fully explain the motives for the 1994 decision. There is compelling evidence to suggest that complex interdependence, weighted heavily on this presidential decision. Channels of formal and informal contacts between and among multinational corporations, international organizations, and the world's elite had factored into the 1994 decision. As well, linkages that had been formed between U.S. and Chinese corporations would have been affected had Clinton decided to base MFN renewal on China's human rights record.

Additionally, economic and ideologic solidarity in the Asian region had a significant effect on the U.S. decision to separate MFN and China's human rights. Asian countries acted as one with regard to their strong stance on an Asian interpretation of human rights. An interpretation which promoted the realist proposition of cultural relativism and which underscored the sovereign rights of nations expressed in Article 2 of the United Nations Charter.[24] It was also found that the Asian region exhibited a high degree of trade and investment interdependency. The U.S. revocation of MFN to China would have threatened the economic security of the entire Asian region because China had become interlinked with her neighbors. The increasingly influential governmental organization, APEC, came to the rescue of China and the Asian region in efforts to keep doors open to free trade and investment. Joining the wishes of the APEC, the ASEAN countries "believed that international isolation of China could lead to a reversal of its open-door policy and to a radicalization of its regional policy" (Jie Chen, 1998, p. 10).

The "new world order" was brought to a climax by the formation of the new WTO, which surpassed the glory of NAFTA tenfold. This new rule-making entity and overseer of world trade made it clear to the global polity that the order of the day was to extend and expand the process of free trade. Despite varying degrees of reservations concerning Western hegemony and trade advantages expressed by leaders from the South, underpinning the goals and principles of the new WTO was a global consensus.

Had President Clinton imposed sanctions on China in 1994, it would have been a move against international opinion. There was also a consensus among APEC, the ASEAN countries, NAFTA, and the EU in 1994, that China should be gradually integrated into the international political economy. As one major U.S. representative explained, "Our goal must be over time to achieve compatibility, compatibility between all countries that are trading, just as we have compatibility between all of the states of the United States" (Gephardt, 1994, p. 63).

Therefore, in the final analysis, it was external environmental factors that shifted U.S.-China policy from linkage of MFN and China's human rights in 1993, to the delinkage of these two factors in 1994. It was, in the end, the global gravitation toward trade liberalization, the formation of regional economic areas, and at the same time, the opening of these regions to one another, and the trend toward multilateralism that ultimately pressured President Clinton to permanently end the ties between China's human rights record and most-favored-nation status. The U.S. support of global trade liberalization was clearly expressed in the Congress in the final debates on the subject.

Endnotes

1   "Few scholars argue that such lobby or organized groups were the sole or dominant force behind these decisions. Indeed, their influence at particular times had depended on fluctuating circumstances, including changes in elite and public opinion, international pressures and opportunities, and other factors. Measuring the influence of individual interest or lobby groups on U.S.-China policy remains a subjective exercise" (Sutter, 1998, p. 3). "Contrary to some popular notions, lobbying, even by rich and powerful domestic interest groups,

seldom causes fundamental shifts in legislation or government decision, studies have found. But marginal shifts can mean life or death for specific interest groups" (Awanohara, 1994a, p. 25).

2   "The growing influence of transnational corporations can be seen in the increase in the stock of foreign direct investment and the growth in the number of transnational corporations and their foreign affiliates. During the 1980s, and especially after 1982, annual foreign-direct-investment flows grew rapidly. By 1992, the global stock of foreign direct investment had reached approximately $2 trillion, which generated about $5.5 trillion in sales by foreign affiliates (compared to world exports of goods and non-factor services of $4 trillion)" (UNCTAD, 1993, p. 4).

3   "Although the evidence of globalization is all around us, it is important to recognize that the impact of this metamorphosis is certainly not all positive. Exposure to global trade and investment can offer hope and opportunity for those countries capable of 'converging'. Unfortunately, nations that have not developed the institutions and human capital necessary to fully benefit from global trade may find themselves falling ever farther behind" (Mascitelli, 1999, p. 47).

4   Yan points out that a wholly-owned Sino-foreign investment project is one that is owned by foreign investment companies; a joint venture is shared and run by a board of directors that act on behalf of shareholders; a cooperative venture is a "partner" venture and is based on contract; whereas an offshore project is based on individual contract rights, and managers act on behalf of the individual project contract.

5   Peter Dicken (1998) clarifies that "in general, we would expect denser and more extensive networks of linkages between TNCs and domestic enterprises in the developed economies than in the developing economies. Within developing countries, such linkages are likely to be greatest in the larger and more industrialized countries than in others" (p. 253).

6   "Government intervention in the sourcing choices of MNEs appears to have been the single most powerful determinant for the creation of local linkages of MNEs. Without such government intervention, it is likely that, despite some market pressure, local MNE linkages would be much less developed than they are today in various countries and industries" (International Labor Organization, 1984, p. 94, as cited by Dicken, 1998, p. 253).

7   "The U.S. Congress refused to ratify GATT's existence when it was formed in 1947, thus the organization was effectively in limbo" (Luce, 1993, p. 12).

8   It should be noted that not all countries benefitted from WTO policies. "Some 30 countries in Africa and 19 in Latin America depend on primary commodity exports for more than half of their export earnings. Yet, these primary commodity exporters were not dealt with in Uruguay Round agreements. These countries suffer from a lack of diversification away from commodity dependence. Primary commodity exporters have faced the worst depression in world markets since the 1920s. Between 1980 and 1993, prices for non-oil primary commodities fell by more than half in relation to prices for manufactured goods. The estimated annual loss to these least developing countries over this period was around US$100 billion, more than twice the total flow of aid in 1990" (LeQuesne, 1996, 12). For original discourse on the terms of trade for developing countries, refer to Raul Prebisch 1959 (pp. 251-73).

9   In most studies, at this time, global income gains had been understated due to the high representation of commodities that were representative of East-Asian economies and natural resource-based economies. As Jeffrey Schott (1994) notes, "Since export expansion of more sophisticated manufactures generates greater export environmental factors, the U.S. (and North American) gains were also under-estimated" (p. 205).

10   "U.S. support for increased global economic liberalization, or 'globalization,' remains strong. During the entire postwar period, the executive branch, whether controlled by the Democrats or the Republicans, acted as a bulwark against congressional demands for increased protection" (Zupnick, 1999, p. 228).

11   The countries in the Cairns group included Australia, New Zealand, Canada, Fiji, Thailand, the Philippines, Malaysia, Argentina, Uruguay, Brazil, Chile, and Colombia, altogether representing 130 million farmers (Foster, 1993, p. 7).

12   China had been an original signatory to the GATT, in 1948, before the communist takeover.

13   "International Governmental Organizations are among the features of the international system that define limits to the maneuverability of the states that governments steer. They offer states a variety of inducements and penalties that enter into the choices governments make among strategies and actions. The way in which IGOs carry out these operations is subject not only to structural and policy variations in the organizations themselves, but also to differential perceptions of their importance by national political actors" (Boardman, 1994, p. 163).

14   The U.N. Sub-Commission on Human Rights, formed in 1979, investigates human rights problems in specific countries.

15   AFP report of Liu Huaqiu interview, June 10, 1993, "La Chine pour des Droits de l'Homme à la Carte", cited by Kent, 1999, p. 173.

16   "The only respect in which the Bangkok Declaration appeared to have retained an influence on the thinking in the Vienna statement was in its itemization of all the rights [self-determination, sovereignty, culture, development] in addition to civil and political rights. As well, the Vienna Declaration, in opposition to the practice of China's human rights, submitted an extensive section on torture, according to which freedom from torture was a 'right which must be protected under all circumstances, including in times of internal or international disturbance or armed conflicts' (sec. II, para. 56) and the need for an independent judiciary and legal profession (sec. I, para. 27)" (Kent, 1999, p. 186).

17   "Maxime Tardu has observed, in his study of the effectiveness of U.N. human rights bodies, that external and internal pressures on human rights reinforce each other to produce compliance" (Tardu, 1993, as cited by Kent, 1999, p. 249).

18   In further evidence of China's continuing influence on U.N. human rights procedures, on April 18, 2000, the United Nations Commission on Human Rights failed to consider a resolution that came from the United States, criticizing China's human rights performance. "The procedural no-action motion was adopted by a vote of 22 supporting the no-action motion to 18 against. Human Rights Watch criticized governments of the European Union, Australia, Canada, and Japan, which had professed concern about the human rights situation in China, but declined to co-sponsor the resolution with the United States or to actively lobby against the no-action motion. . . . The credibility of the U.N. Commission has been seriously damaged by its unwillingness to censure China or even discuss its rights performance" (Human Rights Watch, 2000b).

19   D.M. Gordon notes that "it is perhaps most useful to view the relationship between transnational [corporations] and governments as both cooperative and competing, both supportive and conflictual. They operate in a fully dialectical relationship, locked into unified but contradictory roles and positions, neither the one nor the other partner clearly or completely able to dominate" (Dicken, 1998, p. 243; Gordon, 1998, p. 61).

20   The ASEAN countries, formed in 1967, include Thailand, Malaysia, Singapore, the Philippines, Indonesia, Brunei in 1984, Vietnam in 1995, and Myanmar and Laos in 1997.

21 "The ASEAN consensus on human rights was determined largely by the views of Singapore, Malaysia, and Indonesia. Although the Philippines and Thailand did not share the same convictions, they went along with their ASEAN partners in the interest of group cohesion" (Jie Chen, 1998, pp. 9-10).

22 APEC member countries include: Australia, Brunei, Canada, Chile, Peoples Republic of China, Hong Kong/China, Indonesia, Japan, Republic of Korea, Malaysia, Mexico, New Zealand, Papua New Guinea, Peru, Republic of the Philippines, Russia, Singapore, the Republic of China, Thailand, USA, and Vietnam. These 21-member economies have a combined GDP of US$16 trillion, and in 1998 accounted for 42 percent of global trade ("Asia Pacific Economic Cooperation", n.d., Internet: http://www1.apec.org.sp/member, http://www.apecsec.org.sg).

23 "Asia Pacific Economic Cooperation", n.d., Internet: http://www.apecsec.org.sg/ 97brochures.

24 "The Organization is based on the principle of the sovereign equality of all its Members" (United Nations, 1945, art. 2 [1]).

6 Conclusion

The previous chapter focused on the fourth and final hypothesis of this study. The issue of trade and human rights in the context of the 1994 Clinton decision on China was opened up to a broader perspective. Transnational influences were brought into the argument as causal factors for the delinkage of MFN and China's human rights record. These externalities comprised a complex network of transnational linkages and interdependencies. These linkages included transnational corporate linkages, transnational multilateral institutional linkages, including the linkages between international governmental organizations and international financial institutions. Transnational elite alliances also formed part of this larger political landscape.

This chapter begins with a brief summary of the major findings of the research. I then turn to the major contributions of the research, its limitations, and issues for future investigation. The chapter will then extrapolate the major observations of the study, highlighting the events preceding the 1994 decision, as well as the events that occurred after the decision. The broader implications for both economic and political theory will be defined, as well as implications for U.S. policy formulation. Finally, some recommendations for U.S. foreign policy on human rights will be offered.

Review of Findings

In this project, I have presented and tested four hypotheses. The first hypothesis, premised on realist theory, was that the U.S. intent to sustain and increase power in the Asian region influenced the 1994 Clinton decision to sever the ties between China's human rights record and most-favored-nation status. According to the realist-based argument, the primary obligation of a state is to promote the national interest which is realized by the attainment of power (Keohane and Nye, 1989, p. 11; Kegley, 1995b, pp. 4-5). Therefore, the economic policies of nations are predicated on their contributions to national power.

Concerns for the U.S. national interest were repeatedly evident in the articulations of U.S. leaders in congressional proceedings, debates, and in their speeches to U.S. groups and the public at large. U.S. global economic leadership would be enhanced and expanded by removing obstacles to trade and investment. The deepening of U.S. economic relations with China was thought to improve the economic welfare of U.S. citizens by supplying job growth in the importing, exporting, retailing, and technology sectors of the economy, and by offering quality products on the U.S. market at prices the average U.S. consumer could afford. As well, further entry into the China market would help to build a strong U.S. private sector, which would contribute to the power and wealth of the nation.

The fear of China's threat to the U.S. national security was also revealed in pronouncements on the congressional floor. Such major threats to the U.S. security that were articulated included China's position as a rising economic and military hegemon in the Asian region, conflict on the Korean Peninsula, and the political and economic stability of Cambodia. Closer economic relations with China were looked upon as a deterrent to these perceived threats.

The nationalist argument, however, displayed some shortcomings. The evidence suggested that U.S. policymakers had overestimated China's wealth and national power. It was found that although China enjoyed a positive trade balance with the United States, the United States had increasingly suffered a negative bilateral trade balance with China. China, however, had grown to become one of the largest net debtor nations in the world. Also, when looking at aggregate levels, it was determined that China was not a major source for U.S. job growth in 1994, when compared to other foreign markets. As a result of political and economic transition, China's internal structural impediments undermined the concerns articulated in the Congress of China's immediate threat to U.S. interests. Because of these drawbacks to the realist-based argument, the first hypothesis — that the U.S. intent to sustain and increase power in the Asian region influenced the 1994 Clinton decision — could not be fully accepted.

The second hypothesis was that the U.S. intent to improve the respect for human rights in China through economic engagement was thought to influence the Clinton decision to delink MFN from China's human rights practices. Underlying this liberalist-based philosophy was the notion that the peace and prosperity of nations would be advanced by the removal of economic barriers. U.S. corporations, through individual choice in product selection and management and training techniques, would serve as pathways to democracy and human rights reform by avoiding government constraints and reaching out directly to the people (Clark, 1916; Bernstein and Dicker, 1994/95; Garten, 1997, p. 71). The findings suggest that there were some positive indications of human rights improvements in China. These positive outcomes could be seen in the increasing availability of products on the China market. In the years preceding the Clinton decision, from 1990 to1993, China's standard of living, as measured by key consumer durables, had risen. In particular, such mid-technology products as VCRs, satellite dishes, construction cranes, and facsimile machines, were purchased in greater quantities. These technology products improved the pattern of information flow in China. For example, the facsimile machine helped to spread across the country the word of political arrests that had taken place in Beijing. Additionally, purchases of such lesser value goods as color television sets, bicycles, and washing machines had increasingly risen.

There were some limitations to the liberalist proposition, however. There were, in fact, U.S. policymakers, human rights groups, and citizens who believed that MFN should be contingent upon human rights improvements in China. Contrary to the liberal hypothesis that U.S. economic engagement with China would advance the cause of human rights in China, some U.S. officials felt that only by attaching human rights conditions to MFN renewal could human rights progress, and that the United States should follow the same policy of linkage as past presidential administrations (U.S. Congress, House, 1992 [Committee on Ways and Means, Subcommittee on Trade], p. 41; U.S. Congress, Senate, 1994 [Feingold], p. 8). In a U.S. national poll taken in 1993, for example, it was discerned that 65 percent of the respondents felt that China should improve its human rights practices if China wanted to continue its current trade status with the United States (Bowman, 1994, p. 150). In addition, 276 members of the House of Representatives signed a letter to Secretary of State Warren Christopher demanding that China meet the human rights conditions stipulated in the 1993 Executive Order by the President (Beher, 1994, p. A28). In addition, there was no general consensus on how to improve human rights in China among major human rights groups. For example, the human rights group Asia Watch expressed that human rights would improve in China only through the pressure of the yearly MFN renewal (U.S. Congress, Senate, 1994 [Jendrzejczyk], p. 92). While the human rights group Amnesty International USA did not take a position on linkage, it expressed that the Clinton administration simply did not give human rights issues the significance they deserved in U.S. policy (U.S. Congress, House, 1994 [Jones], p. 171). Because of these discrepancies within the liberal argument, the intent to improve human rights in China by delinking MFN and human rights could not be fully accepted as a motive for the 1994 decision.

The third hypothesis was that U.S. corporations influenced the 1994 decision to end the relationship between China's human rights record and most-favored-nation status. This proposition, premised on radical theory, suggested that corporations exerted a considerable amount of influence on U.S. foreign economic policy. In this economically-determinist perspective, developing countries were believed to be the major targets of an expansionist agenda. This expansionist agenda was guided by an international elite alliance and the needs of monopoly capital (Shambaugh, 1991, pp. 226-27). China therefore, as a developing country, would be considered a target of this expansionist agenda.

U.S. multinational corporations were indeed found to be a significant influence in the 1994 decision regarding China. The growing appearance of business lobbying groups on Capitol Hill gave evidence of the increasing attempts by business groups to influence U.S. foreign policy outcomes. Thousands of small to large firms and trade associations, under the nucleus of the Business Coalition for U.S.-China Trade, came to the forefront of the U.S. congressional agenda to plead their cases for the termination of the linkage between MFN and China's human rights. In particular, U.S. aerospace and defense firms, with key interests in selling to the China market, were vociferous in advocating for delinkage. Armed with public statements before Congress, soft money contributions to congressional Representatives, and letters to and personal meetings with the U.S. president, corporate executives made their positions clear to the U.S. government leadership.

There were some shortcomings to the radical argument, however. Primarily, there was no unified corporate position regarding China's human rights and MFN delinkage in 1994. Many corporations were adamantly against delinking MFN and human rights. Though human rights concerns may or may not have been a reason for their position, these corporations felt that China's practice of forced labor created an unfair trade advantage in China's ability to create quality products at cheaper prices than could the U.S. domestic industry supply, thus supplanting the U.S. home industry. This position was particularly evident in the U.S. textile industry, which argued against China's trade restrictions on U.S. textile imports, among other unfair trade practices.

U.S. corporate interests were not the sole influence in advocating for MFN and human rights delinkage in 1994. U.S. national interests also influenced the Clinton decision regarding China. It was in the best U.S. national interest to build and maintain a strong U.S. private sector that would be enhanced by U.S. corporate expansion into China and the Asian region. Because of these weaknesses in the argument that corporations were the sole influence on U.S.-China policy in 1994, the third hypothesis could not be considered a full explanation for the decision; therefore, a fourth hypothesis was proposed.

In the fourth hypothesis, elements of the preceding hypotheses were argued as partial explanations for the decision. However, a fourth causal factor for the delinkage of MFN and human rights in China was added into the equation, which was complex interdependence. Complex interdependence was defined as "a situation among a number of countries in which multiple channels of contact connect societies, where states do not monopolize these contacts. These multiple channels include formal and informal ties between governmental elites, as well as foreign office arrangements and channels between transnational corporations" (Keohane and Nye, 1989, pp. 24-25).

During the years 1993 and 1994, a significant amount of U.S. intrafirm sales were cross-border with China, Malaysia, and Thailand, where assembly of U.S. goods for export were located, particularly goods pertaining to the electronics industry. U.S. direct investment in China had increased, which in turn increased the mutual dependencies between firms. Many U.S. firms, for example, had come to depend on China's abundant and cheap labor force and the emerging opportunity of China's vast market. U.S. firms looked to the China market as a bridge to other markets in the Asian-Pacific region. Conversely, China's state, collective, and privately-owned enterprises looked to U.S. corporations for the acquisition of knowledge and technology, as well as for entry into the vast U.S. market for its goods. These growing trans-Pacific linkages served to solidify U.S.-China commercial relations that would have otherwise been interrupted had Clinton continued to condition China's MFN on human rights improvements, and had he acted on that claim.

Multilateral institutional linkages also played into the 1994 decision. Major governmental and financial institutions that influenced the opinions of U.S. decision makers included the WTO, the APEC, the IMF, and the World Bank. The end of the Uruguay Round and the formation and solidification of the new WTO in 1994 served to expand the process of trade liberalization and globalization. There was a general consensus among countries, from all corners of the world, that global trade and investment should be liberalized. Any conditions set by the Clinton administration to deter the process of trade liberalization in 1994 would have been a move against the international consensus. Global welfare was thought to be best served by the integration of China into the global marketplace and the international political community.

A major influence on the 1994 U.S. decision was China's linkage to the IMF and the WTO. Throughout the years, China had maintained close connections and good relations with these international trade and financial entities. China had come to rely upon the financial advice and macroeconomic policies of these institutions during the process of modernization. These institutional connections helped to enhance China's leverage in preventing any continued and additional conditions on her trade status with the United States.

Finally, transnational elite alliances had been part of the intricate global web that had influenced the shift in China policy from 1993 to 1994. These international and regional elite alliances had formed between governments, and between business and governments. Asian elites in government and business used their political and financial clout to influence U.S. foreign policy across the Pacific. Through the forum of APEC, for example, international business and government leaders from 21 countries were able to avert any obstruction of China's trade with the United States, which was viewed as an obstacle to the economic development of the Asian region. Such major political elites as Henry Kissinger, Cyrus Vance, and Lawrence Eagleburger, renowned for their expertise on U.S.-China relations, with a history of extensive dealings with leaders in Beijing, advocated for the end of the human rights and MFN linkage. In the final analysis, it was transnational linkages and the global trend toward increased trade and investment liberalization that convinced President Clinton to end the relationship between MFN and China's human rights practices.

Contributions of the Research

This project has sought to enhance the general knowledge of the literature by testing some of the limitations of theories and by improving on traditional theoretical constructs as explanations for U.S. foreign policy outcomes. By applying the case of the U.S. 1994 decision to the three major theoretical schools — realism, liberalism, and radicalism — this study has provided insights into the usefulness of traditional theories for the analysis of foreign economic policy.

By not fully accepting any one theory as an explanation for the motives of the 1994 decision, this research has attempted to kindle the investigation for alternative theories, or perhaps the synthesis of current theories, as foundations on which to assess global revolutionary events at the turn of the century. The resolute insistence of this work on not accepting any one theory in its fullest definition does not, however, imply indecisiveness, or a safer "middle of the road" solution. Rather, by bringing to light the limitations of traditional paradigms as explanations for the 1994 Clinton decision regarding MFN and China's human rights record, the research has served as a caution against viewing events through the narrow lens of a singular theory that has been built upon the circumstances of yesteryear.

This project has contributed to practical value as well. The conclusions and implications which have been presented in this study may provide U.S. decision makers with further insights and knowledge into the relationship between trade and human rights, and the social consequences that the lack of this relationship may cause, particularly as it pertains to human rights abuses in China and elsewhere throughout the world. Through empirical investigation and analysis, this study has strived to provide U.S. policymakers with a greater understanding of the U.S.-China bilateral relationship, so that more fruitful policy choices can be made on future issues on human rights in China, and in all areas of the world.

This research has hopefully brought to light the intricacies involved in upholding international human rights standards through private and intergovernmental and state mechanisms, so that the implementation of U.S. foreign policy on human rights can be more effective. Beyond U.S. policy, the research has also provided the international community with insights into collective policymaking on human rights, and the complexities involved in the formulation of policy within the greater international bureaucracy.

In the broader perspective, this study has underscored the conflicting and complementary issues of the relationship between the economic criterion and ethical issues. Though the debate between the market and ethics has long been ingrained in the rhetoric of scholars throughout history, this research has approached the issue within the context of communism's last major threshold, thus making the contribution to the scholarship all the more timely. In addition, this investigation has brought forward the positive role that corporations can play in promoting and protecting human rights in China, and in all countries in which they operate, provided that human rights monitoring is maintained and that corporate codes of conduct are followed and carried through effectively.

With globalization running at its zenith, this study has stressed the critical issues where commercialism and human rights converge. These issues have included, for example, the relationship between labor conditions and production, between business and freedom of association, and between management and bargaining, and ultimately the relationship between economic relations and human justice. While offering some policy solutions, this work has repeatedly questioned the morality of conducting business in countries where executions for political reasons are a common occurrence. Additionally, the study underscores the fragilities of an international human rights policy in an age when states are redefining themselves and national identities are being rediscovered.

Limitations and Suggestions for Future Research

The greater part of this study has been limited to the confines of propositions that have been based on traditional schools of thought. The theoretical arguments presented, however, were not mutually exclusive. The opinions and testimonials of many U.S. government officials and business leaders involved in the 1994 decision evinced foundations in more than one theoretical school. Therefore, future research may move beyond the boundaries of present theoretical traditions by exploring new qualitative or quantitative foundations on which to base U.S. foreign policy analysis and international politics.

Due to financial and time constraints, this study did not employ survey research or direct interview methods. In the absence of direct interviews, however, enough primary source data was utilized to make convincing arguments and conclusions concerning the motivations of the 1994 presidential decision. Through the employment of the content analysis method, statements by key officials in government and business were repeatedly found, providing insights into the discourse and governmental opinion at the time. Passive research also kept personalities from intervening with objective analysis. A major weakness of the interview method is its "reactivity, where biases may be produced not only by the wording, order or format of the questions, but also by the interaction between interviewer and respondent" (Singleton, Straits, and Straits, 1993, pp. 271-75). Nonetheless, it is suggested that direct interviewing be utilized in future research on the subject of study in order to confirm or deny present deductions.

An additional limitation to the research is that often articulations in congressional proceedings may be emotionally-ridden, or they may serve as a camouflage for other underlying motives for policy. Such is the case where constituent interests may be involved. Although there is no sure method for deciphering the ulterior motives of leaders, it was found that U.S. representatives from key districts and states that were engaged in direct economic relations with China revealed opposing opinions.

Major Observations

This study has concluded that human rights in U.S. foreign policy will be increasingly addressed through the private sector and multilateral institutions. It was also concluded that each hypothesis, premised on competing theoretical perspectives, could not exclusively account for the shift in the Clinton policy on China from 1993 to 1994. It was finally concluded that it was complex interdependence set against the backdrop of global trade liberalization that persuaded President William Clinton and executive leaders at both the national and state levels to cede the connection between MFN and China's human rights transgressions. The decision was influenced not only by national concerns, but also by global concerns for China's integration into the international political economy.

This work has covered a broad range of human rights interests, from the most severe violations of extrajudicial killings, prison torture, arbitrary detentions, and executions to child labor, working conditions, and substandard wages relative to the economy of the host country. Additionally, human rights have been defined and discussed within the classical liberal and western-based tenets of civil and political rights. It should be noted, however, that economic and social rights, which had been stipulated in the Carter/Vance human rights policy position, have not been considered of lesser importance. All of these rights are viewed as mutually reinforcing.

It is predicted that with the ending of ties between MFN and human rights, multinational corporations will become increasingly important global actors in the advancement of human rights throughout the world. This means that in U.S. policy formulation, corporations will work in close concert with U.S. government leaders in transmitting and revealing information on human rights violations in host countries. In addition, based on President Clinton's 1994 decision and his suggestion of the application of corporate codes of conduct, it has been concluded that U.S. corporations will cooperate with local governments in foreign countries in the enforcement of just institutions and the rule of law (DeGeorge, 1993, p. 54). Corporate inclusion in human rights issues is not to suggest, however, that corporations will become involved in "moral crusading". Their private nature guarantees that they are not accountable to the larger public to the extent that a government agency would be. Corporate wealth, resources, and influence, in fact, can be used for self-serving interests that can cause both harm and good in a society. However, the global growth of transnational corporations throughout the past decades gives them more influence over the lives of people. "These consequences entail that corporations are inescapably involved in issues of moral import" (Elfstrom, 1991, p. 32).

With regard to issues pertaining to trade and human rights:

> China, Central and Eastern Europe, and the Republics of the former Soviet Union will enter into greater trade and monetary relations with western Europe, the United States, Japan and other nations. They may join trading groups that will establish international background institutions for firms within those countries as well as for multinationals entering those countries. In the interim, as in the case of developing countries, ethics will have a larger rather than a smaller role to play in international business with formerly communist countries. (DeGeorge, 1993, p. 157)

The conclusion that the role of the private sector will increasingly become an important global actor in the promotion and protection of international human rights does not imply, however, complete acceptance of the liberal explanation for the U.S. policy regarding China and MFN.

The liberal paradigm, which espouses that increased trade with China would in fact lead to increased respect for human rights in China, has not yet been borne out. Clearly, economic reform in China has not yet proven to be a panacea for the widespread political and individual repression that still exists. For example, in infringement of human rights qualifications (iv) and (v) of the 1993 Executive Order, China's prison system, far from humane, continued to practice procedures patterned after the Stalinist camps:

> For every prisoner released, we can name countless others that have been arrested. Thousands of prisoners languish in Chinese prison cells, out of the headlines, isolated and overlooked. They are the nameless victims, shackled and dumped into cold concrete cells, beaten by guards using truncheons, electric prods and bare fists. Deprived of food and relentlessly interrogated, many confess to "crimes" never committed. Such is the fate of thousands in China, despite more than a decade of impressive economic reform. (U.S. Congress, House, 1994 [Zhao], p. 133)

Exhibit A of the appendix provides an example of one of the many accounts of experiences in a Chinese prison. The detailed description of the prison conditions expressed by the prisoner gives evidence that the list of human rights improvements that were to be improved if MFN were to be renewed in 1994, had not been met. Arguments against delinkage were voiced prodigiously in the U.S. political arena. It was expressed in Congress that "there had been no substantive change in China's political life since the protest in 1989, and that the argument that a more open economy will automatically lead to political liberalization had not been borne out". Yet despite the fact that China continued to open the door to trade and foreign investment, the government continued to imprison citizens for their political and religious beliefs (U.S. Congress, House, 1994 [Fan], p. 139).

In fact, 1993 was the worst year for political arrests and trials in China since mid-1990 and the aftermath of the 1989 massacre. Political repression in China was increasing, not decreasing (U.S. Congress, House, 1994 [Jendrzejczyk], pp. 119-21). The U.S. State Department reported that in 1994:

> there continued to be widespread and well-documented human rights abuses in China, in violation of internationally accepted norms, stemming both from the authorities' intolerance of dissent and the inadequacy of legal safeguards for freedom of speech, association and religion. Abuses include arbitrary and lengthy incommunicado detention, torture and mistreatment of prisoners and thousands of prisoners of conscience remain imprisoned or detained. (U.S. Dept. of State, 1995a, China sec.)

U.S. officials communicated that conditioning China's human rights practices on MFN had only resulted in "incremental" improvements. China supplied information on 235 prisoners that the United States had identified, and also promised to provide information on the status of 106 imprisoned Tibetans. A willingness to begin dialogue with the International Red Cross to arrange visits to prisoners of conscience was expressed by Chinese officials, and promises were made to settle certain emigration cases. China also promised to "review interference" with Voice of America (VOA) airwaves (Christopher, 1994a, p. A17).

U.S. Customs inspections of a few Chinese prisons were agreed upon, but only at the request of a 60-day notice from U.S. Customs before the allowance of an onsite inspection (U.S. Congress, Senate, 1994 [Lord], p. 13). Chinese authorities, however, would not permit visits to prisons for which the Ministry of Justice declared there was insufficient evidence, nor access to re-education through labor facilities (U.S. Congress, Senate, 1994 [Bader], p. 21). With regard to the other five rights issued in the 1993 Executive Order, which included adherence to the Universal Declaration of Human Rights, there had only been modest improvements (U.S. Congress, Senate, 1994 [Lord], p. 13). But these "small steps", in the views of some U.S. representatives, in no way warranted the total delinkage of MFN and human rights (U.S. Congress, House, 1994 [Abercrombie], p. 41; [Lantos], p. 11; [Pelosi], p. 28; [Smith], p. 17; [Wolf], p. 21; U.S. Congress, Senate, 1994 [Feingold], p. 9).

In violation of the 1992 U.S.-China bilateral Memorandum of Understanding, Chinese prisoners were still utilized as slave labor for China's export market. More than 100 prisons were disguised by the Chinese government as civilian factories. One prison, for instance, housed more than 7,000 inmates and was called the "Human Heavy Motor Vehicle Factory". Another, a women's prison in Changsha province, was known as the "New Life Cotton Quilt Printing Factory" (Campbell, 1992, pp. 18-19). Coercive birth control practices continued and basic freedoms of speech and assembly were still being denied (U.S. Congress, House, 1994 [Lantos], p. 11). On February 22, 1993, for example, China adopted a new state security law to punish journalists accused of "leaking state secrets abroad" (U.S. Congress, Senate, 1994 [Jendrzejczyk], pp. 78-79). Further restrictions on emigration remained in place for dissidents, and the colonization of Tibet continued (U.S. Congress, House, 1994 [Lantos], p. 11).

Political repression in China also extended to U.S. territory. One of the most outspoken U.S. representatives in support of MFN linkage to human rights articulated of having personal knowledge of Chinese nationals, active in the United States in promoting human rights, who were threatened and harassed by Chinese authorities, which was, according to the spokesperson, in violation of U.S. law. Threats by Chinese government authorities against Chinese human rights activists in the United States were also made to their families and relatives living in China. And in many cases, Chinese human rights activists in the United States were denied re-entry into China (U.S. Congress, House, 1994 [Pelosi], p. 29).

Indeed, the gradual opening of the China market did result in some improvements in the well-being of the Chinese people, particularly during the post-Mao era. The standard of living for many Chinese had risen. More communication with the outside world was possible for a once insular society. China's per capita GDP rose substantially[1] after the 1979 Deng economic reforms and the 1980 granting of conditional MFN by the United States. By the early 1990s, many urban citizens in China could take advantage of new products and technology that increased trade liberalization brought to its eastern seaboard.[2] Although China's economic liberalization was steadily increasing, its human rights record was not progressing as fast. Political repression continued, despite China's market opening and rapid rise onto the global political economy. The 1993 *Country Reports on Human Rights Practices* summarized some of the conditions that were still evident in China: "Hundreds, perhaps thousands of political prisoners remained under detention or in prison. Physical abuse, including torture by the police and prison officials persisted. Criminal defendants continued to be denied legal safeguards such as due process or adequate defense" (U.S. Dept. of State, 1994, China sec.).

Moreover, "in 1995, Chinese diplomats and government officials seemed to intensify their efforts to underscore that good economic relations with the world's largest country would be fostered by decreasing pressure on human rights" (Human Rights Watch, 1997, p. 3). The very freedoms that are outlined in the Universal Declaration and in International Covenants, signed or unsigned by China, have been disregarded by rulers in Beijing.

More recently, China has disregarded Article 5 of the Declaration: "No one shall be subjected to torture or to cruel, inhuman or degrading treatment or punishment" (United Nations, General Assembly, 1948). Human rights violations in China continue to include "extrajudicial killings, tortures and mistreatment of prisoners" (U.S. Dept. of State, 2000, China sec.). Furthermore, China has disregarded Article 9 of the Declaration: "No one shall be subjected to arbitrary arrest, detention or exile" (United Nations, General Assembly, 1948). Human rights violations in China continue to include, "forced confessions, arbitrary arrest and detention, lengthy incommunicado detention and denial of due process" (U.S. Dept. of State, 2000, China sec.). In further violation of international human rights norms, China has lacked adherence to Article 10 of the Declaration: "Everyone is entitled in full equality and to a fair and public hearing by an independent and impartial tribunal of any criminal charges against him" (United Nations, General Assembly, 1948).

Beginning in May of 1999, dozens of China Democratic Party (CDP) members were arrested in a widening crackdown on political expression, and additional CDP leaders were convicted of subversion and sentenced to long prison terms in closed trials that flagrantly violated due process. By the years end, almost all of the key leaders of the CDP were serving long prison terms, and only a handful of dissidents nationwide dared to remain active publicly. (U.S. Dept. of State, 2000, China sec.)

Finally, China has disregarded Article 12 of the Declaration: "No one should be subjected to arbitrary interference with privacy, family, home or correspondence, nor attacks upon his honor or reputation" (United Nations, General Assembly, 1948). During the year 1999, "the Chinese government infringed on citizens' privacy rights, tightened restrictions on freedom of speech and of the press, of assembly and of association, and tightened controls on the Internet. The government continued to restrict freedom of movement" (U.S. Dept. of State, 2000, China sec.). Despite the fact that the present Chinese regime continues to systematically reject Western pressure on its human rights practices, it is concluded that human rights reform in China will, over time, manifest itself through increased economic interdependence with the United States, and other democratic countries. Continued U.S. economic engagement with China would also serve to support grassroots organizations in China that are struggling for both economic and democratic reform. In short, we can expect that the introduction of democratic principles via direct local linkages through multinational corporations would eventually advance the cause of human rights in China.

For human rights advocates and activists, the 1994 decision meant the loss of a powerful bargaining tool to pressure the Chinese regime to comply with international human rights standards and adhere to the 1948 Declaration of Human Rights. As the U.S. government gradually relinquishes part of the burden of global human rights responsibilities, cooperative multilateral efforts at enforcing rights will be increasingly called upon. International governmental organizations such as the WTO, the ILO, the U.N. Commission on Human Rights, and its subcommittees will assume greater responsibility for the protection of human rights in China and around the world. China's claims to cultural relativism and pleas of state sovereignty in the institution of her own human rights practices will eventually give way to WTO pressures and obligations.

China's entrance into the WTO will serve to pressure China's current leaders to adopt universal standards of business conduct, including the conduct of its human citizens engaged in business practice. As yet, however, multilateral institutions have been weak in their ability to respond to human rights violations throughout the global community. Part of this inability is due to a lack of cohesiveness and commitment among member states to support human rights improvements in countries through multilateral mechanisms. Some suggestions are offered with regard to U.S. policies addressing international human rights issues through multilateral institutions in the recommendations section below.

Now that the U.S. government has granted Beijing permanent normal trade relations (PNTR) as a condition of entry into the WTO, the annual executive review of China's human rights performance, based on the Jackson-Vanik Amendment and its requirements regarding emigration, will cease to be an issue. U.S. congressional decision makers have proposed a "substitute" to insure that U.S. concerns about human rights in China will have continued attention. The new U.S. trade bill granting permanent trade relations with China has been augmented by the Levin-Bereuter proposal that would create a special U.S. commission to monitor China's human rights performance (Rogers and Cooper, 2000, pp. A2, A4).

Though well-intentioned, this U.S. unilateral effort could perhaps be a model for a more powerful and persuasive human rights initiative through international institutional procedures, where collective measures in the form of trade sanctions would be a far more effective and persuasive insurance against human rights abuses in China, and elsewhere. In her 1995 speech, the former U.S. ambassador to the United Nations articulated: "One of our top priorities at the U.N. is to build mechanisms that will contribute on a long-term basis to human rights and peace. Accordingly, we were the prime movers behind the successful effort to establish a U.N. High Commissioner for Human Rights" (U.S. Dept. of State, 1995b). In future years, the United Nations will serve not only as a center for international public governance, but also as an important center for pooling expertise and resources needed for dealing with multinational corporations (Elfstrom, 1993, p. 98).

Post-1994 Implications

This case study has significant implications for both economic and political theory, as well as for U.S. foreign policymaking. First, the findings question the plausibility of basing a singular theory, in its traditional definition and perspective, as an underlying framework for understanding U.S. foreign policy behavior. "Given the complexity and open nature of the social world, it is hardly possible that one paradigm could ever be fully explanatory, suggesting the need for a multi-paradigmatic approach to the study of socio-economic events" (Patomaki and Wight, 2000, p. 226). Or, perhaps there is a need to construct an entirely new paradigm, as Kuhn (1970) might advise, on which to study international political behavior.[3] Quite possibly, then, this theoretical impasse implies a transitional phase for present theoretical schools. There is a warning, however, that comes from the radical school of thought with regard to the construction of new paradigms. That is, "a close related error in thinking about theoretical innovation in conjunction with global transformation is to impose Western dichotomies on the Third World, and to seek to universalize them" (Mittelman, 1997, p. 250). From the radical viewpoint, "what we see before us is a new interventionist framework which legalizes international inequality in the guise of a new moral universalism" (Lewis, 1998, p. 97). Radical theory is a constant reminder of the current global trend of "commodity fetishism", or the increasingly widespread commodification of social relations that is partly reflected in the growing conditions and struggles associated with the production of commodities (Gill, 1995, p. 402), and in the global social and macroeconomic imbalances caused by the rapid expansion and exchange of financial capital.

As previously defined in chapter 2, realist theory suggests that human rights would not be a factor in the formulation of U.S. foreign policy. However, the realist assertion that U.S. foreign policy is guided solely by the principles of power and national interests overlooks what has been described as

> a growing recognition of the need for a normative role for ethics in international affairs, and that even the most casual observer must note that today the language of politics and decision making is ridden with references to ethics and moral traditions. From the moral renewal implied in the just war tradition in legitimizing the use of force, the language of ethics carries great political weight. (Goulet, 1992, p. 231)

The language of ethics, however, has become more than just rhetoric, as seen by the fact that even a superpower such as the United States sought to obtain United Nations approval before making the moral decision to deploy the use of force in the Persian Gulf War (p. 231). However, political realists counter that "America may lack the means to conduct these crusades of global meliorism, and should not neglect its own interests in the service of others" (Chomsky, 1998, p. 24). In 1992, the U.S. ambassador to China posed this very same inter-paradigm quandary:

> The new environment summons continued American leadership, albeit of a different kind. What will not change will be the need to fuse realism and idealism to promote our interests and project our values. Free countries respect human dignity, free countries make better economic partners. Of course, we should not press others to adopt the American model. Each nation must find its own path of freedom. (U.S. Congress, Senate, 1992 [Lord], p. 31)

That the liberal paradigm and its principle of altruism was not fully able to account for the 1994 decision challenges liberal theory, as currently defined and practiced, as a basis on which to gauge international political and economic behavior. Has Wilsonian idealism and neoliberal Ricardian economic theory been justified in its promises for peace, utilitarianism, and the betterment of humankind? As mentioned earlier, in the literature review, it has been argued that globalization has caused an asymmetry between owners of capital and un-skilled or semiskilled workers as trade and investment expand across national borders. This would suggest a need for maintaining a balance between the market and society — one that would promote private enterprise without undermining social cohesion (Rodrik, 1997, pp. 4, 13; Ruggie, 1997, p. 92).

The juxtaposition between trade and human rights was clearly exemplified in Keynesian theory. In his 1938 autobiographical essay, "My Early Beliefs", Keynes noted that society overvalues "the economic criterion" in decision making and actions, thus destroying the "quality of the popular ideal" (Keynes, 1938, p. 445). Keynes's notion inevitably led to his thesis that "governments must intervene for the public good" (Keynes, 1935, pp. 135-38). Similarly, Karl Polanyi, in *The Great Transformation* (1957), wrote of the contention between the market and ethics:

> To allow the market mechanism to be sole director of the fate of human beings and their natural environment, indeed, even of the amount and use of purchasing power, would result in the demolition of society. For the alleged commodity "labor power" cannot be shoved about, used indiscriminately, or even left unused, without affecting also the human individual who happens to be the bearer of this peculiar commodity. (p. 73)

In lieu of past theoretical criticisms, it may be considered that present theoretical debates which premise themselves on problems arising from "post-modernist" times may actually be historical repetitions. Perhaps the realist uto-pian vision of unsurpassed state power, the liberal utopian vision of peace through commerce and the radical utopian vision of "pure collectivity" may have been, all along, oversimplifications of evaluating global events since the turn of the twentieth century. With the social complexities brought about by the global transformations of the late 1980s, the search for theoretical explanations for social behavior indeed becomes all the more urgent.

International corporate expansion and the privatization of foreign markets at the turn of the twenty-first century begs the question of what the appropriate role of the transnational corporation is in a liberal society within the context of a global market.

In determining the moral legitimacy of the role of government and the corporation, aggregate social utility is certainly one of the relating considerations. Whether a minimal government with a laissez-faire capitalist market is optimally efficient, whether this arrangement would produce what is best for all, are important considerations, even if not the sole consideration in determining the moral defensibility of a system of political economy. (Danley, 1994, p. 271)

Neoliberal economic theorems based on Pareto efficiency[4] and the attainment of market equilibrium may not be a complete indication of social utility when comparing different economic systems, or when one system is coercive, such is the system of China. This liberal shortcoming may imply the need for a revisionist liberalization that would take into account that human welfare is more than simply the satisfaction of preferences (Danley, 1994, p. 268). Part of this theoretical reassessment would include a reassessment not only of human needs within an economic system, but also of the function of the transnational corporation in upholding international standards of human rights and the Universal Declaration.

Second, the findings of this study demonstrate significant implications for U.S. human rights policy toward China, and for U.S. international human rights policy in general. The U.S. granting of permanent normal trade relations to China in May 2000 has completely and unconditionally liberalized trade between the two countries. Now that trade between China and the United States has become permanently unconditional, and is no longer subject to the yearly MFN renewal process by the U.S. president, the question remains: how will U.S. policy on human rights be adjudicated and implemented? Where will the chips fall in the formulation of U.S. foreign policy on human rights?

More significantly, the findings suggest that the United States will no longer be the sole actor in the formulation of international human rights policy. Such private and nonprivate international actors as multinational corporations and international governmental organizations, will increasingly factor into U.S. policy decisions on human rights. This would further imply a transfer of a certain degree of state sovereignty to other actors within and beyond the state to help advance the cause of human rights in the global polity. The changing role of the state will affect the U.S. decision-making process on human rights policy because it challenges the traditional notion of the state as the sole proprietor of the public good.

Problematic is that

an international law of sovereign equality has always contained the unfortunate implication of providing legitimacy for the national repression of citizens, or at least impunity for its tyrants. The emergence of a body of human rights law may seem to be competing with the traditional principles of respect for sovereign equality of states and non-interference. (Koskenniemi, 1991, p. 398)

The proclamation of the "Charter of Paris for a New Europe", adopted in 1990 at the Conference on Security and Cooperation in Europe, addressed the role of the state in human rights issues: "Human rights and fundamental freedoms are the birthright of all human beings, are inalienable and are guaranteed by law. Their protection and promotion is the first responsibility of government. Respect for them is an essential safeguard against an over-mighty state" (p. 399).[5] This same sentiment had been expressed earlier in U.S. history. Section 502B of the 1975 U.S. Foreign Assistance Act read:

> It is the policy of the United States in accordance with its international obligation as set forth in the Charter of the United Nations and in keeping with the Constitutional heritage and traditions of the United States, to promote and encourage increased respect for human rights and fundamental freedoms for all without distinction as to race, sex, language, or religion. To this end, a principle goal of the foreign policy of the United States is to promote the increased observance of internationally recognized human rights in all countries. (Bitker, 1984, p. 95)

Beyond the implications for state sovereignty, the findings further suggest that in U.S. policy formulation on human rights, greater emphasis will be placed on U.S. corporate involvement and responsibility for the promotion and protection of human rights standards in countries where business is conducted. In the United States, for example, groups such as the National Labor Committee Education Fund in Support of Worker and Human Rights in Central America have already launched protest campaigns designed to oblige corporations to effectively implement their codes of conduct, particularly as they relate to the treatment of workers in Export Processing Zones (EPZs) (Forcese, 1997, p. 11).

To be sure, the first objective of a business is to maximize profit and to satisfy shareholders. Neoclassical economists will argue that the test for "social insurance" lies in the efficiency of the market. As stated by one notable economist: "There is one and only one social responsibility of business — to use its resources and engage in activities designed to increase its profits so long as it stays within the rules of the game, which is to say, engages in open and free competition, without deception or fraud" (Milton Friedman, 1962, p. 133). The global growth of transnational corporations during the past decades, however, gives them more influence over the lives of people. This would suggest that corporations carry the social responsibility that comes with increased global influence.

The rise of the transnational corporation onto the global scene has become a commonly accepted notion as part of the globalization process. Transnational corporations control about five percent of the global workforce and control over 33 percent of global assets. They employ about 72 million people, of whom about 15 million reside in developing countries (United Nations, Research Institute for Social Development, 1994, p. 154, cited in Gill, 1995, pp. 399-423). By 1994, in the financial markets, the daily flow of foreign exchange transactions exceeded US$1 trillion, or "roughly the foreign exchange holdings of all the central banks of the major industrialized nations" (Gill, 1995, pp. 423-25). Multinational corporations, with their close physical proximity and day-to-day interactions with indigenous peoples and local government groups, are at an advantage, relative to the more distant and intermittent contacts by public officials, to assume increased responsibility for upholding human rights standards.

Although many U.S. corporations have instituted codes of conduct in their operations at home and abroad, these codes have not been enforced and have been poorly monitored. For example, in a study conducted by the U.S. Department of Labor of 42 textile firms, it was found that effective monitoring of codes remains uncommon (U.S. Dept. of Labor, 1996, p. v). The lack of enforcement of codes of conduct by corporations presents a challenge to U.S. policymaking on international human rights. In U.S. foreign policymaking, "it is no longer enough to say: 'when in Rome, do as the Romans do.' The question is rather, can companies afford to ignore the human rights which governments violate, despite their claimed international commitment to protect them?" (Forcese, 1997, p. 8)

In addition to the role of the private sector, U.S. policy on human rights in foreign countries will be increasingly addressed through such multilateral avenues as the WTO, the ILO, the U.N. Commission on Human Rights, and its subcommittees. Specifically, with regard to the WTO:

> the entry of China into the WTO, with its requirement for permanent normal trading relations, would make it more difficult for the United States to exercise the economic leverage it has been used to enjoying. Bringing the case to the WTO, with its cumbersome and lengthy adjudication process, with cases judged by international arbitrators, would remove most of the flexibility the United States now exercises to calibrate its pressure and set its own timetable for conflict resolution. (Duesterberg, 1999, p. 17)

On the other hand, U.S. policymakers will come to rely on the WTO to ensure that China complies with international standards of business practices, which would include the abatement of forced or indentured labor in the production and distribution of products. Additionally, U.S. human rights policy toward China will lean more heavily on the ILO and its major ILO Conventions in upholding international labor laws.[6] The "ILO's supervisory machinery is generally acknowledged to be the most sophisticated and its scrutiny the most rigorous and least politicized of any in the U.N. system". Governments have accepted and often ratified their national law and practice after ILO reviews ("International Trade and Labour Standards", 1996, p. 231).

Regarding China, U.S. lawmakers in Washington increasingly will rely on the open market mechanism and direct corporate linkages to help advance the cause of human rights. These direct local corporate linkages include direct contacts with China's local citizenry, through management and training procedures, through technology and resource sharing, through supplier networks, and eventually through greater product choice on the China market. As one corporate executive director of a major U.S. multinational corporation in China verified:

> When Motorola looks at China, we see not only a great commercial market for our technology, but also a social obligation that we are taking very seriously. Motorola exposes its employees to a market-driven business and management practice, core principles of respect for the individual and uncompromising integrity in everything we do. (U.S. Congress, House, 1997 [Younts], p. 103)

Leaders in Beijing continue to reiterate that "China will not adopt foreign models of democracy, and has continued to appeal to fellow Asian nations not to give in to Western pressure" (Hutzler, 2000, p. A1). Undeniably, U.S. policymakers are still faced with the legacy of the Cultural Revolution which firmly denied the freedoms of speech, expression, assembly, and association. The political participation which China had temporarily allowed its citizens proved to be an arbitrary and invalid right (Kent, 1993, p. 139).[7] This revolutionary legacy, still ingrained in Chinese political culture despite the new population of urban "technocrats", makes U.S. policymaking on human rights in China fragile, and at best, tenuous. In broader respects, the China case implies the fragility of a human rights policy at all. This is particularly true when such a policy is applied selectively. This warning came during the Carter administration and is just as applicable to present time. It was said, "the Carter administration runs the risk of dividing the world into two categories: countries unimportant enough to be hectored about human rights, and countries important enough to get away with murder" (Barnet, 1977, quoted in Roberta Cohen, 1979, p. 224). Nonetheless, it is frequently argued that the U.S. policy of economic engagement with China has helped to bring about a Chinese government that is less repressive today than it was twenty years ago. Chinese leaders are more aware of an alternative to a state-controlled economy. They now understand how free enterprise works and know what democracy is about even though it is not practiced. And at least there is an awareness, if not the practice of basic human rights (U.S. Congress, House, 1996 [Moran], p. 16).

The results of this study expose some inherent dangers in the post-1994 era of responsibility-sharing for the protection of human rights in the global polity. The question is, who will step forward first? The U.N. High Commissioner warned of this danger in referring to the tragedy of Kosovo, where:

> the most important lesson to be drawn was that despite ten years of warnings, the international community failed to act in time to prevent tragedy there. Everyone saw the conflict coming, but the political will to do something about it was absent until the situation reached the point where conflict prevention was no longer possible. ("U.N. High Commissioner", 1999, p. 4)

This dilemma would further imply that social accountability in the international community begins at the state level, with individuals assuming responsibility for the implementation and enforcement of international procedures to protect human rights across the globe (p. 4).

The fact that the United States has been, historically and ideologically, a leader in the promotion and protection of individual rights that are ingrained into the American value system,[8] has significant implications for a state's foreign policy that is increasingly shaped by actors beyond the state. It brings to the fore the question of whether the United States will renege on its role as champion of individual freedoms. Will the United States, for example, subsume its human rights responsibilities to multinational corporations and international governmental organizations? Can there be a happy medium amongst these multi-collective avenues of moral responsibility?

An additional problem that is confronted in U.S. policymaking on human rights is the reality that "rights" can be used as a tool for achieving other objectives. Realism contends that moral issues can be used to conceal ulterior motives for actions in international politics (Morganthau, 1967, p. 202). Too often, "ethical and human rights advocacy easily becomes a power play and a lobby game, which makes it difficult to find strategies to implement rights. Strategies which include the institutional procedures and rules as well as criteria for advocating resources". As a result, there is a very mixed record regarding U.S. policy on international human rights (Goulet, 1992, p. 244). In U.S. foreign policymaking, the issue of human rights is a dangerous one because it "touches on the very foundations of a regime, on its sources and exercise of power, and on its links to its citizens" (Hoffman, 1978, p. 8, cited in Farer and Gaer, 1993,

p. 293). When U.S. lawmakers enact the resources to promote and protect basic human rights throughout the world, these issues will remain an ever-present, but necessary challenge.

Recommendations

The conclusion that the respect for fundamental human rights has not yet been witnessed in China, suggests the need for U.S. policymakers to continue to exert pressure on China to improve its human rights practices. The 1994 decision, combined with the more recent May 2000 decision by the U.S. government to grant China permanent normal trade relations, has placed the cause of inter-national human rights in the hands of both private and public international actors. These international actors on human rights issues include U.S. multi-national corporations, their affiliates and suppliers, as well as international governmental organizations.

There are, however, other important national and international actors that can affect the substance of human rights policy. These actors include non-governmental organizations, U.S. investors, constituents, and consumers. It is recommended that U.S. policymakers continue to exert pressure in order to improve human rights conditions in China and in other developing, transitional, and developed countries through all possible avenues.

U.S. policymakers should develop and maintain a nonrelative position toward international human rights. The notion that rights are subject to the inter-pretation of cultures is a detriment to the betterment of human rights around the world. U.S. policymakers should maintain the view that human rights are uni-versal and are subject to the principles of the Universal Declaration of Human Rights set forth in 1948, wherein:

> the Universal Declaration of Human Rights is a common standard of achievement for all nations. (United Nations, General Assembly, 1948, preamble)
>
> ... everyone is entitled to all the rights and freedoms set forth in this Declaration, without distinction of any kind, such as race, colour, sex, language, political or other opinion, national or social origin, property, birth or other status. (Article 2, section 1)
>
> ... no distinction shall be made on the basis of the political, jurisdictional or international status of the country or territory to which a person belongs, whether it be independent, trust, non-self-governing or under any other limitation or sovereignty. (Article 2, section 2)

Second, it is recommended that the view of a duality between civil and political rights and economic, social, and cultural rights, so often utilized in congressional policy debates, be discarded. U.S. lawmakers should adopt and adhere to the international human rights policy that had been recommended by former Secretary of State Cyrus Vance, in 1977. As Secretary Vance had asserted:

> Let me define what we mean by "human rights". First, there is the right to be free from governmental violation of the integrity of the person. Such violations include torture, cruel, inhuman, or degrading treatment or punishment, and arbitrary arrest and imprisonment. And they include the denial of fair public trial and invasion of the home. Second, there is the right to the fulfillment of such vital needs as foods, shelter, health care and education. We recognize that the fulfillment of this right will depend, in part upon the stage of a nation's economic development.
>
> But we also know that this right can be violated by a Government's action or inaction — for example, through corrupt official processes which divert resources to an elite at the expense of the needy, or through indifference to the plight of the poor. Third, there is the right to enjoy civil and political liberties. Our policy is to promote all of these rights. . . I believe that with work, all of these rights can become complementary and mutually enforcing. (U.S. Dept. of State, 1977, p. 1)

It is further recommended that U.S. lawmakers on global human rights issues consider emphasizing the right of physical security, meaning that "no one can fully enjoy any right that is supposedly protected by society if she or he lacks the essentials for a healthy and active life and the right to subsistence" (Shue, 1996, p. 24). However, the right to subsistence need not supplant civil and political rights in U.S. policy on human rights. Particularly, regarding China, it is recommended that the nation's indigenous culture be respected, but that Asian culture not be a justification for lack of civil and political rights, or that the Asian conception of freedom differs from that of the West (p. 66).

Moreover, the international community has decided through a number of covenants and agreements[9] that the protection of human rights transcends national and cultural boundaries. Human rights are designed to protect the inherent dignity of the human person regardless of cultural background. Neither can they be considered an encroachment upon national sovereignty. Without respect for these human rights the rule of law is undermined (Amnesty International, 1998).

Regarding U.S. corporations and their role in human rights, there are a number of recommendations that can be made for U.S. policy on the matter. First, U.S. decision makers should ensure that U.S. corporations comply with the "Nine Principles" that have been developed and suggested by the United

Nations for corporations that operate internationally. These include the following:

1) Identify Human Rights Issues:
That corporations identify human rights issues that are specific to a country. While most companies focus on labor standards, companies in the mineral extraction, apparel, footwear, and agricultural industries have distinct issues that require different approaches.

2) Develop Policy Options
The Universal Declaration of Human Rights and the ILO core labor standards are generally the foundation of a company's policies.

3) Operationalize the Company Policy
Guidelines to aid the implementation from principle to practice and the ability to communicate internally to business and externally to the world by seeking contributions within the company and reaching out to nongovernmental organizations.

4) Dialogue/Outreach/Collaboration
For many companies, this is the first step. It is essential to outreach to academics, as well as to other groups concerned about the corporate approach to human rights issues in advance of policy setting. Consultation with human rights groups and social partners can enhance the basic structure of the company position and will help establish a system of public accountability.

5) Educating and Training Key Staff
To educate the staff about the philosophy and U.N. principles behind the human rights policy to staff from other cultures and from other nations.

6) Develop Appropriate Internal Capacity
Proper expertise on the complex topic of global human rights is necessary to monitor and communicate and manage human rights violations.

7) Communicate effectively with business partners, vendors, subcontractors, and governments on codes of conduct.

8) Develop Internal Accountability
Establish performance benchmarks on human rights with a country to country approach.

9) Independent Verification and Public Reporting
Independent verification is one way that companies can contribute to higher standards of human rights throughout the world. Such independent verification can

be obtained from nongovernmental human rights monitoring groups who possess the experience and expertise to carry out investigative human rights procedures. (United Nations, Global Compact Network, 1999)

U.S. decision makers should also ensure that corporations abide by the ILO Declaration on the "Fundamental Principles and the Rights at Work", which include:

1. freedom of association and the effective recognition of the right to collective bargaining;
2. the elimination of all forms of forced or compulsory labor;[10]
3. the effective abolition of child labor; and
4. the elimination of discrimination with respect to employment and occupation (International Labor Organization, 1998).

Labor standards should not be used for protectionist purposes, and "the comparative advantage"[11] of any country should not be called into question by this Declaration (International Labor Organization, 1998). This recommendation is not to presume that labor standards of developing countries approach Northern levels, but that U.S. policy should promote and protect a "core set of basic labor standards that can be applied to any country, without exception, irrespective of its current state of development" (LeQuesne, 1996, p. 52).

The ILO Conventions on core labor standards for countries are further strengthened by the ILO "Tripartite Declaration of Principles Concerning Multinational Enterprises (MNEs) and Social Policy", which provides guidelines for MNEs, governments, employers, and workers in areas of employment, training, conditions of work and life, and industrial relations. The ILO Tripartite Declaration urges the parties to respect the Universal Declaration of Human Rights and the principles laid down in the Declaration of Philadelphia on freedom and association and collective bargaining.[12]

It is, of course, recommended that the United States adhere to its own "Model Business Principles", adopted in 1995, for U.S. companies operating overseas. These principles serve to reinforce ILO core labor standards at the national level. The U.S. "model" calls for 1) fair employment practices, 2) avoidance of child and forced labor, 3) avoidance of discrimination based on race, gender, national origin or religious beliefs, and 4) respect for the right of association and the right to organize and bargain collectively (OECD, 1996, pp. 190-91).

It is important to consider that business codes of conduct for U.S. corporations have been recommended by the U.S. government on a voluntary basis.

Because of their voluntary nature, business codes of conduct in foreign countries can be subject to implementation at the discretion of the individual corporation. Rather than having business codes of conduct be simply voluntary, they should be adjudicated into U.S. law. The codification of corporate codes of conduct strengthen human rights protections throughout the globe by ensuring that fundamental human rights standards are legally binding.

Infringement of business codes of conduct in countries, once discovered, would then be considered illegal, rather than simply a negligence, and would therefore be subject to legal action in the form of a trade sanction or corporate divestiture from the country in which the infringement is found. More general measures to ensure that human rights standards in host countries are upheld by multinational corporations have been recommended by one author (DeGeorge, 1993, pp. 45-54), and are worthy of consideration when formulating and implementing U.S. global human rights policy. These include the following:

- Multinationals should do no intentional harm.
- Multinationals should produce more good than harm for the host country.
- Multinationals should contribute by their activity to the host country's development.[13]
- Multinationals should respect the human rights of their employees.
- To the extent that local culture does not violate ethical norms, multinationals should respect the local culture and work with and not against it.
- Multinationals should pay their fair share of taxes.
- Multinationals should cooperate with local governments in developing and enforcing just background institutions. (DeGeorge, 1993, pp. 45-54)

This study has also concluded that multilateral institutions increasingly will be called upon in human rights issues throughout the globe. It is, therefore, recommended that U.S. policymakers take the necessary financial, organizational, and support measures to strengthen and solidify the human rights regime within the U.N. system. With a stronger and more effective U.N. human rights regime, human rights violations in various areas of the world may be identified and acted upon more readily. Also suggested is that the United States support and ensure the inclusion of human rights NGOs in the U.N. decision-making process. "International NGOs, through fact-finding, networks, and field work, serve as a bridge between the real world of violations — what happens out there — and legal, political, and bureaucratic institutions in the human rights world" (Brett, 1995, pp. 99-103).

In addition to the above measures, U.S. executive and congressional leaders should encourage a more integrated approach to addressing human rights issues within the U.N. system and its various agencies, such as the United Nations Development Program (UNDP), the ILO, the United Nations Conference on Trade and Development (UNCTAD), the U.N. Human Rights Commission, and the WTO (LeQuesne, 1996, p. 34).

Increased cooperation among multilateral agencies within the United Nations system would serve to lessen the often disjointed and repetitive work of inter-U.N. organizations, which would in turn hasten a unified global human rights strategy. One such recommendation would be that of a joint WTO/ILO advisory body that would review periodically human rights complaints that are justified by countries or persons, with the intention that if no progress is made over a certain period of time, trade penalties would then be applied to the government (p. 34). In further explanation:

> The GATT is the principle body that regulates international trade. Its expertise is in determining the existence of unfair trade practices, such as dumping or subsidies that breach existing GATT/WTO obligations or nullify or impair the receipt of reciprocal trade benefits. It also supervises the cessation of those practices through the imposition of countermeasures and economic penalties. Therefore, the GATT/WTO should bring its expertise on trade practices and its well-developed dispute settlement system and environmental procedures to this joint [WTO/ILO] enforcement regime. (Ehrenberg, 1996, p. 165)

Finally, with regard to the role of multilateral institutions, it is suggested that U.S. policymakers press for a social clause in the WTO to help ensure that core ILO and U.N. labor and human rights standards are met in trading countries, and that economic sanctions be applied in the event that they are not met (Senser, 1998, p. 26). It is, then, further recommended that U.S. policymakers help to assure that these multilateral efforts can be implemented by supporting them at the state level.

Another influential avenue through which the United States can promote and protect human rights throughout the world is by mobilizing U.S. shareholders, consumers, and constituents. The encouragement of socially responsible investment and consumption can be a powerful economic lever in its inherent ability to withhold funds or purchases of products. First, socially responsible investing (SRI) "is a practice in which those who purchase stocks and other securities make their investment decision on the basis of social as well as economic criteria" (OECD, 1996, p. 202). When following this method of investment, capital can be steered to socially responsible firms and diverted from firms that are socially irresponsible, and can thus prove to be a powerful force and economic influence on human rights causes.[14]

Second, the power of consumer sovereignty can be an influential force in the protection of human rights throughout the globe. This basic principle is often called "ethical consumption", which is to "persuade consumers to base their consumption decisions not only on price considerations, but also on moral principles relating to the condition of production" (OECD, 1996, p. 199). This powerful consumer force is realized by boycotting products from countries where ILO and other core labor and human rights standards are not upheld. However, in order to encourage ethical investment and consumption, there must first be a public awareness of the critical and country-specific issues pertaining to the production of products for trade and the social performance of corporations.

To enhance public awareness of global human rights issues before these issues reach the point of tragedy and media attention, U.S. policymakers on Capitol Hill should include a broad range of citizens in the decision-making process on human rights issues, an inclusive range of citizen participation that would reach beyond elite government, business, and academic factions, where the well-honed tools of rhetoric can be used for the purposes of various elite interests, to the public at large (Rieff, 1999, p. 41). An ex-Amnesty International member reflected:

> Twenty years ago, when you went to a meeting at a human rights group, you saw all kinds of people. But these days, you usually find that most of the people there, are either lawyers or human rights professionals. To me, the human rights move-ment has not been successful in capturing the imagination of a broad group of people — the way, whatever I may think of them, a strong civil-society group like the National Rifle Association has done. (p. 41)

Increased economic interdependence among nations at all stages of develop-ment caused by the globalization of physical, financial and human capital necessitates the need for the "globalization of human rights". With regard to U.S. foreign policy on human rights, at least the beginnings of this can be met, with government support, through enforced corporate codes of conduct, col-laborative efforts by international governmental organizations, and the work of concerned citizens throughout the United States and abroad.

Endnotes

1   There are discrepancies over this figure. Most economic analysts agreed, at this time, on the figure US$1,000 for China's per capita GDP.

2   "Out of China's over 1 billion population, only a few tens of millions, mostly in coastal regions and cities, were yet rich enough to become consumers of foreign brands" (*Economist*, 1999c, p. 72).

3   As Kuhn (1970) states, "More is involved, however, than the incommensurability of standards. Since new paradigms are born from old ones, they ordinarily incorporate much of the vocabulary and apparatus, both conceptual and manipulative, that the traditional paradigm had previously employed. But they seldom employ these elements in quite the traditional way" (pp. 148-49).

4   Pareto efficiency refers to "the giving up output of one good in order to get more output of the other good" in order to obtain optimal production efficiency (Appleyard and Field, 1995, p. 75).

5   Note that such a statement returns to the liberal philosophy of John Locke, where Locke contends that "the citizenry retains substantial rights of resistence against the state" (Shapiro, 1986, p. 82).

6   ILO Conventions include: Conventions 87 and 98: freedom of association and the effective recognition of the right to collective bargaining; Conventions 29 and 105: the elimination of all forms of forced or compulsory labor; Convention 138: prohibition of child labor; Convention 111: the elimination of discrimination in respect of employment based on race, color, sex, religion, national origin, or political opinion (International Labor Organization, 1998).

7   One can refer, for example, to the 100 Flowers Movement of 1957, where Chinese intellectuals were advised by the government to speak their views and then years later, were suppressed and reprimanded.

8   "Throughout the history of the United States a broad consensus has existed among the American people in support of liberal, democratic, individualistic, and egalitarian values. These political values and ideals constitute what Gunnar Myrdal termed 'the American Creed,' and they have provided the core of American national identity since the eighteenth century" (Huntington, 1982, p. 1). See also Hartz, 1955.

9   Some of these major international agreements include: the International Covenant on Civil and Political Rights (adopted in 1966 by the U.N. General Assembly); the International Covenant on Economic, Cultural, and Social Rights (adopted in 1966 by the U.N. General Assembly); the Convention on the Elimination of All Forms of Discrimination Against Women (adopted in 1979 by the U.N. General Assembly); the Convention Against Torture and Other Cruel, Inhuman, or Degrading Treatment or Punishment (adopted in 1987 by the Council of Europe); the International Convention on the Elimination of All Forms of Racial Discrimination (adopted in 1965 by the U.N. General Assembly); the Convention on the Rights of the Child (adopted by the U.N. General Assembly); the International Convention on the Rights of Migrant Workers and Members of Their Families (adopted by the U.N. General Assembly) (Humphrey, 1990, annex).

10 For example, "in 1992, Levi Strauss & Co. applied its codes of conduct by employing auditors to inspect the Saipan factories using a questionnaire developed by the company. The company quickly canceled its contract with those suppliers when it was discovered that Saipan factories were operating with forced sale conditions on its employees. Many of the workers were immigrant Filipinos housed in padlocked barracks with their passports confiscated during the contract period. They were working as much as 11 hours a day, seven days a week, for as little as US$1.65 an hour. In addition, contracts with suppliers in the Philippines, Honduras, and Uruguay were terminated when it was found that they were working with a set of ethical values not consistent with those of Levi Strauss & Co. In all,

Levi Strauss terminated contracts with thirty suppliers worldwide and forced reforms in employment practices in over one hundred others" (McCormick and Levinson, 1993, pp. 48-49, cited in Compa and Darrecarrere, 1996, p. 189).

11   For example, the contrary argument is raised by Martin Khor, Director of the influential Southern NGO, "Third World Network", who argues that "the raising of labor standards to Northern levels, or to cross beyond market parameters may well result in more harm than good for the South if it results in closure of industries and thus job retrenchments" (Martin Khor, cited in LeQuesne, 1996, p. 53).

12   "Some workers' organizations reported problems regarding the implementation of the Declaration, such as FDI legislation limiting rights of unions, in particular, Export Processing Zones (EPZs) as well as threats by firms to relocate in an attempt to influence the bargaining process" (OECD, 1996, pp. 190-91).

13   To a certain extent, the contribution to China's development by U.S. corporations has already begun. For example, "The Boeing Company has worked closely with Chinese airlines to develop better air traffic control procedures. Eastman Kodak Company supports cooperative research programs in imaging science and software development at several Chinese universities. Ford Motor Company has established, with a Chinese foundation, the Ford-China Research and Development Fund, which supports 28 three-year grants for advanced research automotive technology. Ford has also supported 125 rural students throughout four years of university, and also supports scholarships for students at Qinghua University. IBM Corporation has established programs in advanced computer technology in over 20 of China's universities, and has contributed US$25 million worth of computer equipment, staff support, scholarships, and grants for this project. The Chubb Corporation has conducted joint research on catastrophe management, with particular emphasis on earthquakes, and has funded visits to the U.S. by senior Chinese scientists. Motorola Inc., has sponsored and estimated 2,000 scholarships for Chinese students in technical universities and has donated more than US$820,000 to the Hope Project (a Chinese charity) to help build rural elementary schools. Amgen Inc. sponsors an award for junior nephrologists, who treat disorders of the kidney, in three Chinese cities. Ameritech is funding GLOBE Program in China, providing students at more than 35 schools with computer and environmental monitoring equipment to enhance learning about the earth and its resources. General Motors Corp., Bristol Meyers Squibb Co., and Pfizer, Inc. donated funds for victims of the Yunnan earthquake" (U.S.-China Business Council, 1996, pp. 4-8).

14   "There are active and growing associations of SRI practitioners who share information and ideas through newsletters, investment clubs, computer networks and organizations such as the Social Investment Forum in the United States and the Ethical Investment Research Service in the United Kingdom. SRI has been expanded to several other countries as well. The International Association of Investors in the Social Economy, founded in 1989, is a Brussels-based organization that has 35 member organizations in 15 countries. Other NGOs and firms involved in this field are located in Austria, Australia, Canada, Germany, and in other countries" (OECD, 1996, p. 202).

Appendix

Letter from China Written to President Clinton, March 18, 1993

"Dear President Clinton:

I am a reporter.

After the Tiananmen massacre my name was placed on the wanted list. I was arrested but the police did not have any evidence against me. The police were determined to discipline me, so under the orders of the provincial party organization and without any respect for the law, I was placed under detention for thirteen and a half months. No reason was given and I never appeared in court.

During my detention I was subjected to all kinds of torture and mistreatment. I was not allowed outside and was not allowed access to sunlight. Even time to use the toilet was strictly controlled to the shortest time possible. The food was never washed and after each meal there was a thick layer of sand and dirt at the bottom of the plate. Over ten prisoners were crammed into a 3 x 12-foot cell. Because food was scarce and there were not enough places for everyone to sleep, there was often fighting among the prisoners. A steel worker (arrested for participation in the June 4th movement) suffered a burst intestine because of a fight over sleeping space.

The physical suffering from poor prison conditions did not compare with the mental suffering. The detention center where I was placed was considered "progressive." Beating of prisoners was a common occurrence. I opposed the guards' personal persecution of me and attempted to stop them from beating the students who were arrested during the June 4th movement. Because of this I was repeatedly hit and kicked and beat with a baton. My hands were placed in handcuffs which were connected to a chain over 100 pounds in weight. I was put in a cold damp cell and was not given humane medical treatment. I became completely paralyzed as a result. Finally, I was given medicine by an untrained prisoner.

Though I can stand now, I still have serious medical problems as a consequence: On cold days and nights my legs and shoulders are lifeless. My memory is greatly affected, my teeth have all rotted, my hands shake constantly, and my waist is

163

constantly in pain due to a spinal injury. The doctor says that if I do not receive proper medical treatment, I could be paralyzed again.

I have brought my case before every level of the judicial branch, but my personal appeal has been ignored. Now, I am not able to work, I do not even have a chance to get a job (since I am a June 4 criminal). I have no money for medical care. I must try and support my family, but I do not have the resources to even take care of myself, much less others too.

Please Mr. President, when giving MFN, remember that China should give me, and others who have been treated like me, at least our minimum human rights so we can keep on living".[1]

Endnote

1   One of the many letters collected by the Independent Federation of Chinese Students and Scholars, of which the names have been deleted for fear of reprisal, submitted before Congress, House, Committee on Ways and Means, Subcommittee on Trade, "United States-China Trade Relations", hearing, 103rd Cong., 2nd sess., February 24, 1994 (Washington, D.C.: GPO, 1994), 236-37.

Bibliography

"50 Governors for Trade Pact"
    1994   *New York Times*, July 19, p. D5.

Almond, Gabriel A.
    1991   "Capitalism and Democracy". *Political Science and Politics* (September), pp. 467-74.

American Electronics Association
    1996   "MFN Fact Sheet". April. Internet: http://aea_web1.aeanet.org/homepge/pubpol/21ae.html.

American Enterprise Institute
    1984   *Proposals to Establish a Department of Trade*. Washington, D.C.: American Enterprise Institute for Public Policy Research.

Amnesty International
    1998   Outreach Work. "General Human Rights Principles for Companies. Report ACT 70/01/98. Internet: http://www.amnesty.it/ailib/1998/ACT.

Appleyard, Dennis R. and Alfred J. Field, Jr.
    1995   *International Economics*. Boston: Irwin.

Arndt, Channing, Thomas Hertal, Betina Dimaranan, Karen Huff, and Robert McDougall
    1997   "China in 2005: Implications for the Rest of the World". *Journal of Economic Integration*, vol. 12, no. 4 (December), pp. 523-25.

Asia Pacific Economic Cooperation
    n.d.   "APEC Member Countries". Internet: http://www.apecsec.org.

Asian Development Bank
    1993   *Asian Development Outlook 1993*. Manila: Oxford University Press.

Auger, Vincent
    1995   *Human Rights and Trade: The Clinton Administration and China*. Pew Case Studies in International Affairs, Instructor Copy 168. Washington, D.C.: Georgetown University, Institute for the Study of Diplomacy Publications, School of Foreign Service.

Awanohara, Susumu
    1993   "Breathing Space: Clinton Delays on Conditions to China's MFN Renewal". *Far Eastern Economic Review* (June 10), pp. 155-56.

1994a   "Asian Lobbies: Cash and Connections". *Far Eastern Economic Review* (June 2), pp. 25-26.

1994b   "The K-Street Crowd". *Far Eastern Economic Review* (June 2), p. 25.

Baldwin, Robert E.
1987   "U.S. and Foreign Competition in the Developing Countries of the Asian Pacific Rim". Working Paper No. 2208. Cambridge: National Bureau of Economic Research.

Barnet, R.J.
1977   "U.S. Needs Modes, Uniform Standard on Human Rights". *Los Angeles Times*, March 12, p. D7.

Bartlett, Bruce
1985   "What's Wrong with Trade Sanctions?" Policy Analysis No. 64. Washington, D.C.: Cato Institute.

Baum, Richard
1994   "The Road to Tiananmen: Chinese Politics in the 1980s", in Roderick MacFarquhar (ed), *The Politics of China 1949-1989.* Cambridge: Press Syndicate of Cambridge, pp. 340-473.

Beher, Peter
1994   "U.S. Business Waged Year-Long Lobbying Effort on China". *Washington Post*, May 27, p. A28.

Berger, Peter
1986   *The Capitalist Revolution.* New York: Basic Books.

Berlau, John
1997   "Lobbyists Spin MFN for Beijing". *Insight on the News*, vol. 13, no. 26 (July 21), pp. 16-20.

Bernstein, Robert L. and Peter Dicker
1994/95 "Human Rights First". *Foreign Policy* (September), pp. 43-47.

Bienefeld, Manfred
1994   "The New World Order: Echoes of a New Imperialism". *Third World Quarterly*, vol. 15, no. 1, pp. 31-48.

Billeness, Simon
1997   Franklin Research and Development. Personal Communication, February 1997 by Craig Forcese.

Bitker, Bruno V.
1984   "The United States and International Codification of Human Rights: A Case of Split Personality", in Natalie Kaufman Hevener (ed), *The Dynamics of Human*

Rights in U.S. Foreign Policy. New Brunswick: Transaction Books [first published in 1981], pp. 77-101.

Blecker, Robert A (ed)
1996   *U.S. Trade Policy and Global Growth.* Armonk: M.E. Sharpe.

Boardman, Robert
1994   *Post-Socialist World Orders: Russia, China and the UN System.* New York: St. Martin's Press.

Bollen, Kenneth A.
1992   "Political Rights and Political Liberties in Nations: An Evaluation of Human Rights Measures 1950-1984", in Thomas B. Jabine and Richard P. Claude (eds), *Human Rights and Statistics: Getting the Record Straight.* Philadelphia: University of Pennsylvania Press, pp. 188-215.

Borrus, Amy and Joyce Barnatham
1992   "Staunching the Flow of China's Gulag Exports". *Business Week* (April 13), pp. 51-52.

Bowman, Karlyn H.
1994   "Public Attitudes Toward the People's Republic of China", in James R. Lilley and Wendell L. Wilkie II (eds), *Beyond MFN: Trade with China and American Interests.* Washington, D.C.: AEI Press, pp. 145-51.

Boyer, Robert and Daniel Drache (eds)
1996   *States Against Markets.* New York: Routledge.

Branigin, William
1994   "Asians Welcome China Decision". *Washington Post*, May 29, p. A8.

Brehm, Carolyn L.
1988   "Bilateral Trade: Countertrade, Offset, Coproduction, and Licensing", in Eugene K. Lawson (ed), *U.S.-China Trade: Problems and Prospects.* New York: Praeger, pp. 143-55.

Brett, Rachel
1995   "The Role and Limits of Human Rights NGOs at the United Nations", in David Beetham (ed), *Politics and Human Rights.* Cambridge: Blackwell Publishers, pp. 96-111.

Brzezinski, Zbigniew
1997/98 "The End of the American Century: The Grand Chessboard: U.S. Geostrategy for Eurasia". *Harvard International Review* vol. 20 (Winter), pp. 48-53.

Burke, William
1972   *The China Trade.* San Francisco: Federal Reserve.

Bush, George. U.S. President
    1990   "Report on Economic Sanctions Against China". May 16. Congress. House Document 101-192. Washington, D.C.: GPO.

Caldwell, John (Colonel, USMC) and Alexander T. Lennon
    1995   "China's Nuclear Modernization Program". *Strategic Review* (Fall), pp. 27-37.

"Campaign '92: Transcript of the First Presidential Debate"
    1991   *Washington Post*, October 12, A16.

Campbell, Todd
    1992   "China, a Favored Nation?" *Scholastic Update*, vol. 125, no. 2 (September 18), pp. 18-20.

Caporaso, James A. and David P. Levine
    1992   *Theories of Political Economy*. Cambridge: Cambridge University Press.

Center For Responsive Politics, Washington, D.C.
    n.d.

Chapman, John W. and Ian Shapiro (eds)
    1993   *Democratic Community*. New York: New York University Press.

Chartier, Charles
    1998   "China: Economic Reforms and WTO Accession". *Thunderbird International Business Review* , vol. 40, no. 3 (May/June), pp. 257-77.

Chen, Edward K.Y. and Teresa Y.C. Wong
    1997   "Hong Kong: Foreign Direct Investment and Trade Linkages in Manufacturing", in Wendy Dobson and Chia Siow Yue (eds), *Multinationals and East-Asian Integration*. Ottawa: International Research Centre, pp. 83-104.

Chen, Jie
    1998   "Tactical Alliance: Southeast Asia and China's Post-1989 Human Rights Diplomacy". *China Rights Forum*, vol. 46 (Fall), pp. 8-11.

Chen, Wenjing
    1996   "The Status Quo and Prospects of Sino-U.S. Trade Relations". *Journal of World Trade*, vol. 30, no. 1, pp. 19-25.

Cheung, Gordon C.K.
    1998   *Market Liberalism: American Foreign Policy Toward China*. New Brunswick: Transaction Publishers.

China Statistical Abstract
    1998

China Statistical Year Book
1995

Cho, George
1995   *Trade, Aid and Global Interdependence.* New York: Routledge.

Chomsky, Noam
1997   "Notes on NAFTA: The Masters of Mankind", September 2. Internet: http://daisy.uwaterloo.ca/~alopez-/politics/chomnafta.html.

1998   "The United States and the Challenge of Relativity", in Tony Evans (ed), *Human Rights Fifty Years On.* New York: Manchester University Press, pp. 24-58.

Christopher, Warren
1993   "Democracy and Human Rights: Where America Stands". Remarks at the World Conference on Human Rights, 14 June. Internet: gopher://gopher.state.gov. PublicAffairs.

1994a   "My Trip to Beijing Was Necessary" (editorial), *Washington Post*, March 22, 1994, p. A17.

1994b   "The U.S.-China Relationship: The Right Balance", *U.S. Department of State Dispatch*, vol. 4, no. 13 (March), p. 191. Internet: gopher://dosfan.lib.vic.edu.

Clark, J.M.
1916   "The Changing Basis of Economic Responsibility". *Journal of Political Economy* (March), pp. 209-29.

Cline, Ray S.
1977   *World Power Assessment: A Calculus of Strategic Drift.* Boulder: Westview Press.

Clinton, William J., U.S. President
1993   Executive Order 12850. "Conditions for Renewal of Most-Favored-Nation Status for the People's Republic of China in 1994". May 28.

1994   Letter to Hon. Thomas S. Foley. "Continuation of Waiver Authority". June 2. House Document 103-266.

Cohen, Ariel
1996   "Engaged Realism". *Harvard International Review* vol. 19, no. 1, pp. 32-EOA.

Cohen, Jerome Alan, Robert F. Dernberger, and John R. Garson (eds)
1971   *China Trade Prospects and U.S. Policy.* New York: Praeger.

Cohen, Roberta
1979   "Human Rights Decision-Making in the Executive Branch: Some Proposals for a Coordinated Strategy", in Donald P. Kommers and Gilburt D. Loescher (eds),

Human Rights and American Foreign Policy. University of Notre Dame Press, pp. 216-47.

Cohen, Stephen D.
    1988   *The Making of United States International Economic Policy*. 3rd ed. New York: Praeger.

Colclough, Christopher and James Manor (eds)
    1991   *States or Markets? Neoliberalism and the Development Policy Debate*. New York: Oxford University Press.

Compa, Lance A. and Tashia Hinchliffe Darrecarrere
    1996   "Private Labor Rights Enforcement Through Corporate Codes of Conduct", in Lance A. Compa and Stephen F. Diamond (eds), *Human Rights, Labor Rights and International Trade*. Philadelphia: University of Pennsylvania Press.

Compa, Lance A. and Stephen F. Diamond (eds)
    1996   *Human Rights, Labor Rights and International Trade*. Philadelphia: University of Pennsylvania Press.

Congressional Quarterly
    1994   Vol. 4, no. 14 (April 15), p. 318.

    1997   "Did China Try to Influence Elections?" (April 26), p. 972.

Congressional Quarterly, Inc.
    1980   *China: U.S. Policy Since 1945*. Washington, D.C.: Congressional Quarterly Inc.

Consumer Asia
    1996   London: Euromonitor.

Corporate Watch
    n.d. Statement of Principles for South Africa. Internet: http://www.igc.org/trac/feature/humanrts/resources/safrica-principles.html.

Cortez, Tricia
    1996   "Cash, Class and Compromise". M.A. thesis, Princeton University.

CQ Researcher
    1992   Vol. 22, no. 44 (November 27), p. 1041.

Dahl, Robert A.
    1998   "Why All Democratic Countries Have Mixed Economies", in John W. Chapman and Ian Shapiro (eds), *Democratic Community*. New York: New York University Press, pp. 266-82

Danitz, Tiffany
1997   "MFN Players Take Position". *Insight on the News*, vol. 13, no. 21 (June 9), pp. 22-24.

Danley, John R.
1994   *The Role of the Modern Corporation in a Free Society*. Notre Dame: University of Notre Dame Press.

Davis, Lester
1996   *U.S. Jobs Supported by Goods and Services Exports 1983-94*. Washington, D.C.: Department of Commerce, Economics and Statistics Administration.

de Mandeville, Bernard
1723   *Fable of the Bees*, n.p.

Defense Daily
1994   Vol. 83, no. 33 (May 18), p. 265.

DeGeorge, Richard T.
1993   *Competing with Integrity in International Business*. New York: Oxford University Press.

DePauw, John W.
1981   *U.S.-Chinese Trade Negotiations*. New York: Praeger.

1988   "The Potential for Military Trade", in Eugene K. Lawson (ed), *China Trade: Problems and Prospects*. New York: Praeger, pp. 247-69.

Dernberger, Robert F.
1971   "Prospects for Trade Between China and the United States", in Jerome Alan Cohen, Robert F. Dernberger, and John R. Garson (eds), *China Trade Prospects and U.S. Policy*. New York: Praeger, pp. 185-321.

Dicken, Peter
1998   *Global Shift*. New York: Guilford Press.

Direction of Trade Statistics
1980-1998   Washington, DC: International Monetary Fund.

Dobson, Wendy
1997a   "Crossing Borders: Multinationals in East Asia", in Wendy Dobson and Chia Siow Yue (eds), *Multinationals and East Asian Integration*. Ottawa: International Development Research Centre.

1997b   "East Asian Integration: Synergies Between Firm Strategies and Government Policies," in Wendy Dobson and Chia Siow Yue (eds), *Multinationals and East Asian Integration*. Ottawa: International Development Research Centre.

Dobson, Wendy and Chia Siow Yue (eds)
  1997   *Multinationals and East-Asian Integration*. Ottawa: International Development
          Research Centre.

Donlan, Thomas
  1997   "Playing Favorites: The World's Freedom Requires Open Borders for Business".
          Barron's, June 2, p. 62.

Dorn, James A.
  1996   "Trade and Human Rights: The Case of China". *Cato Journal*, vol. 16, no. 1
          (Spring/Summer), pp. 77-98.

Doyle, Michael W.
  1997   *Ways of War and Peace*. New York: W.W. Norton.

Drucker, Peter
  1994   "The New Superpower: The Overseas Chinese". *Wall Street Journal*, December
          10, p. A14.

Duesterberg, Thomas
  1999   "Zhu Rongji, Political Magician". *Washington Quarterly*, vol. 22, no. 4 (Autumn),
          pp. 15-20.

Dumbaugh, Kerry
  1994   "China's MFN Status: Implications of the 1994 Decision". August 15.
          Congressional Research Service Report for Congress.

Dunning, J.H.
  1993   *Multinational Enterprises and the Global Economy*. Surrey: Addison-Wesley
          Publishing Ltd..

Eckstein, Alexander
  1971   Introduction, in Jerome A. Cohen, Robert F. Dernberger, and John R. Garson
          (eds), *China Trade Prospects and U.S. Policy*. New York: Praeger, pp. xxi-xxiii.

Eckstein, Harry
  1975   "Case Study and Theory in Political Science", in Fred I. Greenstein and Nelson
          W. Polsby (eds), *Cumulative Index, Handbook of Political Science*. Reading, MA:
          Addison-Wesley, pp. 79-137.

Economist
  1999a   "The Cruel and Ever More Unusual Punishment". May 15, pp. 95-97.

  1999b   "America's Business Lobby: Who Speaks for Main Street?" June 26, pp. 75-76.

  1999c   "Multinationals in China", September 25, pp. 72-74.

  1999d   *Pocket World in Figures*. New York: John Wiley and Sons.

Edel, Abraham, Elizabeth Flower, and Finbarr W. O'Connor
    1989a   "Human Rights, Justice, and Welfare", in Abraham Edel, Elizabeth Flower, and Finbarr W. O'Connor (eds), *Morality, Philosophy and Practice*. Philadelphia: Temple University Press, pp. 586-96.

    1989b   "Marxian Ethics", in Abraham Edel, Elizabeth Flower, and Finbarr W. O'Connor (eds), *Morality, Philosophy and Practice*. Philadelphia: Temple University Press, pp. 390-95.

    1989c   *Morality, Philosophy and Practice*. Philadelphia: Temple University Press.

Eglin, Michaela
    1997   "China's Entry into the WTO with a Little Help from the EU". *International Affairs*, vol. 73, no. 3, pp. 489-508.

Ehrenberg, Daniel
    1996   "From Intention to Action: An ILO-GATT/WTO Enforcement Regime for International Labor Rights", in Lance A. Compa and Stephen F. Diamond (eds), *Human Rights, Labor Rights, and International Trade*. Philadelphia: University of Pennsylvania Press, pp. 163-81

Elfstrom, Gerard
    1991   *Moral Issues and Multinational Corporations*. New York: St. Martin's Press.

    1993   *Contemporary Ethical Issues*. Denver: ABC-CLIO, Inc..

Elliot, Larry
    1994   "U.S. Urged Not to Kill GATT Accord". *Guardian*, November 11, pp. 2-4.

Europa World Yearbook
    1994, 1995

Evans, J.D.G.
    1988   *Moral Philosophy and Contemporary Problems*. New York: Cambridge University Press.

Evans, Tony
    1998   *Human Rights Fifty Years On*. New York: Manchester University Press.

Export-Import Bank Act of 1945
    1945   October. Public Law 95-143. Amended in 1977.

Farer, Tom J. and Felice Gaer
    1993   "The U.N. and Human Rights: At the End of the Beginning", in Adam Roberts and Benedict Kingsbury (eds), *United Nations, Divided World*. Oxford: Clarendon Press, 1993, pp. 240-97.

Fields, Gary S.
1990   "Labor Standards, Economic Development, and International Trade", in Stephen Herzenberg and Jorge F. Perez-Lopez (eds), *Labor Standards and Development in the Global Economy*. Washington, D.C.: Department of Labor, Bureau of International Labor Affairs, pp. 19-20, 22.

Forcese, Craig
1997   *Commerce with Conscience? Human Rights and Business Codes of Conduct*. Montreal: International Centre for Human Rights and Democratic Development.

Foreign Assistance Act of 1961
1961   October. Public Law 94-161. Amended in 1976, 1979.

Forsythe, David P.
1997   "Human Rights Policy: Change and Continuity", in Randell B. Ripley and James M. Lindsay (eds), *U.S. Foreign Policy After the Cold War*. Pittsburgh.: University of Pittsburgh Press, pp. 257-83.

Foster, Catherine
1993   "Cairns Group Anticipates GATT's Agricultural Benefits". *Christian Science Monitor*, December 10, p. 7.

Freedom House
2000   *Freedom in the World 1999-2000*. New York: Heritage Foundation, 2000.

Friedman, Milton
1962   *Capitalism and Freedom*. Chicago: University of Chicago Press.

Friedman, Thomas L.
1994   "Clinton Votes for Business". *New York Times*, May 27, p. A1.

Funabashi, Yoichi, Michel Oksenberg, and Heinrich Weiss
1994   *An Emerging China in a World of Interdependence*. New York: Trilateral Commission.

Fung, K.C. and Lawrence J. Lau
1998   "The China-United States Bilateral Trade Balance: How Big Is It Really?" *Pacific Economic Review*, vol. 3, no. 1, pp. 33-47.

Gadbaw, Michael R. and Michael T. Medwig
1996   "Multinational Enterprises and International Labor Standards: Which Way for Development and Jobs?" in Lance A. Compa and Stephen F. Diamond (eds), *Human Rights, Labor Rights and International Trade*. Philadelphia: University of Pennsylvania Press, pp. 141-63.

Gaddis, John Lewis and Paul Nitze
1980   "NSC 68 and the Soviet Threat Reconsidered". *International Security*, vol. 4, no. 4 (Spring), pp. 164-76.

Gamble, Andrew
1996   *Hayek: The Iron Cage of Liberty.* Boulder: Westview Press.

Garson, John R.
1971   *The Origins of the Embargo: A Short History.* New York: Praeger.

Garten, Jeffrey E.
1997   "Business and Foreign Policy". *Foreign Affairs*, vol. 76, no. 3 (May/June), pp. 67-79.

Garten, Jeffrey and Robert Zoellick
1998   *Riding the Tigers: American Commercial Diplomacy in Asia.* New York: Council on Foreign Relations.

General Administration of Customs of the People's Republic of China
various years *China's Customs Statistics.*

Gephardt, Richard
1994   "NAFTA, APEC, GATT: Top Priority to Global Economics". *Foreign Policy Bulletin* (January/April), p. 63.

Giles, Lionel
1970   *The Analects of Confucius.* New York: Hermitage Press.

Gill, Stephen
1995   "Globalization, Market Civilization, and Disciplinary Neoliberalism". *Millennium*, vol. 24, no. 3, pp. 399-423.

Gordon, D.M.
1998   "The Global Economy: New Edifice or Crumbling Foundations?" *New Left Review*, vol. 168, pp. 24-66.

Goulet, Denis
1992   "International Ethics and Human Rights". *Alternatives*, vol. 17, pp. 231-36.

Graham, Edward M.
1996   *Global Corporations and National Governments.* Washington, D.C.: Institute For International Economics.

Graham, Keith
1988   "Morality, Individuals and Collectives", in J.D.G. Evans (ed), *Moral Philosophy and Contemporary Problems.* New York: Cambridge University Press, pp. 1-18.

Greenberger, Robert S. and Michael K. Frisby
1994   "Clinton's Renewal of Trade Status for China Followed Cabinet Debates, Congress's Sea Change". *Wall Street Journal*, May 31, p. A18.

Greenhouse, Steven
    1992   "China Will Lower Barriers to Trade Accord with U.S". *New York Times*, 10
              October, p. D18.

    1993   "New Tally of World's Economies Catapults China into Third Place". *New York
              Times*, 20 May, p. 1.

Greenstein, Fred I. and Nelson W. Polsby (eds)
    1975   *Cumulative Index, Handbook of Political Science*. Reading: Addison-Wesley.

Gregory, Paul R. and Roy J. Ruffin
    1989   *Basic Macroeconomics*. Boston: Scott, Foresman and Company.

Haass, Richard N.
    1997   "Paradigm Lost: From Containment to Confusion". *Foreign Affairs*, vol. 76, no.2
              (March/April), pp. 43-58.

Harding, Harry
    1994/95   "Asia Policy to the Brink". *Foreign Policy*, vol. 94 (Spring), pp. 74-81.

Harland, Bryce
    1994/95   "For a Strong China". *Foreign Policy*, vol. 94 (Spring), pp. 48-52.

Hartz, Louis
    1955   *The Liberal Tradition in America*. New York: Harcourt, Brace and Company.

Hawkins, William R.
    1997   "For All the Tea in China". *Strategic Review* (Fall), pp. 7-19.

Herzenberg, Stephen and Jorge F. Perez-Lopez (eds)
    1990   *Labor Standards and Development in the Global Economy*. Washington, D.C.:
              Bureau of International Labor Affairs.

Hevener, Natalie Kaufman (ed)
    1984   *The Dynamics of Human Rights in U.S. Foreign Policy*. New Brunswick:
              Transaction Books [first published in 1981].

Hobbes, Thomas
    1994   *Leviathan*. Cambridge: Hackett Publishing (first published in 1668).

Hoffman, Stanley
    1978   "The Hell of Good Intention". *Foreign Policy*, vol. 29 (Spring), pp. 3-26.

Holsti, Ole R.
    1995   "Theories of International Relations and Foreign Policy", in Charles W. Kegley
              (ed), *Controversies in International Relations Theory*. New York: St. Martin's
              Press, 1995, pp. 35-65.

Hong Kong Census and Statistics Department
various years   *Hong Kong External Trade.*

Hook, Sidney
1967   *Human Values and Economic Policy.* New York: New York University Press.

Human Rights Watch
1997   "Chinese Diplomacy, Western Hypocrisy and the U.N. Human Rights
Commission". *Human Rights Watch/Asia Report*, vol. 9, no. 3 (March), pp. 1-14.

1999   "Inquiry Demanded on U.S. Role in Genocide". April 6. Internet:
http://hrwatchnyc.igc.org.

2000a   "More than Sixty Civilians Murdered in Grozny". February 23. Internet:
http://hrwatchnyc.igc.org.

2000b   "Rights Group Deplores U.N. China Move". April 18. Internet: http://
www.hrwatchnyc.igc.org.

Humphrey, John P.
1990   "Human Rights: The Necessary Conditions of Peace". *International Relations,*
vol. 10, no. 2, November, pp. 117-27.

Huntington, Samuel P.
1982   "American Ideals Versus American Institutions". *Political Science Quarterly*, vol.
97, no. 1 (Spring), pp. 1-37.

Huszagh, Sandra M., Frederick W. Huszagh, and Gwen F. Hanks
1992   "Macroeconomic Conditions and International Marketing Management".
International Marketing Review, vol. 9, no. 1, pp. 6-18.

Hutzler, Charles
2000   "U.N. Official Visits China as Groups Report More Crackdowns". *New York
Times*, February 27, p. A1.

International Financial Statistics
1996, 1997

International Labor Organization
1984   *Employment Effects of Multinational Enterprises in Developing Countries.*
Geneva: ILO.

1998   "Declaration on Fundamental Principles and Rights at Work". 86th Sess., June
1998. Internet: http://www.ilo.org.

International Monetary Fund
1992   *Issues and Developments in International Trade Policy.* Washington, D.C.: IMF.

1993   *World Economic Outlook 1992.* Washington, D.C.: IMF.

"International Trade and Labour Standards: The ILO Director-General Speaks Out"
1996   *International Labour Review*, vol. 135, no. 2, pp. 228-38.

Isaac, Jeffrey C.
1996   "A New Guarantee on Earth: Hannah Arendt on Human Dignity and the Politics of Human Rights". *American Political Science Review*, vol. 90, no. 1 (March), pp. 61-73.

Islam, Shada
1994   "Something for Everyone". *Far Eastern Economic Review*, June 2, p. 82.

Jabine, Thomas B. and Richard P. Claude (eds)
1992   *Human Rights and Statistics: Getting the Record Straight.* Philadelphia: University of Pennsylvania Press.

Janis, Mark W.
1988   *An Introduction to International Law.* Boston: Little, Brown and Company.

Jensen, Kenneth M. and Elizabeth P. Faulkner (eds)
1991   *Morality and Foreign Policy: Realpolitik Revisited.* Washington, D.C.: U.S. Institute of Peace.

Jones, Randall, Robert King, and Michael Klein
1992   *The Chinese Economic Area: Economic Integration Without a Free Trade Agreement.* Paris: OECD.

Kagan, Robert
1997   "What China Knows That We Don't". *The Weekly Standard*, January 20, pp. 22-27.

Kant, Immanuel
1970   *Kant on the Foundation of Morality: A Modern Version of the Grundlegung.* Bloomington: Indiana University Press.

1983   *To Perpetual Peace: A Philosophical Sketch.* Indianapolis: Hacket [first published in 1795].

Kanter, Arnold
1992   "U.S. Policy Objectives and MFN for China". *U.S. Department of State Dispatch*, vol. 3, no. 27 (July 6), pp. 551-54.

Kaye, Lincoln
1994   "Commerce Kowtow: Human Rights Concerns Lost in Rush of U.S. Deals". *Far Eastern Economic Review* (September 8), pp. 16-18.

Kaysen, Carl
1967 "The Business Corporation as a Creator of Values", in Sidney Hook (ed), *Human Values and Economic Policy*. New York: New York University Press, pp. 209-24.

Kegley, Charles W.
1995a (ed), *Controversies in International Relations Theory*. New York: St. Martin's Press.

1995b "The Neoliberal Challenge to Realist Theories of World Politics: An Introduction", in Charles W. Kegley (ed), *Controversies in International Relations Theory*. New York: St. Martin's Press, 1995b.

Kennan, George F.
1991 "Morality and Foreign Policy", in Kenneth M. Jensen and Elizabeth P. Faulkner (eds), *Morality and Foreign Policy: Realpolitik Revisited*. Washington, D.C.: U.S. Institute of Peace, pp. 59-77.

Kent, Ann
1993 *Between Freedom and Subsistence: China and Human Rights*. New York: Oxford University Press.

1998 "The Universal Declaration of Human Rights and China: Breaker or Shaper of Norms?" *China Rights Forum* (Fall), pp. 4-7.

1999 *China, the United Nations, and Human Rights: The Limits of Compliance*. Philadelphia: University of Pennsylvania Press.

Keohane, Robert O.
1984 *After Hegemony: Cooperation and Discord in the World Political Economy*. Princeton: Princeton University Press.

1986 *Neorealism and its Critics*. New York: Columbia University Press.

Keohane, Robert O. and Joseph S. Nye
1989 *Power and Interdependence*. Harvard University: HarperCollins.

Keynes, John Maynard
1935 *The General Theory of Employment, Interest and Money*. New York: Harcourt Brace Jovanovich.

1938 *The Collected Writings of John Maynard Keynes*. Vol. 10. New York: St. Martin's Press for the Royal Economic Society.

Kidder, Rushworth M.
1994 "An Ethical Vision of Statecraft". *Foreign Service Journal*, vol. 71 (December), pp. 32-39.

Kim, Samuel (ed)
    1994   *China and the World: Chinese Foreign Relations in the Post-Cold War Era*, 3rd
            ed. Boulder: Westview Press.

Kissinger, Henry
    1979   *White House Years*. Boston: Little, Brown and Company.

    1994   *Diplomacy*. New York: Simon and Schuster.

Kissinger, Henry A. and Cyrus R. Vance
    1994   "The Right Decision on China". *Washington Post*, June 6, p. A19.

Kleckner, Dean
    1997   Statement of the President of the American Farm Bureau Federation. "Regarding
            Clinton's Renewal of Most Favored Nation Status for China". Internet: http://
            www.fb/news/nr/nr97/nr0519.html.

Knorr, Klaus
    1973   *Power and Wealth: The Political Economy of International Power*. New York:
            Basic Books.

    1977   "International Economic Leverage and its Uses", in Klaus Knorr and Frank N.
            Trager (eds), *Economic Issues and National Security*. National Security Education
            Program: Regents Press of Kansas, pp. 99-127.

Knorr, Klaus and Frank N. Trager (eds)
    1977   *Economic Issues and National Security*. National Security Education Program:
            Regents Press of Kansas.

Koskenniemi, Martti
    1991   "Future of Statehood". *Harvard International Law Journal*, vol. 32, no. 2
            (Spring), pp. 397-410.

Krauthammer, Charles
    1990/91 "The Unipolar Moment". *Foreign Affairs* (Winter), pp. 23-33.

Kruger, John and Charles Lewis
    1993   "Bill's Long March". *Washington Post*, November 7, p. C3.

Krugman, Paul R.
    1986   *Strategic Trade Policy and the New International Economics*. Cambridge: MIT
            Press.

Kuhn, Thomas S.
    1970   *The Structure of Scientific Revolutions*. Chicago: University of Chicago Press.

Lampton, David M.
1994   "America's China Policy in the Age of the Finance Minister: Clinton Ends Linkage". *China Quarterly*, vol. 139 (September), pp. 597-621.

1997   "Ending the MFN Battle". *NBR Analysis*, vol. 8, pp. 7-14.

Lardy, Nicholas R.
1994   *China in the World Economy*. Washington, D.C.: Institute for International Economics.

Ledeen, Michael
1997   "A Scandalous Policy". *Wall Street Journal*, March 26, p. A19.

Lee, Gary
1991   "After Intense Lobbying Fight, China Trade Status Vote Likely Today". *Washington Post*, July 23, p. A17.

Lenin, V.I.
1947   *Imperialism: The Highest Stage of Capitalism*. Moscow: Foreign Languages Publishing House [first published in 1916].

LeQuesne, Caroline
1996   *Reforming World Trade: The Social and Environmental Priorities*. Oxford: Oxfam.

Levine, David P.
1996   "Global Interdependence and National Prosperity", in Robert A. Blecker (ed), *U.S. Trade Policy and Global Growth*. Armonk: M.E. Sharpe, pp. 37-57.

Lewis, Norman
1998   "Human Rights, Law and Democracy in an Unfree World", in Tony Evans (ed), *Human Rights Fifty Years On*. New York: Manchester University Press, pp. 77-105.

Lilley, James
1994/95 "Freedom Through Trade". *Foreign Policy*, vol. 94 (Spring), pp. 37-45.

Lilley, James and Wendell L. Wilkie II (eds)
1994   *Beyond MFN: Trade with China and American Interests*. Washington, D.C.: AEI Press.

Lillich, Richard B.
1984   "The Contribution of the United States to the Promotion and Protection of International Human Rights", in Natalie Kaufman Hevener (ed), *The Dynamics of Human Rights in U.S. Foreign Policy*. New Brunswick: Transaction Books, pp. 191-321 [first published in 1981].

Lindsay, James M. and Randall B. Ripley
1997a   (eds), *U.S. Foreign Policy After the Cold War*. Pittsburgh: University of Pittsburgh Press.

1997b   "U.S. Foreign Policy in a Changing World", in James M. Lindsay and Randall B. Ripley (eds), *U.S. Foreign Policy After the Cold War*. Pittsburgh.: University of Pittsburgh Press, pp. 3-21.

Lipsey, Richard G. and Peter O. Steiner
1981   *Economics*. 6th ed. New York: Harper and Row.

Little, David
1991   "Morality and National Security", in Kenneth M. Jensen and Elizabeth P. Faulkner (eds), *Morality and Foreign Policy: Realpolitik Revisited*. Washington, D.C.: U.S. Institute of Peace, pp. 1-21.

Luce, Edward
1993   "Agreement Creates a New Bureaucracy to Back it Up". *Guardian*, December 15, p. 12.

MacFarquhar, Roderick (ed)
1994   *The Politics of China 1949-1989*. Cambridge: Cambridge University Press.

Mann, James
1999   *About Face*. New York: Alfred A. Knopf.

Marx, Karl and Frederick Engels
1994   *The Communist Manifesto*. New York: International Publishers [first published in 1848].

Mascitelli, Ron
1999   *The Growth Warriors*. Northridge: Technology Perspectives.

Mastanduno, Michael
1997   "Preserving the Unipolar Moment: Realist Theories and U.S. Grand Strategy After the Cold War". *International Security*, vol. 21, no. 4 (Spring), pp. 49-78.

Mastel, Greg and Andrew Szamosszegi
1997   "China's Growing Trade Surplus: Why It Matters". *Washington Quarterly*, vol. 20, no. 2, pp. 201-11.

Matsumoto, Morio
1994   "China's Industrial Policy and Participation in the GATT". *JETRO China Newsletter*, vol. 112 (September/October), pp. 2-8.

McCormick, John and Marc Levinson
1993   "The Supply Police". *Newsweek*, February 15, pp. 48-49.

McCormick, Thomas J.
1995   *American's Half-Century: United States Foreign Policy in the Cold War and After*, 2nd ed. Baltimore: Johns Hopkins University Press.

McLennan, A.D.
1997   "Balance, Not Containment: Geopolitical Take from Canberra". *The National Interest* (Fall), pp. 52-63.

Mearsheimer, John J.
1990   "Back to the Future". *International Security* vol. 15, no. 1, pp. 5-56.

Meyers, Robert J.
1991   "After the Cold War". *Society*, vol. 28, no. 3 (March/April), pp. 28-34.

Mill, John Stuart
1848   *Principles of Political Economy*. London: John W. Parker and Sons.

Mittelman, James
1997   "Rethinking Innovation in International Studies: Global Transformation at the Turn of the Millennium", in Stephen Gill and James H. Mittelman (eds), *Innovation and Transformation in International Studies*. Cambridge: Cambridge University Press, 1997, pp. 248-63.

Morganthau, Hans J.
1967   *Politics Among Nations: The Struggle for Power and Peace*. 4th ed. New York: Alfred A. Knopf.

Morrison, David C.
1993   "Capitalist Roaders". *National Journal* (May 29), p. 1283.

Mouat, Lucia
1993   "UN Close to Approval of Human Rights Post". *Christian Science Monitor*, December 10, p. 2.

Muravchik, Joshua
1995   "Clintonism Abroad". *Commentary*, vol. 100, no. 4, pp. 36-40.

Neier, Aryeh
1993   "Asian's Unacceptable Standard". *Foreign Policy* (Fall), pp. 42-51.

1994   "Watching Rights". *The Nation*, vol. 259, no.9 (September 26), pp. 1-2.

"A New China Strategy"
1997   *New Republic*, November 10, pp. 9-10.

Nivola, Pietro
1997   "Commercializing Foreign Affairs?" in Randall B. Ripley and James M. Lindsay

(eds), *U.S. Foreign Policy After the Cold War*. Pittsburgh: University of Pittsburgh Press, pp. 235-57.

Nove, Alec
1992   "Some Thoughts on Plan and Market", in Louis Putterman and Dietrich Rueschemeyer (eds), *State and Market in Development, Synergy or Rivalry?*. Boulder: Lynne Rienner, pp. 39-74.

Nye, Joseph S.
1995   "The Case for Deep Engagement". *Foreign Affairs*, vol. 74, no. 4 (July/August), pp. 90-102.

1997/98 "China's Re-emergence and the Future of the Asia-Pacific". *Survival*, vol. 39, no. 4 (Winter), pp. 66-79.

Oberdorfer, Don and Lena H. Sun
1991   "Chinese Warn U.S. about Trade Status". *Washington Post*, June 16, p. A18.

OECD
1996   *Trade, Employment and Labour Standards*. Paris: OECD.

Ohmae, Kenichi
1991   *The Borderless World: Power and Strategy in the Interlinked Economy*. New York: Harper Perennial.

Orentlicher, Diane F. and Timothy A. Gelatt
1993   "Public Law, Private Actors: The Impact of Human Rights on Business Investors in China". *Northwestern Journal of International Law and Business*, vol. 14, no. 66, pp. 66-129.

Orr, James
1991/92 "Evolution of U.S. Trade with China". *Federal Reserve Bank of New York*, Quarterly Review (Winter), pp. 47-54.

Patomaki, Heikki and Colin Wight
2000   "After Postpositivism? The Promises of Critical Realism". *International Studies Quarterly*, vol. 44, no. 2 (June), pp. 213-39.

Pearson, Margaret M.
1997   *China's New Business Elite: The Political Consequences of Economic Reform*. Los Angeles: University of California Press.

People's Daily
1994   April 15.

Perez, David
1995   "Behind U.S. Trade Sanctions Against China". *Workers World*, February 16, pp. 11-12.

Perez-Lopez, Jorge F.
  1988   "Conditioning Trade on Foreign Labor Law: The U.S. Approach". *Comparative Labor Law Journal*, vol. 9, pp. 253-92.

Perkins, Dwight H.
  1992   *China's Economic Boom and the Integration of the Economics of East Asia*. Washington, D.C.: Institute for International Economics.

"The Peterson Report: Rationale of the New Economic Policy"
  1971   *National Journal*, November 13.

Polachek, Solomon W.
  1997   "Why Democracies Cooperate More and Fight Less: The Relationship Between International Trade and Cooperation". *Review of International Economics*, vol. 5, no. 3, pp. 305-6.

Polanyi, Karl
  1957   *The Great Transformation*. New York: Rinehart and Company, Inc. [first published in 1944].

Prebisch, Raul
  1959   "Commercial Policy in the Underdeveloped Countries". *American Economic Review*, vol. 49 (May), pp. 251-73.

Prybyla, Jan
  1993   "How Should the U.S. Handle Trade Issues with China?" *East Asian Executive Reports* (April), pp. 9-15.

Public Papers of the Presidents of the United States
  1995a   William J. Clinton, "Message to the Congress on the General Agreement on Tariffs and Trade", September 27, 1994. Washington, D.C.: GPO, Book II, August 1 to December 31, 1994.

  1995b   U.S. Press Secretary, "Statement on Support from Economists for Prompt Ratifications of the GATT Agreement". Washington, D.C.: GPO, Book II, August 1 to December 31, 1994.

Putterman, Louis and Dietrich Rueschemeyer (eds)
  1992   *State and Market in Development, Synergy or Rivalry*? Boulder: Lynne Rienner.

Qi, Hong Dong
  1993   "The Welfare Effects of the U.S. Extending Most-Favored-Nation Tariff Preference Treatment to the People's Republic of China: An Empirical Inquiry". Ph.D. diss., Northern Illinois University.

Rawls, John
  1971   *The Theory of Justice*. Cambridge: Belknap Press of Harvard University.

Renteln, Alison Dundes
   1990   *International Human Rights: Universalism Versus Relativism*. Newbury Park: Sage Publications.

Ricardo, David
   1953   *On the Principles of Political Economy and Taxation*. 2 vols. Cambridge: University Press for the Royal Economic Society [first published in 1817].

Richardson, Neil R.
   1991   "International Trade as a Force for Peace", in Christopher Colclough and James Manor (eds), *States or Markets? Neoliberalism and the Development Policy Debate*. New York: Oxford University Press.

Rieff, David
   1999   "The Precarious Triumph of Human Rights". *New York Times Magazine*, 8 August, pp. 36-41.

Roberts, Adam and Benedict Kingsbury (eds)
   1993   *United Nations, Divided World*. Oxford: Clarendon Press.

Robinson, William
   1996   "Globalization, the World System, and Democracy Promotion in U.S. Foreign Policy". *Theory and Society*, vol. 25, pp. 615-55.

Rodrik, Dani
   1997   *Has Globalization Gone Too Far?* Washington, D.C.: Institute for International Economics.

Rogers, Ben
   1999   "Behind the Veil: John Rawls and the Revival of Liberalism". *Lingua franca*, vol. 9, no. 5 (July/August), pp. 57-66.

Rogers, David and Helene Cooper
   2000   "China Trade Bill Gains Strength on Votes by Pivotal Committees". *Wall Street Journal*, May 18, pp. A2, A4.

Rogowski, Ronald
   1987   "Political Cleavages and Changing Exposure to Trade". *American Political Science Review*, vol. 81, no.4 (December), pp. 1124-37.

Rohwer, Jim
   1992   "The Titan Stirs". *Economist* (November 28).

Rosenbaum, David
   1994   "In a Dissonant White House, the Economics Team Hums". *New York Times*, May 27, p. A1.

Rosenberg, Justin
1990   "What's the Matter with Realism?" *Review of International Studies*, vol. 16 (April), pp. 285-303.

Ross, Robert S.
1996   "Enter the Dragon". *Foreign Policy*, vol. 104 (Fall), pp. 16-27.

1997   "Beijing as a Conservative Power". *Foreign Affairs* vol. 76, no. 2 (March/April), pp. 33-44.

Roth, Senator William V. and Senator Abraham Ribicoff
1984   "Bill to Create a New Department of Trade and International Investment". in *Proposals to Establish a Department of Trade*. Washington, D.C: American Institute for Public Policy Research.

Rowen, Hobart
1994   "Administration in Disarray on China Trade Policy". *Washington Post*, March 20, p. H1.

Ruggie, John Gerard
1997   "The Past as Prologue? Interests, Identity, and American Foreign Policy". *International Security*, vol. 21, no. 4 (Spring), pp. 89-123.

Ruigrok W. and R. Van Tulder
1993   "The Ideology of Interdependence". Ph.D. diss., University of Amsterdam (Holland).

Ryan, Alan
1988   "Justice, Exploitation and the End of Morality", in J.D.G. Evans (ed), *Moral Philosophy and Contemporary Problems*. New York: Cambridge University Press.

Samli, Coskun A., Erdener Kaynak, and Haroon Sharif
1996   "Developing Strong International Corporate Alliances: Strategic Implications". *Journal of Euro-Marketing*, vol. 4, nos. 3/4, pp. 23-37.

Schlesinger, Arthur Jr.
1997   "Has Democracy a Future?" *Foreign Affairs* (September/October), pp. 2-12.

Schoenberger, Karl and Leslie Helm
1993   "Clinton Targets Pacific Rim for Trade Crusade". *Los Angeles Times*, November 19, pp. A1, A3.

Schott, Jeffrey J.
1994   *The Uruguay Round: An Assessment*. Washington, D.C.: Institute for International Economics.

Schumpeter, Joseph
    1955   *Imperialism and Social Classes*. Cleveland: World Publishing [first published in 1919].

Sciolino, Elaine
    1994   "Clinton and China: How Promise Self-Destructed". *New York Times,* May 29, p. A8.

"Secretary Christopher's Remarks After Meeting at European Union Headquarters, Brussels"
    1994   *Foreign Policy Bulletin* (January/April), p. 81, excerpt 4.

Segal, Gerald
    1996   "East Asia and the Constrainment of China". *International Security*, vol. 20, no.4 (Spring), pp. 107-35.

Senser, Robert A.
    1998   "Exploring a New Frontier". *China Rights Forum*, vol. 40 (Summer), pp. 24-27.

Seymour, James D.
    1994   "Human Rights in Chinese Foreign Relations", in Samuel Kim (ed), *China and the World: Chinese Foreign Relations in the Post-Cold War Era*. Boulder: Westview Press, pp. 202-26.

Shambaugh, David
    1991   *Beautiful Imperialist*. Princeton: Princeton University Press.

Shapiro, Ian
    1986   *The Evolution of Rights in Liberal Theory*. New York: Cambridge University Press.

Shue, Henry
    1996   *Basic Rights*, 2d ed. Princeton: Princeton University Press [first published in 1980].

Shuman, John R.
    1995   "Global Perspectives: The International Competitiveness of U.S. Banks". *Journal of Commercial Lending*, vol. 77 (August), pp. 10-24.

Silbey, Susan
    1997   "Let Them Eat Cake: Globalization, Postmodern Colonialism, and the Possibilities of Justice". *Law and Society Review*, vol. 31, no. 2, pp. 207-335.

Simon, Sheldon W.
    1996   "Security, Economic Liberalism and Democracy: Asian Elite Perceptions of Post-Cold War Foreign Policy Values". *NBR Analysis*, vol. 7, pp. 5-52.

Singleton, Royce A., Bruce C. Straits, and Margaret Miller Straits
    1993   *Approaches to Social Research*, 2d ed. New York: Oxford University Press.

Smith, Adam
    1994   *An Inquiry into the Nature and Causes of the Wealth of Nations.* New York: Modern Library [first published in 1776].

South China Morning Post
    1984   April 28.

Spiegal, Steven L. and Kenneth N. Waltz (eds)
    1971   *Conflict in World Politics.* Cambridge: Winthrop.

Srinivasan, T.N.
    1998   "Trade and Human Rights", in Alan V. Deardorff and Robert M. Stern (eds), *Constituent Interests and U.S. Trade Policies.* Ann Arbor: University of Michigan Press, pp. 225-53.

Stanley Foundation
    1995   *American Relations with China and India: The Growing Impact of Politics on Foreign Policy: Report of a New American Global Dialogue Conference.* Muscatine: Stanley Foundation.

Stolpher, Wolfgang Friedrich and Paul A. Samuelson
    1944   "Protection and Real Wages". *Review of Economic Studies*, vol. 9, pp. 58-73.

Stone, Peter H.
    1991   "Big Business Favors China Trade". *Legal Times*, May 27.

Streeten, Paul
    1992   "Against Minimalism", in Louis Putterman and Dietrich Rueschemeyer (eds), *State and Market in Development, Synergy or Rivalry?.* Boulder: Lynne Rienner Publishers, pp. 3-38.

Stremlau, John
    1994/95   "Clinton's Dollar Diplomacy". *Foreign Policy* (Winter), pp. 18-35.

Summers, Robert and Alan W. Heston
    1991   "An Expanded Set of International Comparisons, 1950-1988". *Quarterly Journal of Economics*, vol. 106, no. 2 (May), pp. 320-52.

Sung, Yun-Wing
    1991   *The China-Hong Kong Connection: The Key to China's Open-Door Policy.* Cambridge: Cambridge University Press.

Sutherland, Peter
    1993   "If GATT Fails, We All Lose". *Wall Street Journal*, October 19, p. A20.

Sutter, Robert S.
    1998   *U.S. Policy Toward China.* New York: Rowman and Littlefield.

Sweezy, Paul M.
   1989   "U.S. Imperialism in the 1990s". *Review of the Month*, October 16, pp. 1-17.

Tardu, Maxime
   1993   *The Effectiveness of United Nations Methods and Mechanisms in the Field of Human Rights: A Critical Overview.* April 1. U.N. Doc. A/CONF.157/PC/60/ Add.5.

Tyson, Laura D'Andrea
   1997   "Are Economic Sanctions an Effective Tool for Realizing U.S. Interests in China?" *NBR Analysis*, vol. 8 (July), pp. 37-44.

"U.N. High Commissioner Mary Robinson Speaks on Human Rights and Conflict Prevention"
   1999   *WIIS Words*, vol. 8, no. 3 (Fall), pp. 2-4.

U.S.-China Business Council
   1996   *U.S. Corporate Practices in China: A Resource Guide.* Washington, D.C.: U.S.-China Business Council.

U.S.-China Business Council, China Ministry of Foreign Trade and Economic Cooperation
   1998   Internet: http://www.uschina.org.

UNCTAD
   1993   *World Investment Report 1993: Transnational Corporations and Integrated International Production.* New York: United Nations.

   1994   *World Investment Report 1994: Transnational Corporations, Employment, and the Workplace.* New York: United Nations.

United Nations
   1945   *Charter of the United Nations and Statute of the International Court of Justice.* New York: United Nations Department of Public Information.

   1986   *Everyone's United Nations: A Handbook of the Work of the United Nations*, 10th ed. New York: United Nations Department of Public Information.

United Nations. General Assembly
   1948   *Universal Declaration of Human Rights.* New York: United Nations Department of Public Information.

United Nations. Global Compact Network
   1999   "The 9 Principles: From Principles to Practice, Partners and Initiatives 1999. Internet: http://www.globalcompact.org.

United Nations. Organization for Economic Cooperation and Development
   1993   *OECD Economic Outlook 1994.* New York: United Nations.

United Nations. Research Institute for Social Development
1994   *States of Disarray: The Social Effects of Globalization.* Geneva: UNRISD.

United States Congress. House of Representatives
1991   Secretary of State Lawrence Eagleburger Speaking Before the Committee on Foreign Affairs. "Renewal of MFN Trading Status for the People's Republic of China". Hearing, 102nd Cong., 1st sess., June 26, 1991. Washington, D.C.: GPO.

1992   Committee on Ways and Means, Subcommittee on Trade. "Additional Requirements on the Extension of China's Most-favored-nation Trade Status in 1993". Hearing, 102nd Cong., H.R. 5318, 2nd sess., June 29, 1992. Washington, D.C.: GPO.

1992   Mike Jendrzejczyk, Washington Director Human Rights Watch/Asia Speaking Before the Committee on Ways and Means. Subcommittee on Trade. "Additional Requirements on the Extension of China's Most-favored-nation Trade Status in 1993". Hearing, 102nd Cong., 2nd sess., June 29, 1992. Washington, D.C.: GPO.

1992   Arnold Kanter, Under Secretary of State for Political Affairs Speaking Before the Committee on Ways and Means. Subcommittee on Trade. "Additional Requirements on the Extension of China's Most-favored-nation Trade Status in 1993". Hearing, 102nd Cong., 2nd sess., June 29, 1992. Washington, D.C.: GPO.

1992   Congressman Jim Leach of Iowa Speaking Before the Committee on Foreign Affairs. Subcommittees on Human Rights and International Organizations, Asian and Pacific Affairs, and International Economic Policy and Trade. "Most Favored Nation Status for the People's Republic of China". Hearing, 102nd Cong., 1st sess., May 29, 1991. Washington, D.C.: GPO.

1992   Michael H. Moscow, Ambassador and Deputy U.S. Trade Representative Speaking Before the Committee on Ways and Means. Subcommittee on Trade. "Additional Requirements on the Extension of China's Most-favored-nation Trade Status in 1993". Hearing, 102nd Cong. 2nd sess., June 29, 1992. Washington, D.C.: GPO.

1993   Congressman Gary L. Ackerman of New York Speaking Before the Committee on Foreign Affairs. Subcommittees on Economic Policy, Trade and Environment, International Security, International Organizations and Human Rights and Asia and the Pacific. "Future of United States-China Policy". Hearing, 103rd Cong., 1st sess., May 20, 1993. Washington, D.C.: GPO.

1993   Donald Anderson, President United States-China Business Council Speaking Before the Committee on Foreign Affairs. Subcommittees on Economic Policy, Trade and Environment, International Security, International Organizations and Human Rights and Asia and the Pacific. "Future of United States-China Policy". Hearing, 103rd Cong., 1st sess., May 20, 1993. Washington, D.C.: GPO.

1993   Liu Binyan, Publisher of *China Focus*. Committee on Foreign Affairs. Subcommittees on Economic Policy. Trade and Environment, International Security, International Organizations and Human Rights, Asia and the Pacific. "Future of United States-China Policy". Hearing, 103rd Cong., 1st sess., May 20, 1993. Washington, D.C.: GPO.

1993   Committee on Foreign Affairs. Subcommittees on International Security, International Organizations and Human Rights and the Commission on Security and Cooperation in Europe. "Human Rights Policy under the New Administration". Hearing, 104th Cong., 1st sess., June 10, 1993. Washington, D.C.: GPO.

1993   Congressman Tom Lantos of California Speaking Before the Committee on Foreign Affairs. Subcommittees on Economic Policy, Trade and Environment, International Security, International Organizations and Human Rights and Asia and the Pacific. "Future of United States-China Policy". Hearing, 103rd Cong., 1st sess., May 20, 1993. Washington, D.C.: GPO.

1993   Ambassador James Lilley Speaking Before the Committee on Foreign Affairs. Subcommittees on Economic Policy, Trade and Environment, International Security, International Organizations and Human Rights and Asia and the Pacific. "Future of United States-China Policy". Hearing, 103rd Cong., 1st sess., May 20, 1993. Washington, D.C.: GPO.

1993   Thomas W. Robinson, President of American Asian Research Enterprises Speaking Before the Committee on Foreign Relations. Subcommittees on Economic Policy, Trade and Environment, International Security, International Organizations and Human Rights, and Asia and the Pacific. "Future of United States-China Policy". Hearing, 103rd Cong., 1st sess., May 20, 1993. Washington, D.C.: GPO.

1993   Congressman Christopher H. Smith of New Jersey. Committee on Foreign Affairs. Subcommittees on Economic Policy, Trade and Environment, International Security, International Organizations and Human Rights and Asia and the Pacific. "Future of United States-China Policy". Hearing, 103rd Cong., 1st sess., May 20, 1993. Washington, D.C.: GPO.

1994   Congressman Neil Abercrombie of Hawaii Speaking Before the Committee on Ways and Means. Subcommittee on Trade. "United States-China Trade Relations". Hearing, 103rd Cong., 2nd sess., February 24, 1994. Washington, D.C.: GPO.

1994   American Association of Exporters and Importers Speaking Before the Committee on Ways and Means. Subcommittee on Trade. "United States-China Trade Relations". Hearing, 103rd Cong., 2nd sess., February 24, 1994. Washington, D.C.: GPO.

1994   American Chamber of Commerce in Hong Kong Speaking Before the Committee on Ways and Means. Subcommittee on Trade. "United States-China Trade Relations". Hearing, 103rd Cong., 2nd sess, February 24, 1994. Washington, D.C.: GPO.

1994   Charlene Barshefsky, Deputy U.S. Trade Representative Speaking Before the Committee on Ways and Means. Subcommittee on Trade. "H.R. 4590, United States-China Act of 1994". Hearing, 103rd Cong., 2nd sess., July 28, 1994. Washington, D.C.: GPO.

1994   C. Fred Bergsten, Director of the Institute for International Economics Speaking Before the Committee on Ways and Means. Subcommittee on Trade. "United States-China Trade Relations". Hearing, 103rd Cong., 2nd sess., February 24, 1994. Washington, D.C.: GPO, Serial 103-85.

1994   Boeing/McDonnell Douglas Corp. Speaking Before the Committee on Ways and Means. Subcommittee on Trade. "United States-China Trade Relations". Hearing, 103rd Cong., 2nd sess., February 24, 1994. Washington, D.C.: GPO.

1994   Charles V. Bremer, Director of International Trade of the American Textile Manufacturers Institute Speaking Before the Committee on Ways and Means. Subcommittee on Trade. "United States-China Trade Relations". Hearing, 103rd Cong., 2nd sess., February 24, 1994. Washington, D.C.: GPO.

1994   Emergency Committee for American Trade Speaking Before the Committee on Ways and Means. Subcommittee on Trade. "United States-China Trade Relations". Hearing, 103rd Cong., 2nd sess., February 24, 1994. Washington, D.C.: GPO.

1994   Professor Lizhi Fan Speaking Before the Committee on Ways and Means. Subcommittee on Trade. "United States-China Trade Relations". Hearing, 103rd Cong., 2nd sess., February 24, 1994. Washington, D.C.: GPO.

1994   Fashion Accessories Shippers Association Speaking Before the Committee on Ways and Means. Subcommittee on Trade. "United States-China Trade Relations". Hearing, 103rd Cong., 2nd sess., February 24, 1994. Washington, D.C.: GPO.

1994   Fertilizer Institute Speaking Before the Committee on Ways and Means. Subcommittee on Trade. "United States-China Trade Relations". Hearing, 103rd Cong., 2nd sess., February 24, 1994. Washington, D.C.: GPO.

1994   Mike Jendrzejczyk, Washington Director Human Rights Watch/Asia Speaking Before the Committee on Ways and Means. Subcommittee on Trade. "United States-China Trade Relations. Hearing". 103rd Cong., 2nd sess., February 24, 1994. Washington, D.C.: GPO.

1994   Estrellita Jones of Amnesty International USA Speaking Before the Committee on Ways and Means. Subcommittee on Trade. "H.R. 4590, United States-China Act of 1994". Hearing, 103rd Cong., 2nd sess., July 28, 1994. Washington, D.C.: GPO.

1994   Kamm and Associates, Ltd. Speaking Before the Committee on Ways and Means. Subcommittee on Trade. "United States-China Trade Relations". Hearing, 103rd Cong., 2nd sess., February 24, 1994. Washington, D.C.: GPO.

1994   Congressman Jim Kolbe of Arizona Speaking Before the Committee on Ways and Means. Subcommittee on Trade. "United States-China Trade Relations". Hearing, 103rd Cong., 2nd sess., February 24, 1994. Washington, D.C.: GPO.

1994   Congressman Tom Lantos of California Speaking Before the Committee on Ways and Means. Subcommittee on Trade. "United States-China Trade Relations". Hearing, 103rd Cong., 2nd sess., February 24, 1994. Washington, D.C.: GPO.

1994   Leather Apparel Association Speaking Before the Committee on Ways and Means. Subcommittee on Trade. "United States-China Trade Relations". Hearing, 103rd Cong., 2nd sess., February 24, 1994. Washington, D.C.: GPO.

1994   Letters collected by the Independent Federation of Chinese Students and Scholars Submitted Before the Committee on Ways and Means. Subcommittee on Trade. "United States-China Trade Relations". Hearing, 103rd Cong., 2nd sess., February 24, 1994. Washington, D.C.: GPO.

1994   Ambassador Winston Lord Speaking Before the Committee on Ways and Means. Subcommittee on Trade. "United States-China Trade Relations". Hearing, 103rd Cong., 2nd sess., February 24, 1994. Washington, D.C.: GPO.

1994   Mattel, Inc. Speaking Before the Committee on Ways and Means. Subcommittee on Trade. "United States-China Trade Relations". Hearing, 103rd Cong., 2nd sess., February 24, 1994. Washington, D.C.: GPO.

1994   David A. Miller, President of the Toy Manufacturers of America, Inc. Speaking Before the Committee on Ways and Means. Subcommittee on Trade. "United States-China Trade Relations". Hearing, 103rd Cong., 2nd sess., February 24, 1994. Washington, D.C.: GPO.

1994   National Retail Federation (NRF) Speaking Before the Committee on Ways and Means. Subcommittee on Trade. "United States-China Trade Relations". Hearing, 103rd Cong., 2nd sess., February 24, 1994. Washington, D.C.: GPO.

1994   Congresswoman Nancy Pelosi of California Speaking Before the Committee on Ways and Means. Subcommittee on Trade. "United States-China Trade Relations". Hearing, 103rd Cong., 2nd sess., February 24, 1994. Washington, D.C.: GPO.

1994   John Shattuck, Assistant Secretary of State for Human Rights, Speaking Before the Committee on Foreign Affairs. Subcommittees on Economic Policy, Trade and Environment, International Security, International Organizations and Human Rights and Asia and the Pacific. "China, Human Rights and MFN". Hearing, 103rd Cong., 2nd sess., March 24, 1994. Washington, D.C.: GPO.

1994   Congressman Christopher H. Smith of New Jersey Speaking Before the Committee on Ways and Means. Subcommittee on Trade. "United States-China Trade Relations". Hearing, 103rd Cong., 2nd sess., February 24, 1994. Washington, D.C.: GPO.

1994   Christopher H. Smith, Congressman from New Jersey, Speaking Before the Committee on Foreign Affairs. Subcommittee on International Security, International Organizations and Human Rights in China. "China, Human Rights and MFN." Hearing, 103rd Cong., 2nd sess., March 24, 1994. Washington, D.C.: GPO.

1994   U.S. Association of Importers of Textiles and Apparel Speaking Before the Committee on Ways and Means. Subcommittee on Trade. "United States-China Trade Relations". Hearing, 103rd Cong., 2nd sess., February 24, 1994. Washington, D.C.: GPO.

1994   U.S.-China Business Council Speaking Before the Committee on Ways and Means. Subcommittee on Trade. "United States-China Trade Relations". Hearing, 103rd Cong., 2nd sess., February 24, 1994. Washington, D.C.: GPO.

1994   Washington State-China Relations Council Speaking Before the Committee on Ways and Means. Subcommittee on Trade. "United States-China Trade Relations". Hearing, 103rd Cong., 2nd sess., February 24, 1994. Washington, D.C.: GPO.

1994   Congressman Frank R. Wolf of Virginia Speaking Before the Committee on Ways and Means. Subcommittee on Trade. "United States-China Trade Relations". Hearing, 103rd Cong., 2nd sess., February 24, 1994. Washington, D.C.: GPO.

1994   Haiching Zhao, President National Council on Chinese Affairs Speaking Before the Committee on Ways and Means. Subcommittee on Trade. "United-States China Trade Relations". Hearing, 103rd Cong., 2nd sess., February 24, 1994. Washington, D.C.: GPO.

1996   Congressman James P. Moran of Virginia Speaking Before the Committee on International Relations. Subcommittee on International Operations and Human Rights. "China MFN: Human Rights Consequences". Hearing, 104th Cong., 2nd sess., June 18, 1996. Washington, D.C.: GPO.

1997   Peter Tarnoff, U.S. Under Secretary of State for Political Affairs Speaking Before the Committee on International Relations. Subcommittees on International Economic Policy and Trade and Asia and the Pacific. "The Impact of MFN for

China on U.S.-China Economic Relations". Hearing, 104th Cong., 2nd sess., May 16, 1996. Washington, D.C.: GPO.

1997   Executive Vice President and Corporate Executive Director Richard W. Younts, International-Asia and Americas Motorola, Inc. Speaking Before the Committee on Ways and Means. Subcommittee on Trade. "United States-China Trade Relations and Renewal of China's Most-favored-nation Status". Hearing, 104th Cong., 2nd sess., June 11, 1996. Washington, D.C.: GPO.

1998   Stephen Rickard, Director of the Washington D.C. Office of Amnesty International USA, Speaking Before the Committee on International Relations. Subcommittee on International Operations and Human Rights. "Human Rights in China". Hearing, 105th Cong., 2nd sess., June 26, 1998. Washington, D.C.: GPO, pp. 22-26.

United States Congress. Senate
1992   Arnold Kanter, Under Secretary of State for Political Affairs Speaking Before the Committee on Finance. "Extending China's MFN Status". Hearing, 102nd Cong., 2nd sess., July 30, 1992. Washington, D.C.: GPO, S. 2808 and H.R. 5318.

1992   Winston Lord Speaking Before the Committee on Finance, *Extending China's MFN Status.* Hearing, 102nd Cong., 2nd sess., July 30, 1992. Washington, D.C.: GPO.

1992   Assistant U.S. Trade Representative Ira Wolf Speaking Before the Committee on Finance. "Extending China's MFN Status". Hearing, 102nd Cong., 2nd sess., July 30, 1992. Washington, D.C.: GPO, S. 2808 and H.R. 5318.

1994   Jeffrey A. Bader, Deputy Assistant Secretary of State for East Asian and Pacific Affairs Speaking Before the Foreign Relations Committee. Subcommittee on East Asian and Pacific Affairs. "U.S. Policy Toward China". Hearing, 103rd Cong., 2nd sess., May 4, 1994. Washington, D.C.: GPO.

1994   Senator Russel D. Feingold of Wisconsin. Committee on Foreign Relations. Subcommittee on East Asian and Pacific Affairs. "U.S. Policy Toward China". Hearing, 103rd Cong., 2nd sess., May 4, 1994. Washington, D.C.: GPO.

1994   Gerrit W. Gong, Ph.D., Asian Studies Program Director for the Center for Strategic and International Studies Speaking Before the Committee on Foreign Relations. Subcommittee on East Asian and Pacific Affairs. "U.S. Policy Toward China". Hearing, 103rd Cong., 2nd sess., May 4, 1994. Washington, D.C.: GPO.

1994   Mike Jendrzejczyk, Washington Director Human Rights Watch/Asia Speaking Before the Committee on Foreign Relations. Subcommittee on East Asian and Pacific Affairs. "U.S. Policy Toward China". Hearing, 103rd Cong., 2nd sess., May 4, 1994. Washington, D.C.: GPO.

1994   Ambassador Winston Lord Speaking Before the Committee on Foreign Relations. Subcommittee on East Asian and Pacific Affairs. "U.S. Policy Toward China". Hearing, 103rd Cong., 2nd sess., May 4, 1994. Washington, D.C.: GPO, S. HRG. 23.

1994   Senator Larry Pressler of South Dakota Speaking Before the Committee on Foreign Relations. Subcommittee on East Asian and Pacific Affairs. "U.S. Policy Toward China". Hearing, 103rd Cong., 2nd sess., May 4, 1994. Washington, D.C.: GPO.

1994   Senator Charles S. Robb of Virginia Speaking Before the Committee on Foreign Relations. "U.S. Policy Toward China". Hearing, 103rd Cong., 2nd sess., May 4, 1994. Washington, D.C.: GPO, S. HRG 103-723.

United States Department of Commerce
1930   *American Direct Investments in Foreign Countries.* Washington, D.C.: Bureau of Foreign and Domestic Commerce.

1998   *Statistical Abstract of the United States.* Washington, D.C.: Economics and Statistics Administration, Bureau of the Census.

United States Department of Labor
1996   *The Apparel Industry and Codes of Conduct: A Solution to the International Child Labor Problem?* Washington, D.C.: Dept. of Labor.

United States Department of State
1948   Havana Charter for an International Trade Organization. Pub. No. 3206.

1977   Speech by Cyrus R. Vance. "Human Rights Policy". April 3. Washington, D.C.: Bureau of Public Affairs, PR 194.

1992   *Country Reports on Economic Policy and Trade Practices.* Washington, D.C.: GPO.

1994   *Country Reports on Human Rights Practices 1993.*

1995a   *Country Reports on Human Rights Practices 1994.*

1995b   "Madeleine Albright on Human Rights". University of Connecticut. October 17. Office of the U.S. Mission to the United Nations. Internet: gopher:// gopher.state.gove/Public Affairs.

2000   *Country Reports on Human Rights Practices 1999*

United States Department of State. Bureau of Public Affairs
1997a   "Chinese Prison Labor Exports". Fact Sheet. June 17. Internet: http://www.state/ www.regions/eap/fs-china_exp-970617.html.

1997b   "Most-Favored-Nation (MFN) Treatment". Fact Sheet. June 17. Bureau of Public Affairs. Internet: www.state/www./regions/eap/fs-mfn-treatment-970617.html.

"United States Foreign Trade Highlights"
1980-1994   Internet: http://www.ita.doc.gov/industry/otea/usfth/top80cty/china.cp.

Van Ness, Peter
1996   "Addressing the Human Rights Issue in Sino-American Relations". *Journal of International Affairs*, vol. 42, no. 2 (Winter), pp. 309-31.

Vogelgesang, Sandra
1978   "What Price Principle? U.S. Policy on Human Rights". *Foreign Affairs*, vol. 16, pp. 807-22.

Wallerstein, Immanuel
1993   "The World System after the Cold War". *Journal of Peace Research*, vol. 30, no. 1, pp. 1-6.

1994   "The Agonies of Liberalism, What Hope Progress?" *New Left Review,* no. 204 (March), pp. 3-17.

Walt, Stephen M.
1987   *The Origins of Alliances*. Ithaca: Cornell University Press.

Waltz, Kenneth N.
1971   "Conflict in World Politics", in Steven L. Spiegal and Kenneth N. Waltz (eds), *Conflict in World Politics*. Cambridge: Winthrop, pp. 454-73.

1979   *Theory of International Politics*. Reading: Addison Wesley.

1986   "Political Structures", in Robert O. Keohane (ed), *Neorealism and its Critics*. New York: Columbia University Press, 1986, pp, 70-98.

Wang, N.T.
1993   "The Role of Foreign Direct Investment in Reform and Development in China", in *Institute Reports*. New York: Columbia University Press, p. 10.

Wethington, Olin
1988   "The Role of Technology Transfer", in Eugene K. Lawson (ed), *U.S. China Trade: Problems and Prospects*. New York: Praeger, pp. 195-209.

Whitney, Craig R.
1999   "Hands Off: The No Man's Land in the Fight for Human Rights". *New York Times*, 12 December, p. 1.

Wilkins, Mira
1986   "The Impacts of American Multinational Enterprise on American-Chinese Economic Relations 1786-1949", in Ernest R. May and John K. Fairbank (eds),

America's China Trade in Historical Perspective. Cambridge: Harvard University Press, 1986, pp. 259-92.

Williams, Daniel
1994   "U.S. Stress on Rights Gives Way". *Washington Post*, May 27, pp. A1, A28.

Williams, Marc
1999   "The World Trade Organization, Social Movements and Democracy", in Annie Taylor and Caroline Thomas (eds), *Global Trade and Global Social Issues*. New York: Routledge, pp. 151-70.

Wilson, Woodrow
1918   "Fourteen Points Plan". Versailles Peace Conference.

Wogaman, Philip J.
1977   *The Great Economic Debate: An Ethical Analysis*. Philadelphia: Westminster Press.

World Bank
1992   *China: Strategies for Reducing Poverty in the 1990s*. Washington, D.C.: World Bank.

1995   *Global Economic Prospects and the Developing Countries*. Washington, D.C.: International Bank for Reconstruction and Development.

1996   *World Development Report — From Plan to Market*. Washington, D.C.: Oxford University Press.

World Debt Tables
1996, 1997

Yan, Yanni
2000   *International Joint Ventures in China*. New York: St. Martin's Press.

Yang, Yongzheng
1995   "The Uruguay Round Trade Liberalization and Structural Adjustment in Developing Asia". *Journal of Asian Economics*, vol. 6, no.4 (Winter), pp. 493-510.

Yip, George
1992   *Total Global Strategy*. Englewood Cliffs: Prentice Hall.

Yue, Chia Siow and Wendy Dobson
1997   "Harnessing Diversity", in Wendy Dobson and Chia Siow Yue (eds), *Multinationals and East-Asian Integration*. Ottawa: International Research Centre, pp. 229-63.

Zheo, Suisheng
  1994   "Clinton's Human Rights Policy and Beijing's MFN Status". *World Outlook*, vol. 3, no. 22, pp. 6-26.

Zupnick, Elliot
  1999   *Visions and Revisions: The United States in the Global Economy.* Boulder: Westview Press.

Index